P9-CMC-527

Airplanes, Women, and Song

Airplanes, Women, and Song

MEMOIRS OF A FIGHTER ACE, TEST PILOT, AND ADVENTURER **Boris Sergievsky**

EDITED BY **Allan Forsyth** AND **Adam Hochschild**

Syracuse University Press

Copyright © 1999 by Allan Forsyth and Adam Hochschild

All Rights Reserved

First Edition 1999

99 00 01 02 03 04   7 6 5 4 3 2 1

The paper used in this publication meets the minimum requirements of American
National Standard for Information Sciences—Permanence of Paper for Printed Library
Materials, ANSI Z39.48-1984. ∞ ™

Library of Congress Cataloging-in-Publication Data
Sergievskiĭ, Boris Vasil´evich, 1888–1971
    Airplanes, women, and song : memoirs of a fighter ace, test pilot, and adventurer /
Boris Sergievsky ; edited by Allan Forsyth and Adam Hochschild. — 1st ed.
        p.   cm.
    Includes bibliographical references and index.
    ISBN 0-8156-0545-5 (hardcover : alk. paper)
    1. Sergievskiĭ, Boris Vasil´evich, 1888–1971. 2. Air pilots—United States—Biography.
3. Air pilots—Russia (Federation)—Biography. I. Forsyth, Allan. II. Hochschild, Adam.
III. Title.
TL540.S414A3 1998
629.13'092—dc21   98-34258
[B]

Manufactured in the United States of America

Frontispiece: Boris Sergievsky in March 1930, age 42, when he was setting records in the Sikorsky
S-38. *Courtesy of the editors.*

Boris Sergievsky was one of the most colorful of the early aviators. Born in Russia, he learned to fly in 1912. In World War I, he became a much-decorated infantry officer and then a fighter pilot, battling the Austro-Hungarians. During the Russian Civil War that followed, he fought on three fronts against the Bolsheviks. Coming to America in 1923, he joined Igor Sikorsky's airplane company and soon became chief test pilot. In the next decade, he tested the Sikorsky flying boats that Pan American Airways used to establish its worldwide routes, setting seventeen world aviation records along the way. He also flew pioneering flights across uncharted African and Latin American jungles in the 1930s, tested early helicopters and jets, and flew his own flying boat on charter flights until 1965.

Allan Forsyth worked for many years as an editor of college textbooks for Worth Publishers, Academic Press, and McGraw-Hill before becoming a freelance editor and writer. A lifelong aviation enthusiast, he has edited several books about aviation and twentieth-century history, including *The Chinese Communist Air Force* and *End of a War*.

Adam Hochschild is a writer whose books include *The Unquiet Ghost: Russians Remember Stalin*; *King Leopold's Ghost: A Story of Greed, Terror, and Heroism in Colonial Africa*; and *Half the Way Home: A Memoir of Father and Son*, which has been reprinted by Syracuse University Press. His *Finding the Trapdoor: Essays, Portraits, Travels* won the 1998 PEN/Spielvogel-Diamonstein Award for the Art of the Essay; it is also published by Syracuse.

Contents

Illustrations

Acknowledgments

When we began this project in 1991, we had no idea of the pleasures that awaited us. We expected to rummage through dusty archives and their dust-free online equivalents and correspond with far-flung, impersonal research establishments. Because Boris Sergievsky had died twenty years before, we thought that our research would necessarily be based on documents rather than memories.

We found many of the documents we sought—and we also found ourselves welcomed into a community of enthusiasts, men and women who care as passionately as we do about rescuing the story of aviation's beginnings from the perils of fading memories, misinterpretation, and mythmaking. As word of our project spread, strangers called to offer us encouragement and expert advice. These new friends introduced us to others, and our circle of friendships and knowledge widened.

We met people who had known Boris Sergievsky well at various stages of his career, and they gave us vivid recollections that could have come only from firsthand experience. We talked and corresponded with many other people whose knowledge of pioneering airplanes, people, and organizations saved us from many a misinterpretation of documents. We thank all of these friends for their extraordinary and much-appreciated willingness to help us provide the background, sidelights, and historical information necessary to put Boris Sergievsky's memoirs in the context of his time. (We also take responsibility for any errors that may remain.)

Our thanks go first to our editors, without whom this book would not exist. Von Hardesty of the Smithsonian's National Air and Space Museum gave us unstinting support and encouragement throughout our five years of research. Cynthia Maude-Gembler and her colleagues at the Syracuse University Press provided expert, imaginative, and enthusiastic support throughout the publication process. Our special thanks to Syracuse stalwarts John Fruehwirth, Mary

Peterson Moore, Amy Rashap, and Theresa Litz. We are grateful, too, for the copyediting skills of Jeffrey H. Lockridge and Mary Selden Evans and for Pelican Street Studio's ingenious and graceful book design.

Carl Bobrow, our virtual editor, has given us an amazing amount of help over the years, introducing us to people and research sources that have proven invaluable. Among those we met through Carl are Igor I. Sikorsky's sons. Sergei Sikorsky, who sat in his father's lap in the copilot's seat when Sergievsky took the S-42 up on test flights, shared many memories of Sergievsky at work and at play. Igor I. Sikorsky Jr. organized two Sikorsky Symposia in 1994 to encourage researchers to record the history they knew firsthand. We benefited greatly from these symposia and from the assistance and the warm support of both brothers.

Our thanks go also to Sikorsky archivists Harry Pember and Phil Spalla, who have preserved many priceless pieces of Sikorsky history over the years; they responded generously to our many requests for documents and photos. Sikorsky engineer and historian Alan Durkota was equally generous with the information and photos he collected during the years of research that led to the 1995 book, *The Imperial Russian Air Service*, of which he was the lead author.

Many retired Sikorsky workers shared their memories of Sergievsky and the flying-boat days with us, as did several volunteers on the Sikorsky S-44 restoration project. Our special thanks to Harry Hleva, Stratford Town Historian Lewis Knapp, Alec Voight, Zeke Werner, and the late Bob Cowell, Nicholas Glad, and Ray Holland.

Other valued contributions have come to us from farther afield. Elmourza Natirboff of Florida, Sergievsky's copilot in the 1940s and 1950s, gave us many personal recollections of Sergievsky. Romanian pen pal Matei Kiraly provided invaluable information about de Bothezat and his helicopters, as well as the fine drawing of the GB-5 helicopter that appears in this book. Christine White and Sergei Zhuravliev managed to secure many of Sergievsky's service records from the previously inaccessible Russian state archives in Moscow. Ron Wyatt opened the Nassau County Museum Research Library for us, and Lois Lovisolo of Grumman gave us copies of the sales orders for Sergievsky's Grumman Goose and Mallard amphibians.

We also thank Peter Grosz, the dean of World War I aviation researchers; John H. Wright of the Central Intelligence Agency; Bill Camp and Herman Schonenberg of Long Island's Cradle of Aviation Museum; Ellen Scaruffi, Curator of Columbia University's Bakhmeteff Archive; Larry McDonald, Kenneth

Schlessinger, and John Taylor of the National Archives; the late Harvey Lippincott of the New England Air Museum; and Dana Bell, Russell Lee, and Larry Wilson of the National Air and Space Museum for their help and encouragement.

Other researchers have given us valuable leads and information, including Andrei Alexandrov, August Blume, Don Chalif, Peter D. Duz, Nigel Eastaway, Nadja Jernakoff, Norman Malayney, Kurt Tolksdorf, David Winans, and the late Jean Alexander. Barbara Jackson of Meridian Mapping created the two maps in this book. Our thanks to them all, and our apologies to anyone we may have inadvertently omitted from this list of dedicated and generous enthusiasts.

ALLAN FORSYTH
ADAM HOCHSCHILD
MAY 1998

Out of the Blue

Out of the Blue

ADAM HOCHSCHILD

The most vivid memories I have of my childhood are of the summer evenings when Boris Sergievsky's plane took off.

Boris Vasilievich Sergievsky, captain in the Imperial Russian Air Force, World War I fighter pilot, winner of the Order of St. George (which gives you the right to an audience with the Tsar at any time of day or night), test pilot for the Pan American Clippers of the 1930s, tenor, gourmet, lover, horseman, and adventurer, was, miraculously, my uncle. One day years before I was born, he had flown his plane down from the sky and, to the complete shock of all her relatives, had married my father's sister, Gertrude Hochschild. From that point on, life in our family was never the same.

Each summer, my parents and the Sergievskys shared a large house on a lake in the Adirondack Mountains of upstate New York. When I was a boy, in the years right after World War II, Boris Sergievsky was retired from test piloting. He now operated an air charter business in New York City, flying people anywhere they wanted to go in a ten-passenger Grumman Mallard that could put down on land or water. During the summer, he spent his work weeks in New York; for the weekend, he flew north to join his family. Then, on Sunday evenings, with a planeload of houseguests also returning to the city, he took off for New York.

First, a crew of workmen used Jeep, winches, and a huge set of dollies for the landing gear to maneuver the Grumman amphibian out of its lakeside hangar and onto a concrete apron. A short time later, more people began to arrive: passengers, friends, and spectators, coming by motorboat over the lake,

Adapted from *Half the Way Home: a Memoir of Father and Son,* by Adam Hochschild (Syracuse University Press, 1996).

or by horseback, car, or station wagon on the road that ran through the woods to the hangar.

When his passengers had climbed on board, Sergievsky warmed up the plane's engines on shore, watched by a cluster of admiring children. I knelt with my fingers in my ears, a few feet away from the right wingtip. Through the cockpit window I could see the intent faces of Sergievsky and his copilot. Their eyes checked instruments on the panel; their lips mouthed a mysterious technical jargon I could not hear; their hands reached up to adjust a wondrous galaxy of switches and levers. First one motor, then the other gave out a long, shattering roar so loud you felt as if you were standing *inside* the noise. The aircraft rocked and strained at its wheels; the saplings at the edge of the forest behind it bent toward the ground. Finally the engines quieted to a powerful whoosh, and, like an ungainly three-legged duck, the plane rolled down the beach and into the water.

Sergievsky taxied out to the middle of the lake, the propellers blowing a wet wind back over us on shore. Suddenly, a great white tail of spray spread out behind the plane. The Mallard, its wheels now folded into its belly, lifted higher and higher in the water, transformed into a shape of sleek grace. A motorboat or two raced alongside, then were quickly left behind. At last, triumphantly, the plane broke free of the water and rose into the dusk. The engines' roar echoed off the lake; the very mountains vibrated. A plume of water drops trailed from the fuselage, then faded to a fine mist, then to nothing. On the ground, people quietly began talking again, moving slowly, reluctantly, toward the waiting cars. High in the sky, Sergievsky dipped a wing and turned toward New York.

There could have been no more improbable addition to our rather formal and reserved family than Boris Sergievsky. He dropped out of the sky in 1930. Someone had suggested to my father and his brother that they buy a small plane with which to commute on weekends between Manhattan, where they both worked, and their summer home in the Adirondacks. They called the Sikorsky Aviation Corporation. Hard hit by the Great Depression, the company was so eager to sell an aircraft that it sent a pilot to fly these potential customers from New York to the mountains as a free demonstration. And so Boris Sergievsky descended out of the clouds at the controls of a Sikorsky S-38, saw

1. Boris Sergievsky at the controls of the Chilean S-38 over Central America, 1931, photographed by his copilot, Igor Sikorsky. *Courtesy of Igor I. Sikorsky Historical Archives, Inc.*

a large country home like those of his beloved pre-Revolutionary Russia, and, among the crowd of curious onlookers gathered on the shore to meet the plane, an unmarried sister.

For the next five years, Sergievsky courted my aunt Gertrude secretly. She waited until two weeks before the wedding to tell her brothers that she was marrying him, for she was certain they would disapprove. They did. Sergievsky had been married twice before, and, to top it off, he was late for the wedding because he had to finish off a test-piloting assignment. My father loyally kept his sister company while they watched Sergievsky's stalls and spins from the ground.

The life Sergievsky recounts in the following pages was one of extraordinary adventure. As an officer of the Tsar's infantry in World War I, he won Imperial Russia's highest medal by leading his company of soldiers uphill to capture a fortified mountaintop. Charging over the last wall, they fought hand to hand with Austro-Hungarian soldiers, Sergievsky slashing with his sword.

Midway through the war, Sergievsky transferred to the Russian air force, where he eventually commanded a fighter squadron and is credited with shooting down eleven German planes and three observation balloons. After Russia withdrew from World War I in the wake of the Revolution, he made his way to England and trained pilots for the Royal Air Force. Later, when the Russian Civil War was under way, Sergievsky returned to Russia and fought on the White side, both on foot and in the air. He was captured, escaped from prison, worked his way through Europe as a gymnastics instructor and cabaret singer, and came to the United States in 1923.

The first job he could find in New York was with a pick and shovel, digging the Holland Tunnel ("I felt marvelous," he said later. "The physical work was just what I needed.")[1] Soon, though, he went to work for another recent immigrant to the United States, his old schoolmate from the Polytechnic Institute of Kiev, the distinguished aircraft designer Igor Sikorsky. For most of the 1920s and 1930s, Sergievsky was Sikorsky's chief test pilot, and was the first man to fly many of the principal flying boats and amphibians of that era.

In interludes when there were no new planes to test at the Sikorsky factory, Sergievsky flew oil prospectors up Colombia's turbulent, alligator-ridden Magdalena River, and flew cargoes of live boa constrictors downriver, to be made into snakeskin shoes and handbags. He flew with Lindbergh. In Africa, he landed his plane on lakes where no plane had ever landed before.

Sergievsky was surely one of the few aviators in history to have served in three air forces: the Russian (in 1916–17), the British (in 1918–19), and the American (in World War II), and to have once worn the uniform of a fourth—the Chilean. Chile bought a Sikorsky plane to fly the Prince of Wales around the country on a royal visit there in 1931, but had no one qualified to pilot the aircraft. So they dressed Sergievsky in a military uniform while he trained Chilean pilots and attempted, as a *New Yorker* journalist later wrote, to look "as Chilean as possible."[2]

2. Sergievsky, an expert horseman, loved to ride the trails of his wife Gertrude's family estate. Here, in a competition elsewhere, he is flying to an altitude he rarely reached in the ill-fated GB-5 helicopter. *Courtesy of the editors.*

During those magical summers when my parents and I lived in the same house with Boris Sergievsky and his family, he was always returning from somewhere exciting: from test-flying captured Nazi jet fighters at the end of World War II, from flying moose hunters to the Canadian North, from landing in a rough sea to pick up films of the *Andrea Doria* shipwreck for CBS. He usually brought a planeload of friends with him, and the pace of our household turned festive as they arrived.

Sergievsky knew everybody, from Commander Whitehead of the Schweppes advertisements to the man who ran the restaurant in the Eiffel Tower. But his closest friends were all Russians. Many were former aristocrats or officers, born to lead hussars on parade, now growing old in a foreign land. We children took horseback riding lessons, for example, from Colonel Kadir Azamat Guirey, a Circassian cavalryman who ran a riding school in New York. Among the other guests were Colonel Zouboff, who gave Russian lessons at Berlitz; Lonya Kalbouss, who played the accordion at a Russian restaurant in New York; Prince and Princess Bagration—the prince was a relative of the General Bagration who appears in *War and Peace;* Countess Alexandra Tolstoy, the great man's youngest daughter; and Nicholas de Transehe, who had been, I was told, an Arctic explorer in old Russia. One noblewoman, a relative of the Imperial family, signed our bilingual guest book simply as "Vera of Russia."

Orest Sergievsky, Sergievsky's grown son by his first marriage in Russia, visited on occasional weekends. A ballet dancer, he danced for a time with the Metropolitan Opera Ballet and various other companies, then later had his own teaching studio. He was a warm, ebullient man with a wide circle of friends—artists, musicians, singers, dancers.

To feed all of these people, the Sergievskys hired a Russian cook who made delicious *piroshki, kasha, shashlik,* and the cold creamy soup called *okroshka.* My own favorite was broth filled with *pelmeni,* Siberian dumplings filled with seasoned chopped meat. Sergievsky, who cheerfully claimed that everything important had been invented by Russians, described *pelmeni*'s history:

"See, you make big pot of *pelmeni.* Then you put them in a sack on the back of your sleigh. You set off across the steppe. They freeze. You stop for dinner and take out as many *pelmeni* as you want. You put them in boiling water, and there you have it—the world's first frozen food!"

He also claimed *pelmeni* as the ancestors of wonton, ravioli, and other inferior imitations: "The Chinese, the Italians, they all got the idea from us in Russia!"

3. Kira and Orest Sergievsky, Boris Sergievsky's two children, around 1960. *Courtesy of the editors.*

Sergievsky's sturdy, tree-trunk torso exuded strength and health. He had a superb tenor voice, and, after dinner when the mood was right, he stood by the piano, fixed his blue eyes intently on first one, then another woman among the assembled guests, and sang arias from *La Belle Hélène, La Traviata,* and other operas and operettas.

Only when pressed did Sergievsky talk about his past, but then it was with an earthy gusto. I remember one time when he was telling me about some battle he had fought in, during which a bullet had grazed a friend standing next to him, nicking an artery. "His blood was all over me!" He slapped his leg and roared with laughter. "I was *red* from head to foot!"

4. Boris and Gertrude Sergievsky and their daughter, Kira, about 1940. *Courtesy of the editors.*

Sergievsky loved friends, airplanes, champagne, horses, steak tartare, and, above all, beautiful women. When he made a much-noted twenty-eight-hour small-plane crossing of the North Atlantic,[3] a newspaper headline read: "Sergievsky, Wife, and Ballerina Fly to London 'Just for Fun.'" In a natural, almost animal way, he was the most masculine man I ever knew. I do not mean that robust sexuality and physical bravery are the province of men only, but merely that, having lived the life he had, Sergievsky had no need for any macho pretense. He was at ease with himself.

Boris Sergievsky flew for more than half a century, from 1912 until 1965. Finally, when he was seventy-seven, the doctors made him stop. He sold his beloved Grumman Mallard. From all the flying, he had grown deaf. Or *said* he had grown deaf, for he seemed to hear well if someone spoke to him in Russian, or called to him using the Russian pronunciation of his name, "BahREES!" With no battles to fight or planes to fly, he sat in his living room like a caged lion, although he came to life instantly, eyes wide, head thrown back, nostrils flaring, if an attractive young woman entered the room.

For his eightieth birthday, in 1968, there was a big party in New York City. Sergievsky had recently had an operation to implant a pacemaker for his heart. His cheerful, soldierly directness was unchanged. "It's good," he told me between waltzes, proudly tapping the metallic bulge beneath his shirt. "It will give me another two or three years." He was exactly right.

A year or two after that, I wrote to him that I had learned to fly a glider. He wrote back a beautiful note in the handwriting of Russian émigrés: many curls on the letters, and false starts where Cyrillic characters had been reluctantly converted in mid-stroke to Roman ones. He said that he, too, had flown gliders and appreciated "the beauty and the silence," although perhaps someday I would learn to fly power planes as well: then I would no longer be limited by the air currents, and the whole world would be mine.

On a visit home a few months later, I went to see him and my aunt. We had just had our first child, and Sergievsky grunted with satisfaction as he watched my wife nurse the baby, "just like we used to in Russia." As with wonton, ravioli, and most advances in aviation, he seemed about to claim that Russians had invented breast-feeding.

Then he and I went off to a corner. His frame was as broad as ever, but he moved very slowly. We talked for an hour or so, probably the only time we had talked alone for so long. We both knew it would be the last. It was then that he told me the whole story of his life, which up until that point I had heard only in fragments from others. He finished by describing the great Russian Civil War battle in 1919 when the White army almost captured Petrograd. "We were so close. We were so close, I could see the golden towers of St. Peter and St. Paul. And then, outside Petrograd, we were met by a much larger army under the command of Trotsky himself.

"There were lice everywhere, carrying typhus. There was much dying. I was one of the lucky ones." He looked out the window through the trees onto the lake where he had first landed in our lives some forty years before. "I have had a good life. I have no regrets." Boris Sergievsky died a few months after that conversation, at the end of 1971. He was eighty-three years old.

It was not until after Sergievsky's death that I learned that, decades before, he had composed his memoirs. They date from 1934. Sergievsky gave a number of public lectures that year, arranged by F. Leslie Fairchild, an agent in Bridgeport, Connecticut, where the Sikorsky plant was then located. It was apparently Fairchild who persuaded Sergievsky to sit down with a stenographer for a dozen or so sessions during the summer of 1934, to dictate the story of his life up to then. The only surviving correspondence about this is a letter from Fairchild beginning "Dear Captain" and saying that what Sergievsky had produced so far was not yet enough to show to a publisher.[4] The letter urges Sergievsky and his family to come over to Fairchild's house for more dictation.

Fairchild's hand is also visible in an effusive article in the *Bridgeport Post* in August 1934, where a reporter describes the "thrilling tales" and the "sensational story" the public would soon be able to read in Sergievsky's "vital, turbulent" memoirs. But no vital and turbulent book appeared, perhaps because it was hard to find a publisher during the Depression, perhaps because Sergievsky's marriage to Gertrude Hochschild the following year relieved him of financial worries.

The transcript Sergievsky dictated sat in a drawer for more than thirty-five years. After his death, most of it was translated into Russian and published as part of a memorial booklet, *Boris Vasilievich Sergievskii 1888–1971*. This booklet, privately printed for Sergievsky's many friends in New York's Tsarist émigré community, also contains some reminiscences of him by others, and a list of his Russian military postings and decorations.

Now, more than sixty years after he was persuaded to tell it, Sergievsky's life story appears for the first time in English, just as he first dictated it. He spoke six languages and, by the time Fairchild got him to tell his story, had been in the United States for more than a decade and knew English well.

Sergievsky seems to have produced the chapter about flying Martin and Osa

Johnson around Africa (pp. 183–207) at a different time than the rest of his story, for at the point where it should appear, there is a note in the manuscript: "Insert Story of the Trip." Perhaps the decision to tell it was an afterthought, to satisfy Fairchild's demand for more material. The editors of the Russian-language memorial booklet included it. But the original English manuscript of this chapter has disappeared, and so I have translated the Russian text back into English for this volume. The chapter about Sergievsky's first flight to Chile (p. 00) was also written at a different time. A longer version of it appears over his byline in the May 1931 issue of the *Sportsman Pilot.* A note in the dictated manuscript says that this article is to be inserted at that point.

We have divided Sergievsky's story into chapters; otherwise, except for minimal copyediting, adding some explanatory footnotes and modernizing proper name spellings, we have left the manuscript unchanged. Sergievsky was a natural storyteller, and despite its being a dictated first draft, his memoir is as clear and vivid as any reader could hope for. Montaigne once wrote that the directness of good prose is "not pedantical, nor friar-like, nor lawyer-like, but rather downright, soldier-like." Sergievsky, a professional soldier much of his life, gives happy proof of this.

Sergievsky's book, however, is much more than the story of one man's adventurous life. For the historical record, its significance is twofold. First, despite the millions of Russian, German, Romanian, and Austro-Hungarian soldiers who met their deaths there, virtually no books about the Eastern Front in World War I are now in print in English. For a theater of fighting that accounted for nearly half the casualties, in a war whose shadow still hangs over this century, this is an amazing lacuna. Sergievsky describes what it was like to fight in that immense but forgotten conflict—both on the ground and in the sky.

Second, Boris Sergievsky's years in the air covered a key period in the history of aviation. He made his first flight less than ten years after the Wright brothers made theirs; he made his last only four years before the first Concorde took off. During that time Sergievsky fought biplane aerial dogfights in World War I, test piloted the great flying boats of the 1930s, mapped and explored Africa and Latin America from the air, and was one of the handful of Allied pilots who tried out the world's first fighter jets. Few, if any, aviators so often managed to be in the right place at the right time, and to survive to tell the tale.

Some years after Sergievsky's death, I managed to find the house where he had grown up, in Odessa. It was on a lovely, quiet street bordered with poplars, along a high cliff overlooking the Black Sea. From the windows, you can see ships at anchor and the long, curving breakwater of the harbor. Today the building is subdivided into apartments, and some twenty people live there.

The house where Sergievsky lived in Kiev is no more. But, outside the city that has taken back its original name of St. Petersburg, I was able to visit the old battlefield at Pulkovo Heights. Today it is a placid meadow of wildflowers. Sergievsky was right: from this spot, you can see flashes of gold on the distant city roofs on the horizon. On that day in 1919, those golden towers remained out of reach of the army Boris Sergievsky was with; the city was never captured, and the Russia of the Tsars was never restored. But in the memoir on the pages that follow, he captures that Russia for us, and many more parts of the world his remarkable life crossed as well. It is a pleasure to help put this work before English-speaking readers for the first time.

The Memoirs

A Russian Youth

The family of my father, Vasily Sergievsky, comes from Saratov, on the River Volga.

All my ancestors on my father's side were in the Army, and one of my great-grandfathers distinguished himself in the famous Battle of Moscow against Napoleon. Some members of his family were Cossacks of the Don River. My father was the first one in many generations who was a civilian. He was a civil engineer, working on what we call in Russia "Ways and Communications."

All of my mother's ancestors were also in the military service. Probably this family background accounts for my inclination toward military service and my keen insight in military affairs. I got my education as a civil engineer, but after my obligatory army training (which, for the educated class in Russia, was one year after reaching the age of twenty-one), I liked military life so much that I decided to stay in the service. Also, I knew that through the Army I could get into aviation more easily than as a private citizen, because at this early stage, aviation was a very expensive game. I could not afford to do it on my own.

Speaking of family, I remember stories my mother told me as a child, of her grandfather playing a very important part in the war against the Turks that led to the conquest of the Caucasus Mountains for Russia. I remember often reading a very official-looking paper, yellow from age, that gave a dry account of such and such villages being captured by Colonel Tomashevsky (which was my mother's maiden name). These villages were taken in the heart of the Caucasus.

The Colonel's son, Pavel Savich Tomashevsky, was a very capable and brilliant officer in the Horse Guards in St. Petersburg. As a young colonel of the Imperial Guards, he played a joke on Tsar Nicholas I—who did not like having jokes played on him! He was one of the most serious Tsars in the history of Russia. Nicholas I was a soldier himself and extremely strict about requirements and regulations covering discipline, the uniform, and such. One of the rules of the Russian Army was that an officer never had the right to wear rubber overshoes. The climate in St. Petersburg is cold and wet, and my grandfather, who was always very smartly dressed, wanted to preserve his shoes and keep them clean. Violating the rule, he had rubber overshoes made with special slits in them to put his spurs through, to make it hard to see that he had overshoes on.

When an officer met the Tsar on the street, he was supposed to immediately stand still and salute. My grandfather, out for a walk with his rubber overshoes on, almost collided with the Tsar and, stopping in front of him, saluted. The Tsar looked him over from head to foot and, in his typically abrupt way, commanded, "Rubber shoes, to Jail!" My grandfather obeyed the Tsar's order very strictly. He took his rubber shoes and deposited them in the Military Jail, reporting, "The rubber shoes are brought here by the order of His Majesty," and then he went quietly home!

In a few hours, the Tsar sent one of his aides to the Military Jail with an order to release the colonel of the Horse Guards sent there by him for wearing overshoes. The Commandant had to tell the aide that the overshoes were there but the colonel was not. In spite of my grandfather's explanation that he actually had carried out the exact order given to him, the Tsar got very angry and exiled him to Fortress Kerch, on the Black Sea.

My grandfather was appointed commandant of the fortress, but despite the honor, he was considered to be in disgrace as he had disobeyed the Tsar.

My mother was only three years old when my grandfather died in Kerch from a sickness that would probably now be called appendicitis; the quiet young man had to die simply because medical science was not advanced.

Relatives of my mother took her back to St. Petersburg, as her mother had died soon after her birth and there was no one to take care of her. These relatives also took her only brother, later my uncle, who was two years older than she. Mother was put in an exclusive girl's college in St. Petersburg, called the "Smolny Institute for Girls of Noble Birth." (By the irony of fate, the name "Smolny" became infamous as the headquarters of the Bolshevik party during the revolution in Russia, when all the girls of noble birth were thrown out into the streets to give place to the drunken sailors who were in power in St. Petersburg. That place which had had such a retiring and special atmosphere for many, many generations of our great-grandmothers became a place of extreme cruelty and torture.)

My mother's brother Boris, in whose honor I was named, was placed in a similar institution for boys, situated in the little town of Gatchina, a summer resort about two hours distant from St. Petersburg.

As the Smolny Institute for Girls was what we called "closed" the whole year round—even visitors were allowed there only on big holidays—the relatives who were taking care of the Tomashevsky children moved out to Gatchina. During one vacation, my mother went from St. Petersburg to Gatchina to join the family. There she met my father, who had just graduated from the Engineering College and had his first job, straightening out the streets of Gatchina. They were married the year that my mother graduated from the Smolny Institute and the next year I was born, on February 20, 1888.*

I was still a small boy when my father was transferred to Odessa on the Black Sea, where he was in charge of the construction of the harbor. Here I received my early schooling, corresponding to the American high school and known as "real school." In Russia we had two sorts of schools. Classical school, called the "gymnasium", focused on ancient languages and moral literature. The "real school" had no Greek or Latin but two modern languages were obligatory. Great stress was put on the study of mathematics and physics. Those graduating from the "real school" were qualified for engineering and technical vocations.

I graduated from the "real school" in 1906 and at graduation I maintained the same standard I had set during my seven years there: first in my class in science and last in behavior!

What I remember of those days in school is a great interest in all sorts of sports. Studying took a very little part of my life; it seemed that it just came to me. I was more for listening to what was going on during class than studying at home. Most of my time at home I devoted to physical exercises and games, especially to bicycle racing and racing on skates. At sixteen, I was a champion in both. I took part in several public contests. I was also threatened with expulsion several times, as pupils were not allowed to take part in public contests. Only my extremely good standing in science saved me from being expelled.

My two young brothers were in the same school—one two years and the other four years lower in grade than I. My second brother, Gleb, had much more inclination for music than for sports, but our third brother, Roman, liked aquatic sports more than anything else. From his early childhood, he was allowed to spend all his time away from school in a boat. We were all good swimmers and we spent much of our time in sailboats; our house was close to the seashore.

* When dating events in his Russian years, Sergievsky uses Imperial Russia's Julian or Old Style calendar, which lagged the West's by thirteen days.

We played many interesting and thrilling games together. One of the most popular was the "war" between the English and the Boers, which was raging then in South Africa. The trouble was that no one wanted to be English; everyone wanted to be Boer. The sympathies of the Russians were entirely on the side of the Boers. I still remember that the youngest brother, who couldn't help being "English" in the game, was beaten several times by the two older "Boers."

At this period of my life I met Sergei Utochkin, who was then the World Champion of bicycle racing and was considered almost a "God Almighty" by all the youth of Russia. He stuttered slightly and boys wanted so much to be like him that many of those interested in bicycling began stuttering. I did not follow this habit, even though I became closely acquainted with this extremely interesting man, who was not only a champion cyclist but very capable in everything he was doing in life, and he took a great interest in me.

Utochkin later became one of the first men to go up in a plane. Like all the pioneers, he had no one to teach him how to fly. He bought a plane and flew it without knowing how! He gave me my first few flying lessons, and it was largely through this friendship that I became so interested in aviation.

When I was sixteen, and still in the Sixth Class, I saved the life of a boy who was swimming in a very rough sea off the coast of Odessa. This was a spectacular event. It looked as if the boy could not be saved and was about to drown, as nobody dared go out in such a rough sea. After several attempts to put out boats from the lifeguard station were unsuccessful, as the boats were thrown back to shore by the surf, I succeeded in swimming out to him and bringing him to shore. The event was reported to St. Petersburg and, quite unexpectedly, the head of my school gave me a silver medal with a black and red ribbon, awarded to me by Tsar Nicholas II for saving the boy. At the time I did not think of the rescue as outstanding. To me, it was only natural to help a pal who was not doing so well fighting the waves. But of course such an award for a boy of sixteen from the Tsar was thrilling! I still have this medal and though since then I have received most of the medals and decorations that a Russian officer can receive, I still value this little silver medal very much.

After graduating from the "real school" I had a summer of extremely hard work, studying for a competitive examination for college. We organized a group of six young men and took a cottage on the shore of the Black Sea, where we worked eighteen hours a day, helping each other with difficult mathematical problems and getting ready for this severe competitive examination, which took place that autumn.

For my examination I went to the Polytechnic Institute of Kiev. There were 864 applications for sixty vacancies. The exam covered four subjects, worth a total of 20 points. One boy received 20 points; I was second, with 19.5 points. On being admitted to the Institute, I selected the Division of Civil Engineering. I wanted to follow the profession of my father.

My mother decided to move to Kiev with me. She left her two younger boys in the care of servants in Odessa because she was afraid to leave me alone, knowing my character. She thought I was going to get into trouble if she left me alone, but her presence did not help much! I was in trouble constantly.

I fell in love with a Polish girl and naturally, being eighteen, I thought that we had to marry immediately. Her parents felt quite differently, for two reasons: They thought we were too young, and they would never consent to the marriage of a Catholic Polish girl to an Orthodox Russian boy. The fact that we were not allowed to see each other made it much more romantic and interesting, and I started neglecting my studies, inventing different ways to meet the girl.

Her parents were annoyed by this, and decided to send her off to some relatives in the country. Of course I found out when the train was going to leave and went to bid her good-bye with a big bunch of flowers and a box of candies. I was in the same car with all her relatives; I could only say, "Farewell," and give her the flowers and candies. I was standing at the end of the platform when the train started to move; as the last carriage was passing I jumped in. For a long time I saw her father and two cousins running behind the train, waving their fists in the air and shouting unpleasant things. When I entered my sweetheart's compartment, she actually fainted on seeing me. I came back the next day as I had to report for my studies at the Institute, but that unexpected trip is one of the sweet memories of my life.

During my second year in college I met a student by the name of Igor Sikorsky, who had just entered the mechanical engineering school at the Institute. We met in a so-called Aviation Students' Club. That club had no planes and no one knew how to fly, but we were interested in aviation, making drawings of planes, building models, and discussing the flights of those fliers who were pioneering the new way of transportation through the air.

Even then, Mr. Sikorsky wanted to build large planes with several engines.

Loves and a Marriage

Sergievsky's pursuit of the Polish girl established a lifelong pattern of unruly romantic pursuits and conquests, often accompanied by choruses of outraged relatives. His range of romantic possibilities was expanded in 1910, when his father died after a long and costly illness. Relieved of the hospital expenses, granted an ample pension by the Tsar, and thriving as a private tutor, Sergievsky's mother, Katerina, bought a mansion in Kiev.

The scale was grand. The central room, with its crystal chandelier, had French doors opening onto a forty-foot porch where parties and lunches were held in the summer. The front courtyard was flanked by small buildings for the staff and a few working-class tenants. The enclosed garden, occupying a whole city block, was laced with paths that wandered among the fruit trees and berry bushes. Orest Sergievsky, Boris's son by his first marriage, conjured up the scene decades later in his autobiography.

> Roman, Boris's youngest brother, was still like a colt—all arms and legs. Only after his teens did he become a competition to his brother with his good looks.
>
> Gleb, the second son, was a quieter personally—an artist. Music was his life. Some people thought he was better looking than Boris; in his own calm way, Gleb attracted attention at the grand piano, creating magic with his music.
>
> Boris, the eldest, was usually the life of any party, charming the guests with his looks, love of life, and enchanting voice. He fell in love with a lovely young lady named Yadviga, who was often among the guests who used to attend the *vecherinki*—the evenings of talk, music, and singing at which tea was served with the ever-popular *piroshki.* Looking back on this—Boris's first passionate encounter with a woman—it is easy enough to see the pattern which their love would soon take: the inner storms, the unseen wounds which would fortunately dissolve with time, and the many things which remained unspoken but still created shadows on family relations. Before graduation and receiving his diploma as an engineer, Boris had to acquire practical experience, to gain firsthand knowledge in different parts of the country. When Boris was leaving to spend several months in Odessa, Baku, Sevastopol, and other places, he asked his brother Gleb to keep the young fiancée, Yadviga, company. Gleb was asked to accompany her to concerts and parties so that she would not be lonely. But even before Boris left, the subtle charm, the deeper personality of Gleb, started to intrigue and fascinate the young woman.
>
> The mother of the family, and gradually a few others, began to realize with uneasiness the possibility of drama in the near future.
>
> Gleb did not encourage Yadviga; he was a gallant escort, but ever conscious that he was with his brother's fiancée. Nevertheless, by the time Boris returned, Yadviga was hopelessly in love with Gleb.
>
> After a few weeks of polite coolness and uneasy silence, Gleb left to visit a friend outside of Kiev. Boris had to go to Odessa; his mother wrote to the Bergau family in Odessa to try to cheer Boris up when he visited them. The Bergaus had been neighbors of the Sergievskys; their sons and daughter Ella had been playmates of the Sergievsky boys during their childhood.
>
> The "cheering up" of Boris led to his engagement and later marriage to Ella. I, their son, arrived upon the scene in August 1911.[1]

AF

He was thinking of an airplane as a real flying ship—he called it a "flying truck." Safety was his main aim in his projects. I was more interested in the art of flying and my dream plane was a single-seater, so small that the pilot flying it would feel like a bird. The wings of the plane would become his own wings and he would feel himself not as flying a "machine" in the air, but flying as a bird flies.

Flying at this time was a very expensive game and no private individual with limited means could afford to buy a plane. Almost every flight, if not actually every flight, would end in some sort of a crash. Then the plane would have to be rebuilt or repaired and that would involve additional expense. Mr. Sikorsky's father, a well-known Professor at the University of Kiev, helped him financially to carry on his projects. Not having the money to buy a plane for myself, I thought of joining the Army and starting to fly as a military pilot. Then I was called up for my year of obligatory military service.

After completing this year, I took an officer's examination and was commissioned on December 6, 1912. As I was not quite through with my studies at the Polytechnic Institute, I went into the Reserves in order to finish college.

In 1912, I took my first few lessons in flying from my friend Sergei Utochkin. After about three lessons he gave me an antiquated plane which had a sixty-horsepower Gnome engine, with an elevator in front and the pilot sitting between the wings. The engine was behind his neck. I made my first solo flight on March 16, 1912.

I graduated from the Polytechnic in 1913 and that summer went back to active service in the Army. There were so many applications for the Air Force and their forces were then so small that I did not succeed in securing a transfer from the Infantry to the Air Force. Disgusted by this fact, I returned to the Reserves and got a position in the city of Kiev as an engineer, constructing reinforced concrete bridges.

I was peacefully building bridges in the summer of 1914 when one beautiful night, about 3 o'clock in the morning (and three days before the official mobilization of the Russian Army was declared), there was a strong knock at my door and I was handed a sealed package. When I opened it, I found an order to report immediately for active duty with the 125th Kursk Infantry Regiment, which was stationed at Rovno—about eighty kilometers from the western border. I had twenty-four hours to arrange my personal affairs, say good-bye to my family, and leave the peaceful life of Kiev forever.

Sikorsky I: The Russian Years

Igor Ivanovich Sikorsky (1889–1972) spent the years 1903–6 at the Imperial Russian Naval Academy in St. Petersburg and six months after that studying in Paris. Shortly after he entered the Kiev Polytechnic Institute in 1907, aged eighteen, to study engineering, he organized and headed the Aviation Students' Club there. Such leadership was predictable in a young man who literally had been pursuing his dream of flight since 1900. Sikorsky later described the dream that had inspired his life's work:

> I saw myself walking along a narrow, luxuriously decorated passageway. On both sides were walnut doors, similar to the stateroom doors of a steamer. The floor was covered with an attractive carpet. A spherical electric light from the ceiling produced a pleasant bluish illumination. Walking slowly, I felt a slight vibration under my feet and was not surprised to find that the feeling was different from that experienced on a steamer or on a railroad train. I took this for granted, because in my dream I knew that I was on board a large flying ship in the air. Just as I reached the end of the corridor and opened a door to enter a decorated lounge, I woke up.
>
> Everything was over. The palatial flying ship was only a beautiful creation of the imagination. At that age I had been told that man had never produced a successful flying machine and that it was considered impossible.[1]

By the time his fellow student Boris Sergievsky met him in 1907, Sikorsky knew that his dream was not impossible. In France, accounts of the Wright brothers' flights, published in *L'Aérophile* in December 1905, had stirred a frenzy of aerial experimentation by such pioneers as Santos-Dumont, Blériot, Farman, and Voisin. In January 1909, Sikorsky returned to France, by then the center of the aviation

world, where he learned much hard-won knowledge from the leading aviators and designers of the day. Thanks to his sister Olga's generosity, he also managed to buy one of the first engines designed for airplanes, a twenty-five-horsepower, three-cylinder Anzani like the one used by Blériot in the first flight across the English Channel that same year.

Sikorsky came back to Kiev in May 1909, determined to build a helicopter, but after two unmanned test models barely got off the ground, he returned to his concept of the "flying truck." As Sergievsky notes, Sikorsky taught himself to fly by the pioneers' method of building and test-flying a series of his own designs. He built four biplanes in 1910, wrecking the S-1 and S-2 during his tests, but his S-5 was a success; he taught himself to fly in it and earned Pilot's License No. 64 in 1911. Sikorsky later attributed the rapid advance of aviation to the fact that mediocre designers were soon killed by their own flawed designs, leaving the field and the financing clear for the more talented and skilled survivors.

Sikorsky's genius as a designer flowered quickly. On May 26, 1913, less than ten years after the Wrights' first flight, Sikorsky's giant passenger transport, the *Grand*, soared above St. Petersburg. The *Grand*, with its spacious enclosed cabin for crew and passengers, was the first four-engined airplane in the world—in part because other designers feared that an engine failure would make such a plane uncontrollable. Sikorsky proceeded to demonstrate that the Grand could be flown safely even with two engines shut down on the same side. One year later, Sikorsky flew an even more advanced successor, the *Ilya Mourometz*, on an epic voyage from St. Petersburg to Kiev and back—2,400 miles in less than 26 hours' flying time. Later versions of these four-engined giants gave Russia an almost invincible long-range bombing and reconnaissance force in World War I.[2]

The small border town of Rovno lies on the railroad from Warsaw to Kiev. At the moment when the general mobilization of the Russian Army was ordered, a train occupied by a musical comedy troupe was traveling from Warsaw to Kiev. It was stopped in Rovno, and as no civilian travelers were allowed to go anywhere during the period of mobilization (all the trains and carriages being needed for transportation of troops), the musical troupe had to stay in Rovno for a few days. They hired a theater (a moving picture house) and gave marvelous performances there. The leading lady of the musical comedy was one of the most beautiful women I have ever seen in my long life.

After long hours of training with the regiment in the field, preparing for our march to the western border, we hurried to the theater. Three young men, all with college educations and all second lieutenants* (among them myself) sent their cards backstage asking the leading lady to have supper after the performance. Our invitation was accepted. All three of us fell in love!

At the next performance, the leading lady sang for each of us our favorite song. We knew that the regiment's stay in Russia was limited to a matter of hours, or a few days at most. There was no time to lose and we knew also that three of us could not succeed together, so we wrote our names on three pieces of paper. Then a fourth officer (an impartial one) drew the name of the lucky fellow who was supposed to invite our "queen" for the next supper. We agreed that if, in the course of the evening, she showed that she didn't love him, he was eliminated from the race! For the next evening, it would be one of the two remaining officers whose name would be drawn.

The first night, neither of us slept. We were waiting for the return of the lucky boy. When he arrived about 3 o'clock in the morning at the barracks, we did not have to ask any questions. He was unlucky. He almost fell down on his cot and told us, "She doesn't love me."

The second night my friend Stefan was the lucky man, and he invited the fair lady for supper. I stayed awake alone, again waiting for my friend's return. When he came back, also at three in the morning, my first impression was that he had been successful. His face was radiating happiness. He came straight to my cot and told me that he was extremely happy because he loved such a wonderful person. But then he said he thought that the girl was interested in me,

* Here and throughout his memoirs, Sergievsky uses the equivalent U.S. Army rank rather than the Russian original.

More Loves, Another Marriage

By the time of his romantic interlude with the musical comedy star on the way to war in August 1914 (p. 23), Sergievsky had a new wife. His first wife, Ella Bergau, had gone back to her parents' home in Odessa for good in 1913, leaving their two-year-old son, Orest, with his grandmother, Katerina, in Kiev. Orest described in his autobiography how this situation came about:

> Our neighbor, Dr. Kotchoubey, and his wife, Alexandra, shared our garden; their house was on one side of our block, and her music room had windows overlooking the garden. During my father's visits home there would be small parties, singing. I would wake up and listen to the melodies of *Rigoletto* and *Traviata*. It was Father singing the operatic duets with Mme. Kotchoubey. I heard these melodies many times without knowing their names.
>
> Dr. Kotchoubey was constantly away and the three handsome men [the Sergievsky brothers], Boris, Roman, and Gleb, were tempting company for the future opera star. But Roman was always misbehaving. For example, he would start sneezing when a much-perfumed lady would pass the veranda. Gleb was too busy with his music. But Boris, a gallant officer who loved to sing, would oblige willingly and sing a duet or two.
>
> The duets were followed by other meetings.

> In the evenings one could hear the melody of a then-popular romance, with a definite message in the lyric: "Sunset is beautiful across the river, the perfume of flowers fills the air; meet me, my dear, in the garden. . . ." Relations became more personal. As I write this, I still cannot understand why Dr. Kotchoubey used to give me chocolate candies. Was it because we two were left out—he by his wife and I by my father? I remember the Doctor telling Granny during the war (1914) that he was actually grateful to my father for "taking away" his wife. I remember, too, overhearing that Alexandra threw the doctor's wedding rings out of the train window on their honeymoon.
>
> Grandmother had tried to call the romancing couple to reason. She had a talk with Mme. Alexandra, reminding her that Boris was a married man, that there was duty to the family in married life. But Mme. Alexandra's answer was: "Until one is thirty, life is ruled, experienced by the heart and senses; after thirty it is governed by brain and duty." Father was then twenty-three years old.[1]

Sergievsky divorced Ella Bergau, and then married the newly divorced Alexandra Kotchoubey on November 21, 1913.

AF

because several times during the evening she asked where I had gone. My first friend had said the same thing the night before.

As there was no more drawing of names, the next night was my turn to invite the lady for supper after the performance. That same night, we got orders to start the march to the western border at five the next morning.

Before going for dinner I packed my few belongings and told my orderly to bring my pistol and my possessions straight to the place where the battalions were to assemble at 5 A.M. I had a hope that I would not have to return to the barracks that night—and that hope was justified.

The regiment lined up in front of the barracks, officers on the right flanks of their companies, the whole regiment of four thousand men standing in the courtyard. It was a beautiful sight. Sharply at 5 A.M., General Ruzski, commanding the Third Russian Army, arrived. He was a thin tall man, with a little gray moustache. He went to the middle of the courtyard and in a few words, in a clear loud voice, explained why Russia had to go to war. He asked that we have faith in the high command, telling us that they had studied the problems of this war for many years, knowing that it was coming. He said that we should do everything in our power to spare the lives of every soldier; that in a war mistakes are unavoidable, and we should not judge anyone too severely for mistakes and for losses that were unavoidable. Instead of everyone judging or finding fault with others, he asked each of us to think of his own immediate duty and be the most severe judge of himself. If everyone did his duty to the fullest extent, said the General, success would come.

After this speech we started for Austria.

War in the Mountains

The 125th Kursk Infantry Regiment was one of the so-called first-line regiments. The first-line regiments were stationed within one hundred kilometers of the border. They were supposed, in case of war, to receive or to deliver the first shot at the enemy, keeping the enemy busy while the mobilization went on under their protection.

For this reason my regiment did not detach from itself any reserve battalions, which was the custom for the rest of the army. Reserve battalions were supposed to be a sort of training school for men drafted during the mobilization and, after repeated mobilizations, for new men to replace the casualties.

Within a few hours of the first mobilization, the first-line regiments received a number of additional men from the last two years of service, and a few selected reserve officers also joined their ranks. Then the orders came to march to the front. On this day, August 5, our regiment started its march, having in its ranks 4,000 men and 77 officers.

During the days of training in Rovno, I had no chance to get well acquainted with the rest of the officers of the regiment. I knew only my company commander, a battalion commanding officer, and the officers of my company, totaling three besides myself. But from the beginning of the march I got to know almost every one of the officers more intimately because from that time on we led a common life like one family. We had all our meals together in the officers' mess and, whenever possible, gathered at every stop. It was a group of men of an exceptionally high quality as officers. Later on I will describe in more detail some of the striking characteristics of the officers and men I met at this period of my life.

When the command to march rang out, the fine regimental band played the regimental march and, with parade-ground precision, the ranks started to move. It was just like a peacetime parade, except that little crowds of relatives, mothers, and wives, were standing on the sidewalks. Some of them were running along trying to keep step with the marching men, trying to shout the last few words of farewell to them. The tragedy of separation, which meant separation forever for many of them, was quite striking.

In my company there was a very young second lieutenant who had married just a few days before. He was so young he looked like a girl himself, having very light hair and rosy plump cheeks. He was about twenty-one, his bride of a few days was perhaps eighteen, and she also looked like a child. This pair could not tear themselves from each other. He never left his place in the ranks, but she ran along as the regiment marched on. When all the rest of the relatives who went out with the regiment were returning to their homes, this young lady was still marching on, in spite of the insistence of her husband, and the repeated insistence of the battalion commander to her, to turn back home. She went on and on for about two hours, until she fell on the side of the road entirely exhausted. But we were going to war, and no one was allowed to step out and attend to her. We had to look only forward, and march on.

The young woman probably had a premonition that she would never see her husband again, and that was why she could not bear to separate herself from him. In our very first engagement, a few days later, the young lieutenant was shot through the heart. I believe he was the first officer of our regiment who was killed in the war.

A regular day's march for an infantry regiment in Russia is twenty-five kilometers. It is not easy for the men to march twenty-five kilometers, when they have to carry on their backs not only all their personal belongings necessary for all kinds of weather to come—a spare pair of boots, a change of underwear—but also a heavy rifle with a bayonet and 140 cartridges for the rifle. The officers had the right to accompany the march on horseback, but before we started out we agreed that, to set an example for the men, all the officers except the colonel, his staff, and the battalion commanders would go on foot, together with the men in the ranks. Even so, the officers' load was much lighter because the only things we had to carry were a service pistol, a sword, a leather container for maps, and a pad of paper for a field book of reports.

The day was extremely hot. After every hour of march there was a ten-minute rest. During these ten minutes the men were allowed to sit down or lie down, without actually leaving the ranks. Everybody was very tired after the

5. The Eastern Front in World War I. During the war and the Russian Civil War that followed it, Sergievsky fought over much of this vast area, from Ivano-Frankovsk in the south to the outskirts of St. Petersburg in the north. *Courtesy of Barbara Jackson, Meridian Mapping, Oakland, Calif.*

WAR IN THE MOUNTAINS

first day's march, and after a good meal everybody went immediately to sleep, after an advance guard was spread in a fan-like fashion in front of the regiment.

Now there was nothing between us and the enemy, and his appearance could be expected at any minute of the day or night. It was a strange feeling that you are facing, unknown to the rest, the Austrian Army advancing on you, and that you are the living wall protecting Russia from invasion. Almost everybody felt an unusual sense of responsibility. In listening to the conversation of the men, I understood that this feeling was common, and was not just a privilege of the educated part the army.

On the third day of our march we crossed the Austrian border. My company was in the vanguard on that day, and I remember jumping on the border post, painted black and white with the Austrian two-headed eagle on top of it, and pulling that post down. I hoped that the new border post, whenever it was going to be erected, would be much further west. It was not that we had an imperialistic feeling for expansion, but we were entering the part of Austria called Galicia, which was once, many centuries ago, a part of Holy Russia. The people there spoke our language and had our religion, and their natural inclination was toward reunion with Russia.

By the way we were greeted in the Galician villages, how the people rushed out offering our men refreshments and food, which we had plenty of ourselves and did not need, we understood that we were entering really friendly territory. Still it was Austria, and we were in enemy country. The strictest orders were issued not to offend any of the civilians and never to take anything from them without paying money for it. It was made clear that the slightest attempt to abuse the rights of the people would be punished by immediate death.

An entirely different attitude toward our invasion was shown by the people in the Galician towns. This change of attitude was especially visible in towns where the majority of the people were Jewish merchants. They were very much for Austria and very much against us. They had all the rights of citizens in Austria, and they knew that in Russia their rights would be limited and they would be persecuted. In one of these towns, volleys of shots were fired on our columns from several houses. When we entered the buildings we found young Jews, armed with antiquated rifles, revolvers, and hunting guns, all rather harmless in fighting against a well-equipped army.

Such attempts to resist our progress by unorganized civilians in little towns were repeated on quite a few occasions, but our casualties from them were negligible.

We still did not meet any resistance from the Austrian Army. Clearly, the mobilization plan of Austria was to concentrate some of her forces further back in their country, and strike when they were ready.

The first blow, and a very violent one, fell on August 26, 1914. That day we will remember forever. The head of our column was approaching a village named Skvarzava. Right behind our first battalion of infantry, a battery of the 33rd Field Artillery Brigade was moving up. Then came the second battalion, followed by one more battery. Our scouts reported the village unoccupied. But as the first battery was passing over a narrow bridge over a creek, all of a sudden, like a thunderbolt on a clear day, a terrific artillery fire started, covering almost the entire column. The first heavy shells fell right on the bridge, overthrowing guns, killing horses and men. In the first few seconds the battery was destroyed, before the men even had time to dismount. The enemy was invisible.

I remember that at the moment of this first blow, I had taken out of my bag half of a roast chicken and had started to eat it. It is funny that I remember that I had only time to eat one leg of it when the firing started, and I had to throw away the rest.

The command was given and repeated along the column, "Regiment to battalion formation." A second command was given by the battalion commanders: "Battalion to company formation." The third command, distinctly shouted by the company captain, was, "Company to platoon formation," and that was the signal for me to act.

I had the Third Platoon of the 14th Company. My order was, "Interval two paces, on the village, march!" Taking out my sword I ran at the head of my platoon, which consisted of sixty-five men. We ran half way to the village without casualties, and approached the village cemetery. Then, to the artillery fire, which was still going on, was added another sound, of rifle and machine gun fire, and my men started to fall to the left and right of me.

Stopping my platoon sharply, and ordering the men to lie down, I remained standing, trying to see where the fire was coming from. Then I saw the blue-gray uniforms of the Austrians, who were hidden behind some of the monuments of the cemetery, and behind the stone wall surrounding it. Giving a few words of command to the men to direct their fire, I lay down myself in the tall grass surrounding the cemetery. Shooting broke out all along the line to the left and right, growing louder and louder, and in about five minutes the first shells of the Russian artillery started to fall in the cemetery, destroying the simple crosses and monuments, and crushing the little stone wall behind which the Austrian infantry was hidden.

It is unbelievable what moral support the infantry feels when even a few shells from our artillery strike where they really should strike. The state of surprise and uncertainty which everybody felt at the beginning of the engagement changed to an assurance that our superiors knew what they were doing, and that the whole advance was well organized. Things that every officer and man were taught to do during training came back to our minds. It was exactly like the previous year during the maneuvers near Kiev; the only difference was that the shots exchanged between the rifles were real shots, and human life did not count much from that moment on.

Right behind me arose the huge figure of Lieutenant Colonel Kanzerov, my battalion commander. He passed right by me, telling me, "Lieutenant, get up. Let's go forward and see what is to be done about this." He was as calm and self-possessed as if it were a training exercise. We advanced about one hundred meters, followed only by four privates, who were ordered never to leave the battalion commander, except to carry his orders to the various companies.

Then a new machine gun joined in very sharply and this one sounded very near. My first instinct was to drop to the ground, and so I did. I heard the tall grass around me being cut as though by a thresher. Fortunately I was lying in a small gully. The battalion commander was shot twice through the chest, once through the stomach and through both legs. He could not be removed immediately, two of his orderlies being killed right beside us. The few minutes that I lay there, right beside my heavily wounded commander, under the terrific fire of this machine gun so close by, seemed like hours of agony.

Then very close on my right I heard the high-pitched voice of an old gentleman, which I recognized immediately as the voice of Brigadier General Behr. Over his general's uniform he wore a khaki raincoat without epaulettes. He carried a small stick in his hand and no sword. In a very calm voice he was directing one of the platoons of my company, which was crawling in the grass behind him. Pointing with his stick he told the soldiers, "Now aim well at that machine gun that is doing this damage. We are flanking it, don't be afraid of it. We will have them in a minute." Then I heard a very loud "Hurrah!" and the men of the platoon led by the General seized the first machine gun nest in the cemetery, and by flanking fire cleared that first stand of the Austrians. The machine gun fire ceased immediately. We all stood up and went in pursuit of the Austrians, who were rapidly retreating.

We advanced at least two kilometers at a rapid pace, straightening out our line and getting our formations in a better order. Then a second, very heavy fire met us from behind a railroad line running from north to south. The fight for the possession of this railroad line lasted until dark. We gradually crawled forward, sometimes getting up, running a few paces, falling down again, and shooting, but steadily advancing toward the railroad, which was shelled by our field artillery very successfully. With the coming of the dark we stopped shooting and at the command, "Bayonets, rush the line!" we charged in, but there was nobody behind it. The last Austrian companies were rapidly retreating in the dark. They did not accept the bayonet fight.

Pursuit in the dark was impossible. We could not see the enemy, and we were in such a state of nervous and physical exhaustion after this first battle that the moment the Austrian position was actually taken, the men began falling asleep where they were lying with their guns aimed in the dark. I had to apply all my willpower, and to call on my sense of duty and responsibility as the only officer in the company who was not wounded, to stay awake and see that every tenth man in the rank would stay awake during the coming night, and be relieved every two hours by somebody else. There was no question of going anywhere to sleep; we slept right on the field in the same fighting line where we were caught by the dark in our advance.

One of the staff officers arrived at my position, and informed me that I was in command of the company. He said that I was responsible for a line about half a kilometer in length, and told me also where the headquarters of the regiment were, to send my reports to.

When daylight came, in front of us was an empty field covered with killed and wounded Austrians; there was no sign of the Austrian Army. That was our first victory.

In the morning we were all summoned to regimental headquarters, where a division general congratulated the regiment for its outstanding success, and regretted only the regiment's losses, which were 20 percent of the men and 40 percent of the officers. He emphasized that the proportion of losses among the officers was too high, that 40 percent in the first encounter proved that the officers did not take proper care of themselves. They obviously were exposing themselves too much, and a real sense of duty and bravery would make them more careful, keeping in mind that the war could not be won in one or two battles, but had to last perhaps several months. Who could tell then that it would last four years?

The next day's march was only about ten kilometers, and that was only to straighten out the front of the neighboring divisions and the army corps, which had fought an engagement on the same day. Then we were ordered to halt, rest, and reorganize because a reorganization was needed. In that first encounter we lost three out of our four battalion commanders, and the new battalion commanders, who were formerly company captains, had to get acquainted with their new duties and appoint new company leaders in place of those killed, wounded, and promoted to battalion commanders.

On this day we saw a plane fly over our heads. Nobody had any idea whether the plane was Russian or Austrian. The air forces of both countries were so negligible that not only the men but even the officers were not acquainted with the distinguishing marks of their own forces. In a general panic some of the men started to shoot at the plane, and when we saw distinctly the Russian three-colored markings under the wings it was too late to stop the firing. The plane, which was flying rather low, came to a landing right near the headquarters of the regiment.

Out of it stepped the familiar (to me) figure of our foremost pilot, Captain Nesterov, whom I had known in Kiev, in the prewar days. Using tremendously strong language, he lectured the embarrassed staff officers of our regiment on how to tell the difference between an Austrian and a Russian plane. Very fortunately, only his gas tank was shot through.

Captain Nesterov was one of the world pioneers in aviation. Considered the first Army flyer of Russia, he was actually the first man in the world to loop the loop in a plane, which he did in a Nieuport monoplane in 1912. After this feat he was arrested for violating the regulation against stunt flying in an Army plane. Later on, some people believed that the French aviator Pégoud was the first one to loop the loop. Years later, I had a chance to ask Pégoud himself about it. He readily admitted that he was experimenting with preliminary steep "S" turns when Nesterov looped the loop. Learning about Nesterov's success, Pégoud looped the loop himself, knowing that it could be done.

At this early stage of the war, planes were not equipped with any means of attack or defense. Their duties were strictly scouting; they were simply the eyes of the Army. When our pilots met an Austrian or a German plane in the air, they would wave to each other and proceed on their tasks, flying in opposite directions. The planes were not strong or powerful enough to carry machine guns, so the observers were ordered to bring along Mauser carbines and try to shoot their aerial enemies down. To my knowledge, no one succeeded in doing it; aerial shooting is a difficult art.

On September 5, 1914, Captain Nesterov made the first real attempt at an aerial fight. He went up in a single-seat monoplane after seeing a larger Austrian biplane flying over our lines, declaring that he planned to destroy the Austrian by striking him with his own undercarriage.

His fellow officers and men watched Nesterov's faster plane quickly climb, approach the Austrian plane, and make several attempts at collision, which the Austrian plane tried to avoid. Finally there was a terrific crash. The wings of the Austrian plane collapsed and it fell down in flames. For a moment the little Russian monoplane fell together with it in one mass, then it disentangled itself and appeared above the flying field, gracefully coming down with its undercarriage entirely gone. It made as good a landing as possible without an undercarriage. A few minutes after the landing Captain Nesterov died of a broken spine, his last conscious movement being to land the plane at its airfield.

Until we had to leave Russia after the revolution, all air-minded Russians considered September 5 a day of national mourning. Nesterov's tomb in the historic cemetery of Askold in Kiev, on the bank of the Dnieper River, was always a place of pilgrimage on September 5, and was covered with flowers. Captain Nesterov will live in history, not only as the first pilot to loop the loop, but also as the first pilot to bring down an enemy plane down in an aerial fight [on the Eastern Front].*

Coming back from this aerial diversion to the advance of my regiment, I recall that for the first few days after the battle of Skvarzava my battalion was marching constantly in the vanguard. I had maps of the country in front, I had exact directions from our headquarters as to the point we should reach, and in going forward I was taking my own precautions against a sudden ambush. I suppose that such a responsible appointment, that of actually leading our regiment by the maps, was given to me because I could read the maps of this hilly

* Nesterov's heroism was also celebrated in Soviet Russia. In 1951, both a town and a region were renamed Nesterov, and in 1962, the Central Aero Club of Russia sponsored the Nesterov Cup, to be awarded to winners of World Aerobatic Championships.

6. Nesterov's wrecked Morane-Saulnier G, No. 281. It crashed nose-first, with its undercarriage still attached and pieces of the Austrian Albatros two-seater entangled in its propeller. Nesterov fell out of the plane before it hit the ground. Sergievsky did not witness Nesterov's crash; his different account sounds like the kind of mythmaking that often followed the deaths of World War I air aces. *Courtesy of Alan Durkota.*

part of the country unusually well, due to my previous engineering education. The colonel of the regiment, after finding that out, developed a great trust in me, not only in my ability to read the complicated maps well, but also in my judgment about when to stop and investigate the unknown country ahead of us.

In the early morning of September 3, 1914, we entered the historic old city of Lemberg after an all-night march.* No resistance was offered. We had had only one engagement, lasting about three hours, on the previous day, but without big casualties on our side. Evidently, this was just an Austrian maneuver to delay our advance; apparently they had decided to abandon Lemberg without serious resistance. That surprised us at the time, because Lemberg, the capital of Galicia, is a large and beautiful city. Later we found out that the Austrians made this decision because of the extremely difficult situation on their left flank, where they had been in a disorderly and rapid retreat. I believe that I was actually the first Russian officer to enter the city of Lemberg.

* Like much of the area where Sergievsky fought, Lemberg later changed hands—and names— several times. Lemberg was the city's name under the Austro-Hungarian Empire. Between the World Wars it became part of newly independent Poland, as Lwów. After 1945, it was absorbed into the Soviet Union as Lvov. Today, part of Ukraine, it is called L'viv.

7. Russian troops of the 33rd Infantry Division enter Lemberg on September 3, 1914; they could well be members of Sergievsky's 125th Kursk Infantry Regiment, which he led into the city. *Courtesy of Corbis-Bettmann.*

With many precautions we passed the first few houses. Women were standing on the balconies throwing flowers to our soldiers and shouting "Hail Russia!" As soon as I saw this, I sent a report to the colonel briefly outlining the situation. In a few minutes he rode up on his handsome horse, followed by his staff officers, and the band began to play our beautiful regimental march. With flying banners and beautiful music, we entered the city of Lemberg in parade formation.

On this memorable day I was the regimental officer of the day, and therefore I was in the regimental headquarters tent, situated in a central plaza of the city, where the regiment was in bivouac. No one was allowed inside the houses. At every stop, connection with the field telephone was established immediately.

A War of Movement

Unlike the trench warfare on the Western Front, where an advance of a few hundred yards was regularly proclaimed as a major victory, World War I on the Eastern Front was a war of maneuver. Vast armies moved back and forth over hundreds of miles, advancing and wheeling and encircling as they seldom did on the blood-soaked fields of France and Flanders. Boris Sergievsky took part in three of these great military movements: two were advances of the Imperial Russian forces, one a retreat.

The 1914 Galician Campaign was Russia's major success of the war. It was fought against Austria-Hungary, another shaky multiethnic empire, and the only major belligerent whose bumbling army was even more incompetent than Russia's own. Some of Austria-Hungary's rifles were obsolete single-shooters; its cavalrymen made easy targets in their brilliant red and blue uniforms; and units of Slav soldiers surrendered by the thousands to their ethnic brethren, the Russians. Reflecting the empire's power relations, three-fourths of Austria-Hungary's officers were of German-speaking stock, but only one enlisted man in four even spoke the language.[1] The resulting muddle was immortalized in Jaroslav Hašek's classic novel, *The Good Soldier Schweik.*

During the opening months of the war, despite being soundly defeated by the Germans farther north, the Russians pushed deep into Austria-Hungary. Russian forces swept southwest across the plains of Galicia—land that today lies mostly in Poland and Ukraine. They seized thousands of square miles of territory and the region's major city, Lemberg, into which Sergievsky led a vanguard unit of Russian troops in September 1914 (see p. 36). Galicia's largely Slavic population often welcomed the arriving Russians. By the end of the year, though, the Tsar's troops had reached the natural barrier of the Carpathian Mountains. Fierce fighting (pp. 46–67) continued, but for some months terrain and winter stopped the war movement.

The 1915 Retreat was the war's biggest defeat for the Russians, a humiliating disaster that evoked in the Army the first signs of the mutinous discontent that would later topple the Tsar. The Russians were crippled by supply shortages and by artillery that was sometimes more than fifty years old. The inept Austro-Hungarian troops were stiffened with German reinforcements and state-of-the-art big guns from Prague's famous Skoda works. The Central Powers forces rolled back the Russian armies, including Sergievsky's regiment (p. 67), by several hundred miles, taking Warsaw, Vilnius, Pinsk, and other major cities that had been within the Russian Empire's borders. Between May 1 and November 1, 1915, the Russian armies lost an estimated 1.4 million soldiers killed and wounded, or more than 7,500 *a day*.[2]

One Russian general described the scene:

Creeping like some huge beast, the German army would move its advanced units close to the Russian trenches. . . . Next, that gigantic beast would draw its tail, the heavy artillery, toward the trenches. That heavy artillery would take up positions in places which were almost or entirely beyond the range of the Russian field artillery, and the heavy guns would start to shower their shells on the Russian trenches, doing it methodically, as was characteristic of the Germans. That hammering would go on until nothing of the trenches remained, and their defenders would be destroyed. Then the beast would cautiously stretch out its paws, the infantry units, which would seize the demolished trenches. . . . During . . . counter attacks the Russians would suffer enormous losses, since the German infantry, halting its advance, would take cover in the shell holes which were everywhere, and open fire from close range. Having gained full possession of the Russian trenches the "beast" would draw up its tail again, and its heavy guns would start their methodical hammering of the next Russian line of defense.[3]

Another general wrote: "The retreat from Galicia was one vast tragedy for the Russian army. No cartridges, no shells. Bloody fighting and difficult marches day after day. No end to weariness, physical as well as moral. Faint hopes followed by sinister dread. . . . Blood flowed unendingly, the ranks became thinner and thinner, the number of graves constantly multiplied."[4]

The Brusilov Offensive in the summer of 1916, in which Sergievsky took part as an airman (p. 73) was the last major Russian advance of the war. At the cost of nearly half a million casualties,[5] troops commanded by General Alexei Brusilov managed to recapture a swath of enemy-held territory, mostly in much fought-over Galicia. For the first time, Russian aircraft used radios to direct artillery fire. The offensive helped the Western allies by diverting German and Austro-Hungarian troops. But the Russians' success was far less dramatic than their Galician conquests of 1914, and, in the end, was not enough to change the course of the war in the east.

AH

One of the duties of the officer of the day was to write down the important messages received over the field telephone.

We were not an hour in Lemberg when the following order from General Lutsky was received: "The 33rd Division immediately to march a forced march to Rava-Russkaya." That was all.

Before transferring that order to the regimental commander, I looked at the map. To my surprise, I found that the march ordered for this day was seventy kilometers. I carried the order into the colonel's tent. The general commanding the division, the four colonels of the regiment, and the two brigadier generals assembled in a few minutes in our regimental tent. After a brief conference, I was handed a message signed by the division commander, asking General Lutsky for a confirmation of his order, and informing him that the 33rd Division was exhausted beyond description after making a previous day's march of forty-five kilometers, and having engaged in several skirmishes in the course of this advance. The message added that most of the men were already asleep, that they had not yet been fed, and if possible a postponement of the march should be granted until the next day.

No sooner was my message sent than I received General Lutsky's answer, every word of which I still remember: "The state of the 33rd Division is known to me, but the aim of the march is so important that it must start immediately."

That was the longest march I ever made without a stop. On a forced march you do not observe the ten-minute intervals after every hour, or the midday

An Austrian Defeat

Stanley Washburn, the *Times of London* correspondent in Russia, witnessed the aftermath of the Russian victory over the Austro-Hungarians at Rava-Russkaya, the destination of the forced march Sergievsky describes on pp. 39–41.

The Austrians, let it be said, were in an extremely strong position round this quaint little town, and were prepared to defend themselves to the last ditch, which in fact they did. . . .

Each trench tells its own story of defence. Piles and piles of empty cartridges, accoutrements and knick-knacks are heaped in every ditch. Right across the field between their positions is written their hurried change of line, with new graves and hundreds of haversacks scattered in between. Then comes another trench with the same signs of patient endurance under shot and shell. . . . One can walk for hundreds of yards stepping from one shell hole into another, each five feet deep and perhaps ten feet across. One can pick up the dirt of the trenches and sift the shrapnel balls out in handfuls. . . . In every direction from each shell hole are strewn the fragments of blue cloth of the Austrian uniform, torn into shreds and ribbons by the force of the explosive; and all about the field are still bits of arms, a leg in a boot, or some other ghastly token of soldiers, true to discipline, holding on to a position that was alive with bursting shells and flying shrapnel.

Beyond this line was the artillery position of the Austrians, and here again we find heaps upon heaps of brass shrapnel shells, with shattered wheels and splinters of caissons in every direction. This last stand finally caved in, and the next field, dotted with dead horses, shows where the remnant of the Austrian artillery took its way.[1]

AH

one-hour break. In ordering the march, the general of the division, the two brigadier generals, and all the colonels of the division gave orders to send all the officers' horses, including their own horses, back to the train. Their decision was to go on foot together with the men and suffer with them the difficulties of the march, setting an example of endurance and devotion to duty.

After the first two hours of the march, men started to drop from exhaustion. The others would step right over them and go on at the same quick pace set by the head column. By the time night arrived I was so tired that I actually fell asleep while walking, and woke up only when I bumped into the rear man of the company ahead. I never before believed that a man could be fast asleep while walking, but it is a fact that at least half of the men were walking in their sleep.

When we reported that we had reached our destination, Rava-Russkaya, I do not believe that 10 percent of the division actually had reached it; Rava-Russkaya was occupied by this 10 percent. The remaining men kept coming on, following after they had a few minutes' rest on the road and had regained their strength after falling down. They kept coming for hours, on into the following day.

The day after we occupied Rava-Russkaya, we realized what drove the commander of our army, General Lutsky, to give such an order and force us to such a superhuman effort. By occupying Rava-Russkaya, we cut the path of retreat of the Austrian army operating in Poland. As a result of our march, 270,000 prisoners were taken the next day. Many batteries of Austrian artillery, being cut off, surrendered without a shot. A few score Austrian general staff officers were led into the headquarters of our division general. That day was actually a defeat for the whole Austrian Army; after that, the Austrians never offered serious resistance to our Army without the help of German armies.

General Lutsky was a real hero, adored by his officers and men. Everybody had complete faith in his judgment, knowledge, and military genius. Our own losses were negligible. There was hardly any fighting, it was all done by maneuvers, which cut the lines of retreat and made fighting useless and impossible for the Austrians.

To our great disappointment, immediately after this operation, which put Galicia under Russian control, General Lutsky was promoted to command of a group of armies on the Northern Front and a Bulgarian, General Radko-Dimitriev, was appointed commander of our Third Army.

The career of General Radko-Dimitriev was startling. He rose to great prominence in the Balkan War of 1912 and was considered one of the national heroes of Bulgaria, but when the Great War of 1914 started and Bulgaria joined the Central Powers, General Radko-Dimitriev fled with several other Bulgarian high officers and they all joined the Russians as volunteers. General Radko-Dimitriev had been educated at the Russian Military Academy, knew Russian military ways and the Russian language very well, and brought with him his splendid record in the Balkan War of 1912. He soon was promoted from command of a brigade to a division, then a corps, and succeeded General Lutsky in command of the Third Russian Army.

Apparently the Balkan War was different from the one against Austria and Germany. Despite General Radko-Dimitriev's personal bravery, and his honest efforts to maintain the standard of success of the Third Army which General Lutsky had established, every officer and man of the Third Army felt the difference in his handling of difficult situations. The command of General Radko-Dimitriev was unlucky for him and for us.

After we captured Rava-Russkaya, our advance through Galicia met hardly any resistance. Quite a few days (or rather nights, because from that time on we were ordered to advance at night to elude the vigilant Austro-German air observers) we marched on, making our twenty-five kilometers daily, and soon reached the slopes of the Carpathian Mountains. From some of the summits of the Carpathian Mountains we were looking already into Hungary. Our division had advanced far into western Galicia, in the direction of Kraków.

I remember spending one night in the little town of Wieliczka, which is the distance of a gunshot from the forts of Kraków. Wieliczka is famous for its salt mines, but, unfortunately, we had no time to inspect them. The morning after we entered it, we received a rush order for a flanking movement to the south. The Austrians were making a general advance, reinforced by the Bavarian Guards taken off the Western Front, and fierce fighting began.

Through beautiful forests and valleys of the lower Carpathian Mountains we marched day and night, directed to a destination where fierce fighting was going on. In the early hours of December 9, 1914, our hurried march stopped. An officer from the 164th Regiment met us on the road and transmitted his commanding officer's urgent request for a battalion to reinforce their position, because the Bavarian Guards were advancing toward them. My battalion was sent to follow this messenger.

Almost running, we went about two kilometers forward, where we were met by a colonel of the 164th Regiment, who was in a highly nervous state. He was standing at the left flank of his regiment, which was spread in battle formation on a hillside. Hurriedly he told me, as the first officer to reach him, that his left flank was exposed, and toward his left was moving a great number of the Bavarian Guards. If we did not stop them, it could be a disaster because his regiment was at the left flank of the army and his defeat would mean the defeat of the army. Giving me the general direction, he told me, "Now, do your duty as you see best. I must attend to my own regiment." With these words he left me.

Looking across the valley through my field glasses, I saw, at a distance of about one kilometer, several battalions of Germans moving through the forest clearings in closed columns. Something had to be done immediately. I advanced to a place in the forest where I could hide my men in the thick underbrush. There was a wide clearing at the front, beyond which stood scattered pine trees. We were in the direct path of the advancing German battalions if they did not change their direction.

8. Russian ski troops advance through a forest in the Carpathian Mountains late in 1914. Sergievsky's battle with the Bavarian Guards took place in woods like these. *Courtesy of Corbis-Bettmann.*

I had time enough to see each soldier of my company properly placed, and to say a few words to each group of them, telling them that in such a situation, discipline of fire is most important and not a shot should be fired without my command. Then I ascertained that the next company of my battalion was to my left, so that my flank was properly protected, and went to my observation point right in the middle of the company, any second expecting the appearance of the first Germans on the far side of the clearing.

At this moment, when everything was in tense readiness, from under the pine trees on the other side of the clearing I heard moans and shouts in Russian.

I did not dare to go very far forward toward them because the Germans would appear any moment, and I might find myself between the firing line of my own company and the Germans. But I advanced, running forward as fast as I could, trying to see what was going on. There, scattered under the trees in the grass, lay about twenty men of the 164th Regiment, who had been patrolling the left flank of their regiment and were wounded encountering an advance German patrol. Hearing the branches crack under the columns of the Bavarian Guards on one side of the clearing and seeing our fighting formation on the other, they realized the danger of their situation, and begged me in the name of God to remove them before we started firing.

Through the trees I could already distinguish in my field glasses the first advancing columns of Germans. To give in to my pity for the wounded soldiers would be to lose the battle not only for myself, but very probably for the army. Several of my soldiers volunteered to take a chance and run forward and drag their wounded comrades to our line. I had to order everybody to remain at their stations and crawled back to my position in the center of my company. Then I stood up there, hidden by the thick underbrush, looking at the advancing line of Germans and trying to estimate the distance and the exact time to give the order for the first volley.

The first battalion of Germans to appear was moving in a rather careless manner, evidently unaware of our presence. Their patrol that had met and defeated the patrol of the 164th Regiment had reported the road clear and the Germans believed they were making an unopposed flanking movement.

I could clearly see an older gentleman, probably the commander of the battalion, and about twenty officers in single file behind him, and then a solid column of the Guards Regiment behind them, marching with their rifles on their shoulders.

When they were about 500 paces from our line I gave the order for the first volley. After that, I could not control the fire of my company. A few men took aim before shooting, while most of them fired without aiming. But their fire was so intense that not only the advance column fell under it, but also the high pine trees on the other side of the clearing; cut through at their roots by our bullets, they fell together with the German soldiers.

It is hard for me to say how long the shooting lasted. The surviving Germans all fell to the ground, along with the killed and wounded, and started to fire at our positions. But we were well hidden in our bushes, and they were firing without seeing us, being well exposed themselves. I believe the whole fight lasted not more than ten minutes. In this time my company used up most of its ammunition. I had sent for some more cases when I realized the number of Germans advancing on us, and I knew that there was going to be a lot of shooting.

Now I eagerly awaited the arrival of the ammunition, seeing that the last cartridges were being shot away in a panicky fire which I could not stop. But when the cases of ammunition arrived we did not need them. I could walk right over the place where the Germans were a few minutes ago. The twenty wounded men of the 164th Regiment, lying between the Germans and ourselves, were of course instantly killed by the first volley.

I could not count the number of killed in this encounter. It was not a fight, our casualties were negligible; it was almost a slaughter. More than two thousand men were piled up one on top of another under our fire, and now were lying there in this clearing in the Carpathian Mountains.

In the previous few months, my nerves had become well acquainted with the horrors of war, but on this particular day there were actually moments when I could not stand it. I was on the verge of a nervous breakdown when a messenger from headquarters arrived to tell me that, following the report of the colonel of the 164th Regiment, the commander of our division congratulated me for saving the whole situation on this front, and said that on his report I was going to be awarded some sort of a high medal or decoration by the Tsar of Russia.

When the tension of these minutes of waiting and panicky firing was over, the soldiers of my company were extremely happy. They immediately wanted to rush over and find some sort of booty on the dead Guardsmen. The only thing we allowed them to take, and even ordered them to take was the rifles. I took as souvenirs several engraved officers' swords for myself. But the amount of rifles and ammunition piled up with the dead bodies of the Bavarian Guards was so great that it could not be carried by one company. I had to send for wagons and trucks to come haul it away.

We had to remain in this position for one more day, but no more attacks were made on this front, the attack of the Bavarian Guards having been checked right there.

My experience, as I found out later, was not unique. The same picture was presented down the line for several kilometers. Transferred from the French Front, the Bavarian Guards were misinformed as to the quality of the Russian

Army and the intensity of our fire. As a result, the division we encountered ceased to exist on that chilly December day.

After the battle of Mukhovka with the Bavarian Guards, we continued our march to the south, mainly going along the eastern slopes of the Carpathian Mountains and marching at night to hide from enemy aerial observation. Around December 20, we approached a place where very fierce fighting was going on. The infantry division we were about to replace had already lost several of its battalions in the fighting over one key mountain, referred to as "384". If, during the day, the Russian Army took possession of this mountain, towards morning it would be taken away again in fierce attacks by the Austro-Hungarian Army.

My battalion was kept in reserve when the First Battalion of my regiment was sent to attack the mountain. In command of the First Battalion was my former battalion commander, Colonel Kanzerov, who had been so severely wounded in the first battle, and who had just returned from the hospital. He led his battalion splendidly, and took possession of Mountain 384, taking quite a number of prisoners and machine guns.

That was in the afternoon of December 21, 1914. Just before daybreak a messenger from regimental headquarters woke me up, and when I reported to headquarters I was told that our battalion had to start immediately for Mountain 384, where something strange had happened to the First Battalion. Nobody seemed to know what actually had happened there, but the telephone communication was interrupted and they could not get in touch with Colonel Kanzerov.

Taking the usual precautions, we started for Mountain 384. At the foot of it we found Colonel Kanzerov in a little abandoned hut with two men of his liaison service. In the few months I had known Colonel Kanzerov, I had never seen him in such a state of depression and collapse. When I asked him where his battalion was, what had happened, with eyes full of tears he pointed at the two men who were with him and told me in a broken voice that that was all that was left of the First Battalion. Then he sat down at the table and put his head down on his crossed hands. No further inquiries were necessary. We all understood that by a sudden night attack, Mountain 384 had been recaptured by the Austrians, and the Colonel and his two men were the only ones who had escaped death or capture. From the men we learned that the Colonel had actually cleared a way out for himself and his two men with a bayonet. We found out also that Mountain 384 was now held by one of the crack Hungarian regiments.

At this time my battalion, the Fourth, was commanded by Lieutenant Gladkovsky. A few months before the start of the war he had gone to a sanatorium, having tuberculosis, and was considering retirement from the Army due to ill health. When war broke out he returned to active duty, declaring that the doctors had pronounced his death sentence anyway, and he preferred to die like a soldier rather than in bed in some sanatorium. In all the previous engagements, he had showed that he meant what he said. He never tried to seek any protection from danger, never tried to be careful about his own person. We all had the impression that he wanted to get killed in action because be was getting weaker every day, his sickness progressing rapidly under the stresses of military life.

On this particular day he was feeling quite weak. He came to my company and told me frankly that his physical condition would be a serious handicap to the task before us, that he was not able to move and walk fast enough to be where he would be most needed, and as the task of our battalion was to recapture and retain Mountain 384 at any cost, he was entrusting his battalion to me.

I reminded him that I was not next in command, as two other company captains in the battalion were superior to me in rank and length of service. His answer was that he trusted my judgment, and that he believed that I would be better able to fulfill the difficult task ahead of us than any other officer of his battalion.

We had a short conference right there because by the growing light of the dawn, we could already make out the approaches to Mountain 384. Between the place where we were standing, hidden by the forest, and the steep slopes of Mountain 384 was a deep valley with a creek running through it. The slopes had patches of trees and bushes but were generally bare. On top of the mountain we could distinguish through our field glasses a rather primitive barbed-wire entanglement, partly destroyed by previous fighting, and trenches now occupied by the Hungarian regiment.

Following the order of my battalion commander, I took over the command and made an exact disposition of each company, and what paths they were to follow. The three companies were to attack simultaneously. The Fourth Company, which I retained under my personal command, was to follow behind, and strike at the moment and place I would choose.

Before it got quite light, the three companies rapidly marched out in battle formation. Remaining on the opposite slope and watching through field glasses, I saw their rapid progress up the steep sides of Mountain 384. They were about halfway up when they were noticed by the defenders of the mountain and a rapid rifle and machine gun fire started. By this time I was joined by a lieutenant of our artillery brigade, sent forward to correct the fire of our batteries by telephone. As it grew lighter we could easily tell where the most deadly machine-gun fire was coming from, and where the few field guns were situated that had been brought up during the night to help the Hungarian infantry. Our artillery fire was very successfully concentrated on these points, facilitating the advance of my three companies. From my observation point, it looked as if they were almost at the top when their forward motion was checked by enemy fire.

I could not expect that soldiers who had already gone such a long distance under fire, and now were digging in almost under the barbed wire of the Hungarian position, could get up again and gather enough momentum to drive forward for the final attack. It was time for the reserve company to act quickly.

When I took command of the battalion, I retained two messengers from each company, who were to be near me all the time. Three of them now were sent with orders for each company in the front lines not to move until my arrival, but on my signal, they were to open up the heaviest fire that they could maintain and keep it up as long as they could, not aiming at any particular thing but just covering the Hungarian trenches. I made the same request to our artillery officer, who was next to me. I asked him to telephone all the batteries that were in shelling range of our mountain to direct the heaviest frequent possible fire at the trenches and to keep it up until they were told to stop it entirely. Then we agreed on the signals I would give from the mountain, when I threw my men over the top for the final attack, to stop the shelling so that our artillery would not continue firing when we were on top of the trenches ourselves.

Everything was ready, and fierce fire started from our artillery and the three companies in front. My reserve company rapidly marched down the creek and up the slope. Our losses were negligible because the Hungarians could not see our advance, all their attention being concentrated on the three companies that were right in front of them. We halted at the last little forest on the slope of the mountain so that my soldiers could catch their breath and gather their strength. Then we started at a run, dashing up the mountain, and as we passed over the place occupied by our advance companies they joined us, getting up rapidly, and everybody made a rush for the top of the mountain. At this time I gave the appointed signal to our artillery observer, and our artillery fire stopped.

Hilltop Battlefields

From December 1914 through March 1915, Boris Sergievsky fought in the Carpathian Mountains, near where the borders of today's Ukraine, Poland, and Slovakia meet. It was here that Sergievsky won his Order of St. George (p. 52) for capturing a fortified mountain top, was wounded (p. 58), and took part in many other battles as well.

Bernard Pares, later knighted for his scholarly writings about Russia, was an official British observer with the Russian armies. In early 1915, he toured the Carpathian front. There is a tantalizing possibility that he met Sergievsky, for he describes the vivid impression made on him by a young officer who—exactly like Sergievsky—led the storming of a mountain crest, "was the first man into the [enemy] trenches"[1] and received the Order of St. George for this exploit. He describes this officer as "young, but dark and sallow, . . . to whom this part of the front had been entrusted. When I said I should like to visit it, he said, 'You'll be killed.' . . . He struck me and others as bearing a hard burden, and bearing it well."[2]

Pares's account of his visit, however, was published under wartime censorship, and Pares was not allowed to identify any Russian officers or units by name. So we will never know whether the dark, sallow, young officer was Sergievsky. In any case, Pares describes exactly the kind of fighting for strategic hills that Sergievsky took part in:

My orderly told me with pride that this was the best fighting Division in the army; certainly it has that reputation in other quarters and has three times in this campaign done decisive work against superior odds. It has rushed the Austrians from point to point, and would do so still unless they had taken refuge in the hill country before the Carpathians, where every hill has to be won in turn. . . .[3]

We had to climb one of the steepest hills I have ever gone up. Fortunately it was covered with light scrub: otherwise I should never have got to the top, for the frozen and clouted soil was so slippery that one slid back at every step. Yet up this hill the Russian troops had gone at night under the fire of the defending Austrians not many days before, and I was told that the ground was then in even worse condition. The storming of these hills one after the other calls for the most reckless courage.[4]

Pares watched the Russians repulse an Austrian attempt to recapture one hill:

In all some eight hundred shells must have been lodged on the hill on this day. . . . No fewer shots were fired the next day, and when I was later able to get to this ground, it was all harrowed up with enormous holes even in the gullies that ran crosswise through the hill itself. The [Russian] men crouched in the trenches where death threatened any exposed movement. . . .

A whole division of gallant Tirolese advanced on the projecting angle of the line. These are the best troops that Austria has left, and they were opposed to parts of two Russian regiments. They ensconced themselves at night in rifle pits on a lower ridge of the hill. . . .

And now came the reply. Standing up under the cannonade the Russian infantry, with the support of its machine guns, poured in such volleys that everything in front went down . . . the trenches occupied by the Tirolese became a line of corpses; no attempt was made to resist the bayonet . . . the whole attack . . . rolled down the hill, leaving 1,300 corpses in the wood and in the open; a number of prisoners, wounded and Red Cross men were left behind; and next day retreating columns, without even their baggage, were seen marching off into the hills beyond the river."[5]

AH

Not being so heavily loaded with ammunition as the soldiers, I ran a little faster than they could, and I actually found myself alone for a few seconds standing on top of Mountain 384. Several Hungarians rushed in my direction with their bayonets pointed at me, ready to throw me down the mountain slopes. I fought them off with my sword. The shooting ceased entirely and my soldiers appeared on all sides of the mountain. The real bayonet fight started then. It was the first one I had been in since the beginning of the war. In every previous engagement, when it came to the bayonet attack, our adversary had turned and run.

This time the Hungarians, being surrounded on all sides, put up a fierce bayonet fight. During this engagement, I delivered about twenty blows with my sword and emptied two loads of my service pistol at very close range.

When everything was over, and the remaining Hungarians threw down their rifles and raised their hands in surrender, I made a rough count of them and, giving them a small escort of my soldiers, I sent 570 prisoners to our division headquarters. Besides this, twelve machine guns and four pieces of field artillery were captured there. My service overcoat was ripped in many places by bullets and bayonets, but I had not a scratch on myself.

From the top of Mountain 384 I saw very clearly the whole line of the Austro-Hungarian position extending south. I was on their left flank and slightly behind it. All their barbed wire and trenches were directed east, and they were unprotected from the spot I was occupying. The opportunity of cleaning up a considerable part of their position by a flanking movement was so striking and so tempting that I did not wait for orders from headquarters, or for confirmation of my plan of action, which I rapidly drew in my field book and sent with the escort of prisoners to our division headquarters.

I left one company to hold the top of Mountain 384 and, with three companies in a very rapid march, started my flanking invasion of the Austro-Hungarian position, which I approached from their left and behind. Practically no resistance was offered. As we took one hill after another I sent my messengers to the Russian Army units across the valley, stating that the division front ahead of them was clear of the enemy and would they please advance as there would be no resistance ahead of them.

I proceeded in this way for almost ten kilometers along the Austro-Hungarian line until it grew dark. Then I called it a day and returned to my original Mountain 384, following the trenches occupied already by the battalions and regiments formerly facing this position.

At Mountain 384 I found an order from the colonel of my regiment to hold our position and to start an advance at daybreak. He already knew about my flanking attack and stated that due to its success he could not blame me for assuming too much responsibility.

The Austrians attempted to recapture Mountain 384 that same night, but we were well on the lookout and used the captured machine guns to repulse the attack.

The next morning at daybreak we started west, rapidly passing through a small town whose name I do not remember now, and which was almost completely abandoned by the population. We crossed two or three valleys during the day and in the evening found ourselves before another stronghold, shown on the map as Mountain 415.

Looking at the steep eastern slopes of this mountain I understood that it would be very difficult to take it from this direction. The western slopes of the mountain were gentle, and it occurred to me that if I could manage to go around the mountain and attack from the west, it would be a much easier task. But to do so we would have to cross the Austro-Hungarian lines somehow.

To the south of Mountain 415 was a narrow river with a thick growth of reeds on both banks and in the water. With a small party of scouts I went down to explore it and found that the river was about chest deep and had a hard bottom. But we could not proceed very far because the Austro-Hungarian lines extended right down to the river and, noticing our scouting party, they started shooting.

After it got dark I chose two companies and ordered them to take everything in their equipment that would make any sort of noise and tie it tightly with string and soft rags. Then without a sound we slipped into the river in single file.

We marched chest deep in the water, and passed along the Austro-Hungarian line unnoticed. We were well hidden by the reeds, and after I was sure that we had gone at least half a kilometer behind the Austro-Hungarian lines, we climbed out of the water. We were all very cold and uncomfortable, but the idea of the surprise we were going to give the enemy in the morning warmed us.

At daybreak, without a single shot we rushed the position on Mountain 415 from behind. It was a very easy, almost bloodless victory. From the top of Mountain 415 I sent a report that it was in our possession. I accompanied my report with almost 1,000 prisoners.

I received word that my capture of Mountain 415, and my flanking movement of the previous day, had forced a general retreat of several Austro-

Hungarian army corps from this sector. My reports from my field book, telling other regiments along the line that they could safely advance, that I had cleared the hills in front of them, were forwarded to army headquarters, and our army commander sent a telegram to the Tsar of Russia, requesting that I be awarded the Officers' Cross of Saint George.

This decoration was created by Catherine the Great, and it was considered the highest award that anyone could receive. It could not be given by a simple order, even of the Tsar. Every time the award of this decoration was considered, a commission of high-ranking officers and representatives of the general staff had to investigate and report, because personal bravery was not sufficient to earn the Order of Saint George. There had to be clear proof that the actions of an officer being nominated had positively affected the outcome of a major battle.

As an example of how highly prized that decoration was and how unusual it was to receive it, one of the first Orders of Saint George in the war was conferred on General Joffre after be had won the battle of the Marne. Every other military decoration was a part of the imperial privileges of the Tsar, but the Order of Saint George was awarded to Nicholas II only late in 1916, after the great advance of General Brusilov, when Nicholas II was in supreme command. The Tsar of Russia valued this decoration so much that he never parted with it, even after the Revolution. It was the only decoration that he always wore, and it was on his chest when he was executed with his family in 1918.

The Order of Saint George is a simple-looking golden cross covered by white enamel, with a black and yellow ribbon. In Imperial Russia it gave tremendous privileges to the few who were lucky enough to have it. One of the privileges was the right to call on the Tsar and speak to him at any time of day or night. To an Officer of the Cross of Saint George, access to the Tsar could not be denied. There were many other privileges in the service and also in private life, and to receive the Order of Saint George was the ultimate dream of everyone in the Army.

A few days later a telegraphic reply arrived from Army headquarters. At about lunchtime an orderly from the colonel came to summon me to regimental headquarters. When I arrived there I found all the officers assembled, and at my entrance the colonel ordered everybody to stand up. I was standing at attention when he came toward me and read the telegraphic order signed by the Tsar himself, which awarded me the Order of Saint George and promoted me one rank higher, to first lieutenant.

The colonel unfastened from his chest the Order of Saint George that he had received in the Japanese campaign of 1904 and pinned it on my uniform.

A few weeks later my own decoration arrived from headquarters together with all the necessary accompanying papers. But this little weather-beaten white cross that my colonel had worn since the campaign of 1904 is still one of my most valued possessions.

The next few days of December we marched south again. At Christmas we reached the banks of the River San in Galicia. There we fought a fierce battle that lasted three days for possession of the western shore. In this battle I lost one of my very best friends, whom I had known since my student days in Kiev, and who was my partner in the last carefree days in Rovno, when we both fell in love with the musical comedy star.

9. Sergievsky treasured this blurred photo because it caught the moment when his colonel pinned his own Order of Saint George on Sergievsky's uniform. *Courtesy of the editors.*

Although he was reported killed, I did not want to believe it unless I could find his body. After the battle at the San was over I searched the field myself for many, many hours until I found him with a bullet wound right through his heart. His left hand was still grasping his pistol, and his right hand was holding his sword.

My friend's death was a very heavy blow to me, although he must have died instantly because his face did not express any suffering or pain. I arranged for a separate grave for him, having in mind that perhaps his relatives, who were very dear friends of mine, would later want to take his body back to Russia.

Although we took possession of the western shore of the River San, it was not considered safe for the whole army to remain there, having the river right in back of us, and a river which was not easily crossed.

The roads in Galicia were almost impassable in winter, and as the weather grew worse and worse, it was quite apparent that there was going to be a standstill, probably until spring. We withdrew to the eastern shore of the River San, while holding the bridges, and building on the western shore in front of each bridge a small fortification called a bridgehead. This sort of arrangement allows the whole army to be more comfortable behind a river that is difficult to cross. At the same time it makes it easy to advance to the other side without having to force the river crossing again in difficult and heavy battles.

Naturally, the enemy always concentrates on these bridgeheads, and does all in its power to sieze the bridges. Holding these fanlike fortifications in front of bridges is a very strenuous and responsible task, and the battalions assigned to it have to be relieved, as a rule, every three days. When my battalion occupied one of these fortifications on the River San it was Christmas. The trenches in the very low ground were half full of mud and water. The shooting never let up. In some spots the German lines were as close to our fortifications as seventy paces. Constant vigilance was necessary. Only a third of the men were allowed to sleep, and they had to sleep fully dressed with rifles in their hands. The rest of the men were actually standing knee deep in mud and water with their eyes fixed on the enemy line. Not one of the officers slept at night. We took turns napping once in a while only during the day.

The narrow bridge we were holding was under constant fire day and night. Every attempt to cross it during the day, even by single soldiers, was unsuccessful. The distance was so short that sharpshooters could shoot anyone who tried to cross it while it was light enough to see. Communication with the other shore was made only at night. At night also the engineers repaired the damage done to the bridge during the day by the constant firing.

The Germans continued to fire at the bridge at night, but that was blind shooting; they could not see what was going on and could not aim. They simply knew the direction and fired at intervals of a few minutes.

Food supplies were carried across the bridge only by men on foot. On the first night, we attempted to take across a field kitchen, but a rocket flare illuminated the bridge long enough for the enemy artillery to destroy the kitchen. After that, we did not dare to send a field kitchen across, and our food supply was rather irregular.

The shooting in this particular section was so intense that it was decided not to attempt to relieve the battalion at the bridgehead, because that would necessitate one battalion crossing west and another crossing east, and heavy losses would result from such a movement. Therefore, my battalion remained at the bridgehead for forty days.

We did not have heavy losses during this time, but at the end of forty days I myself, and all the officers and men of the battalion were exhausted from lack of sleep and from not having a chance to wash or change our clothes; we were awfully dirty and very uncomfortable. It was a great relief when we were sent back to rest in the reserve.

The second day after we were relieved, I was called to the regimental headquarters and the Colonel informed me that I was going to be sent to Kiev, my hometown, for two weeks on special duty. This was before regular leaves were allowed in the Army, and I was very fortunate to receive such an assignment. I don't think it took me more than half an hour to get ready after I had received this order.

In the fighting zone all the railroads were damaged, and I had to go about 100 kilometers on horseback before I could board a train. I traveled this 100 kilometers at such a pace that when I arrived at the station my horse fell dead. This horse was not my regular regimental horse—I used one of the captured Austrian horses—but I felt very sorry for it.

The train that took me from this unknown little town in Galicia to Lemberg was traveling about thirty kilometers an hour and some of the stops were unbearably long. From Lemberg to Kiev there was regular railroad communication, fast and efficient.

I was not expected at home, and it was a great joy and a great surprise to my family when I arrived. The two weeks of my special duties in Kiev went by too quickly for me.

Nobody was ever allowed to know the location of any particular part of the Army. Returning to the front, I was instructed not to go to the same station I started from, but to report first to Army headquarters. From Army headquarters I was sent to corps area headquarters, then to division headquarters. The location of my regiment was revealed to me only at division headquarters. I realized that it had shifted considerably south.

When I finally found my regiment it was high in the Carpathian Mountains, many miles south of where I had left it two weeks before. The winter weather made maneuvers impossible; everything was at a standstill. On both the Austrian and our sides the roads were almost impassable. Ammunition could not be brought forward fast enough, artillery could not move, and the only thing we could do was to make our trenches as comfortable as possible for the duration of the winter.

Once in a while we would try to seize some mountaintop which would offer certain advantages of shooting and observation, but such activities were only of local value.

In one of the engagements in this mountain warfare, when I was leading my company in a local attack, an Austrian shell burst right in front of me and ripped the holster of my pistol to pieces, at the same time wounding one of the soldiers right beside me. The Austrians mounted a swift counterattack, led by a *Jaeger* regiment. As we were heavily outnumbered, we had to retreat rapidly to our trenches.

For a moment I was left alone with the soldier who had just been wounded and had fallen in my path. This man was one of my orderlies who carried orders to other companies. I knew him by name and by face and I hated the idea of leaving him wounded there. I picked him up and carried him for quite a distance down the hill until I found some soldiers to help me, and then we turned him over to the stretcher bearers. At the time I did not attach any importance to the incident, and eventually forgot the man's name. After he got well he was sent to some other regiment, which often happened. I did not see him again until a very strange and tragic moment during the revolution, when he had an opportunity to fully repay me for what I had done for him.

In November of 1918, I went alone to the airport a few miles out of Kiev to put a few shots into the engine of my special single-seat fighter, which was liable to be captured by the Bolsheviks at any moment. I did not want them to have such a fine plane as my especially fast and well-armed fighter.

I was almost too late. The advancing lines of Bolsheviks were already around the airport. When they heard the two shots I put through the engine of my plane, several men rushed to the hangar, pursuing me and shooting at me when I ran out the back door of the hangar and across the field toward the railroad station. We exchanged several shots, but I had only an automatic pistol and they had rifles, and there were hundreds of them against me.

When I reached the railroad station the Reds came running from almost every direction, attracted by the shooting, and I considered myself lost. I had no ammunition left, I was exhausted from running, and I had no place to hide.

Then from one of the locomotives standing near the platform I heard a surprised shout, "Is that you, Captain Sergievsky?" I lifted my head and saw the engineer's familiar face, but I could not locate where I had seen it before. He shouted to me, "Come up here, quick!" I climbed up on the locomotive without asking any further questions. He gave full steam ahead and through volleys of shots from the Reds we swept on to Kiev.

This man was the same soldier I had carried down the side of a mountain in Galicia in one of the battles of February 1915. His debt to me was paid in full.

Easter of 1915 found us in trenches in southern Galicia. The roads were still in an impossible state, and most of our time was devoted to trying to make the trenches as dry and comfortable as possible.

In early March 1915, I heard the excited voice of our colonel on the phone. He was congratulating everybody on the line for the capture of Fortress Przemýsl, considered impregnable by military authorites. From the very outbreak of the war it was surrounded by the Russian Army. Several attempts were made to capture it by force, but the Russian Army had heavy losses and no success. In March of 1915, due to lack of food and ammunition, a white flag was displayed on the fort, and the garrison of Przemýsl surrendered. It was a very pleasant and unexpected surprise, which was celebrated throughout Russia as one of the greatest victories of this campaign.

Inspired by this success, our high command suggested an advance in the Carpathian Mountains, in order to occupy a higher ridge which was looming in front of us.

On March 28, 1915, I led an attack of my company up the steep hill of the mountain. My target was a Hungarian artillery battery. Following the terrain, we were able to approach the battery with almost no losses. But we had to rush the few remaining meters in the open. I started to run as fast as I could, closely followed by the soldiers of my company, whom I had ordered to leave all their bags and most of their ammunition in the trench in order to be faster and lighter. I thought we would get all our supplies after we captured the battery. The infantrymen who were supposed to protect the battery had already run away in a panic, fleeing our bayonet attack, but the artillerymen remained at their stations.

I heard the command in German of, "Battery, fire!" and immediately felt a severe pain in my right elbow, right side, and forehead and blood streaming down my face.

I fell down from the shock, but immediately got up again and saw that no one was around me. The moment that I was shot down my men turned and retreated behind the first little hill to give them protection from the fire.

The second lieutenant of my company rushed to my side and helped me out; then I was turned over to stretcher bearers and carried down to our trenches. I did not find any actual wounds on my right side or my right elbow, but my coat and shirt were ripped to shreds on both my right side and sleeve, and my skin was actually torn off. I am sure that the whole artillery shell went under my arm, ripping my clothes, and taking off the skin on my right side and on the inner side of my arm.

A fragment of steel was deep in my forehead above my left eye. The doctor in the hospital later found out it stopped very close to the brain after damaging the nerve of the left eye (at that time I was blind in my left eye).

There was no way to get from our trenches to the regiment's headquarters except on horseback or on foot. In the state I was in, I could not very well go on foot, and could not safely ride, but somehow I got astride a very quiet horse and two of my men walked on either side to catch me if I should fall or faint. It took me a whole day to reach regimental headquarters.

There the regimental surgeon discovered, in addition to the wounds I already knew about, that I had a shell fragment deep in the calf of my right leg, my boot being actually filled with blood. The pain in my forehead and my skinned side and arm had been so great that for almost twenty-four hours I did not notice the wound in the leg.

The regimental surgeon made an attempt to extricate the shrapnel in my forehead, but he found the operation too complicated to be performed in the field hospital. He suggested that I go as quickly as possible to the division post. He treated all my other wounds very efficiently.

In a hospital wagon I was sent to the town of Ivano-Frankovsk where the big Army hospital base was. Just a few days before a serious engagement had started near Ivano-Frankovsk, and all the hospitals were full of wounded, the doctors and nurses working twenty-four hours a day. The doctor who examined my wound told me that the reason the operation was so complicated was due to the fact that my optic nerve was damaged. He warned me that if I did not have this operation I would remain blind. He knew of only one surgeon who could do this operation successfully, and that surgeon was in the Red Cross Hospital in Kiev.

I asked to be evacuated to Kiev immediately. I got all the necessary papers, but I found out that I would have to wait at least one week. All the Red Cross trains were fully occupied. So I decided to travel on my own.

I went to the railroad station, where I found out that all the places in the trains were taken for the next three days, but that I could reserve a place on the fourth day if I wished. I knew from the previous conversation with the doctors that by that time I would have no hope of restoring my eyesight. I went to the military commander of the station. To my surprise I recognized him as an officer of my own regiment who had been badly wounded in one of the first battles and, as he remained an invalid, had been assigned to this post.

In a few words I explained my situation to him. He went with me to the train and found a compartment occupied by two generals of the General Staff who were going to Kiev on some sort of special mission. When we told the generals what was at stake if I did not get passage on this train, they were perfectly willing to share their compartment with me.

I think that I offered a very pitiful sight. My whole head was bandaged, leaving only my right eye open. My right arm was in a sling, and I was very badly lamed by the shot through my right leg. My orderly was traveling with me to help me to walk around and take care of my baggage.

When I arrived in Kiev, before going to the hospital I went straight home. My son, who was four then, tells me now that his first memory in life is my arrival, all bandaged, at the house. This sight of his father struck his young imagination so strongly that he does not remember anything before or after, but he still clearly remembers that homecoming.

The next day I reported to the famous surgeon, who performed the operation

While Rome Burned

Seldom has a large army gone to war as ill prepared and as incompetently led as the Imperial Russian forces in World War I.

Like the other major belligerents, Russia assumed the war would be short. But, unlike them, it did not have the factories to make arms for a long one. When Russia ran short of supplies, it turned to England and France for help. But Allied supply ships had to dock at icebound ports in the Russian Arctic or at Vladivostok on the Pacific, a third of the way around the world from the front lines in Europe.[1] Railway service was chaotic, locomotives broke down, and trainloads of key munitions got forgotten on remote sidings. Months after Russia withdrew from the war, crates of disassembled Sopwith and Nieuport fighter planes and other war supplies were found that had been sitting near the docks at Murmansk for years.

The Russian military was rife with featherbedding. "Senior officers were never retired, but hung about the barracks gambling and drawing full pay," writes Alan Clark.[2] Bribery was endemic: "A celebrated story recounts how a French businessman, seeking a contract to supply 10,000 platoon tents, was duly placing his bribes in the Ministry of War. Finally he came to the highest point, the minister's personal secretary. . . . To the businessman's alarm the private secretary insisted on a personal 'gratuity' equal in size to all the lesser disbursements which he had been obliged to make on the way up. He protested that, if this last sum were paid out, he would have no profit left on the order. 'Ah,' replied the secretary with a silky smile, 'I understand. But why deliver the tents?'"[3]

Top army commanders got their jobs for their connections at Court. One army corps, according to historian W. Bruce Lincoln, was commanded by a general who "was unable to conduct operations because his nerves could not stand the sound of rifle fire."[4] While Russian soldiers died by the hundreds of thousands in late 1914, special trains still brought fresh flowers each week from the Crimea to the Tsarina's palace in St. Petersburg. When the catastrophic defeats at the hands of the Germans could no longer be concealed, authorities turned on the traditional scapegoat for all Russia's troubles, the Jews. Pillaging, whip-wielding Cossacks and other troops brutally drove some 800,000 Jews from their homes.[5]

After the Russian Army, reeling from the Germans, managed to capture some territory from the weaker Austro-Hungarians, officials with little sense of priorities sent priests to convert newly conquered subjects to Russian Orthodoxy. "Here I am expecting trainloads of ammunition," fumed Army Commander-in-Chief Grand Duke Nicholas Nikolaevich, "And they send me trainloads of priests!"[6]

The Grand Duke had an odd sense of priorities himself. He let it be known that after-dinner conversation at his headquarters should be on "diversionary themes not concerning the conduct of the war."[7] Nicholas Nikoaevich's main military qualifications appeared to be royal blood and height: at 6 feet 6 inches, he towered impressively over all other officers, which was considered a great asset. At Army headquarters, the Grand Duke kept hitting his head on door frames. Aides pinned pieces of paper to them, to warn him to duck.

After still more defeats, Tsar Nicholas II himself took over as commander-in-chief. But he knew even less of military matters than his uncle, the Grand Duke. He watched parades, toured the countryside near headquarters in his Rolls-Royce, played dominoes, and issued odd orders, such as one promoting all the officers who happened to attend a ceremonial dinner. "My brain is resting here . . . no troublesome questions demanding thought,"[8] he wrote.

Added to these woes were Russia's size and primitiveness. At the start of the war, Russian troops tended to fire on all airplanes; not having seen any before, they believed such exotic machinery must be German.[9] Barbara Tuchman writes: "The essence of the problem, as the Grand Duke once confessed to

Poincaré, was that in an empire as vast as Russia when an order was given no one was ever sure whether it had been delivered."[10]

"Telegraphs would suddenly stop working," writes Norman Stone, "and investigation of the lines to the rear would reveal a party of soldiers cooking their tea with pieces of telegraph-pole."[11] There was also a shortage of wire, and telegraphed orders to field commanders often traveled the last part of the way on foot. When exasperated officers resorted to radios instead, operators would forget their codebooks in the excitement of combat, and broadcast uncoded orders and pleas for help. The amazed Germans listened in, and what they learned helped them inflict several disastrous defeats on the Russians.[12]

"In the days when people expected the war to be short," writes Stone, "there was a rush of charitable offers: rich ladies would run hospital-trains and their daughters would do the nursing. . . . Each [nurse] had her own coupé, and the trains had a way of finding themselves in the rear of the ultra-marriageable Guards Corps . . . the nurses were allowed to accommodate only 'cases of light wounds, above the belt.'"[13]

Invisible to the upper-class nurses and to the aristocrats who had enough pull to get into the exclusive Guards or cavalry regiments, the ordinary, underequipped infantry units did the great bulk of the fighting and dying. In the mountainside trenches of the Carpathians, some men froze to death. In December 1915, with no boots to be had, part of the Russian Seventh Army marched to their battle positions barefoot.[14] Sometimes the only rifles available were those that could be gathered from the battlefield dead, and so some infantry units moved up to the front carrying only axes. In the war as a whole, calculates historian and former Lt. Gen. Nicholas N. Golovine, 36.9 percent of Russian infantry soldiers were killed or wounded, and 56.5 percent of Russian infantry officers.[15]

AH

10. Tsar Nicholas II, center with beard, reviews a 1911 parade while his much taller uncle, Grand Duke Nicholas Nicholaevich, salutes him. The Grand Duke's height and many medals gave him a commanding presence, but the war soon revealed his incompetence. *Courtesy of the editors.*

immediately. I still don't know why, but he declared that no anesthetic could be used. I think I can still hear the scratching sound of his instruments on my skull.

The operation did not last very long, but was very painful. At the end of it he showed me the queer-looking piece of steel that he had extricated from my head. In order to get it out he had to make the wound in my forehead much larger than it was before the operation, but very gradually the optic nerve healed up and I regained the sight of my left eye.

Under the rules of the Russian Army, we had to appear before a medical commission every two weeks, and the commission would decide whether we still should remain at the hospital or under a physician's care, or could return to the front. When the third commission in six weeks ruled that I should remain at least one more month in Kiev, to heal all my wounds and to compensate for the great loss of blood I had suffered, I did not agree with their opinion. I was feeling strong enough to go back and did so on my own accord.

When I finally found my regiment it was again in a different place. In trying to locate it I met three other officers of my regiment who were also returning after healing their wounds, and we traveled together from the army head-quarters to the corps area headquarters. When we arrived and asked the chief of staff, a smart-looking young general, for the location of our regiment, he looked at the three of us and replied, "The 125th Regiment? Well, half of it is right here in this room."

That was a terrible shock to us. We knew that some dreadful disaster must have struck our regiment. Fortunately, the opinion of the chief of staff was ex-aggerated, but it was true that of seventy-seven officers who marched out at the declaration of war, only seventeen remained alive.

When we finally located the regiment's headquarters, the colonel welcomed us with the words, "We need you now more than ever."

We were expecting new reinforcements for our regiment and could not do anything before we trained them well enough so that they would fit in with the few remaining men in each company.

I was put in command of three companies, being the only senior officer who could be trusted with the command of a company. The other officers of these three companies had just arrived from the military academy and had no war ex-perience whatever. This practice of putting one of the more experienced officers in command of several companies had to be adopted due to the very heavy losses which we suffered in the spring of 1915.

For quite a few weeks after my return to the regiment's headquarters we were kept in the rear of the battle front, getting reinforcements, training them, and breaking them in. Then the order came to move forward again.

Spring was coming along pretty fast in this beautiful part of southern Galicia. Our front then was on the river called the "Golden Lipa." The riverbanks were hilly and covered by beautiful trees. It was a rather inactive part of the front because forcing a river crossing would not be easy and would entail heavy losses. On both sides, the positions were strongly fortified by several lines of barbed wire and trenches.

In the section of the front assigned to my three companies, the river made a sharp U-turn, and if the Austrians kept their position along the riverbank they would be under our flanking fire. Therefore, they had to abandon the riverbank and keep a more or less straight line across the U-turn. This had certain advantages for us across the river. We had built a temporary bridge over it, and my task was to occupy the Austrian bank of the river, with strict instructions not to undertake any fight that would endanger the companies under my command. We were to be on the lookout, make constant scouting patrols, and once in a while provide our command with prisoners, who would show what kind of troops were opposing us. In case of any advance by the Austrians, we were to withdraw to the other bank of the river and take up our fortified positions.

This particular spot was a very favorable one to send over and to receive spies. The Russian Army's secret service was using the place very extensively. During this period it was quite the usual thing for a staff officer to arrive with some odd-looking Galician peasant or a woman, and turn the agent over to me with instructions to make some sort of a maneuver in front of the Austrian lines, and find a way to put this agent across the lines.

The Unknown War

Almost all the thousands of histories, novels, and memoirs in English about World War I treat only the fighting in France and Belgium. A mere handful deal with that war's Eastern Front. This is all the more surprising because the war in the east between the Central Powers and Russia redrew the map of Europe far more drastically than did the fighting in the west: It shattered the centuries-old Hapsburg and Romanov Empires, brought half a dozen new nations into being, and ignited the Russian Revolution.

In 1914 Russia sent into battle the largest army that history had yet seen. Russia suffered more war deaths than either England or France. Because of the collapse of the tsarist government, statistics are somewhat imprecise, but a careful reckoning has been done by the commander-turned-historian Lieutenant General Nicholas N. Golovine. According to Golovine's figures, by the time Russia pulled out of the war in 1917, a staggering *7.9 million* Russian soldiers were dead, wounded, or (a fortunate minority) taken prisoner.[1] Some other estimates place the number higher still.

One Westerner who realized the immensity of the Eastern Front slaughter was Winston Churchill, whose *The Unknown War* is one of the relatively few books on the subject. "The tale is one," he wrote, "of hideous tragedy and measureless and largely unrecorded suffering."[2]

AH

I was also instructed on several occasions to be on the lookout for spies coming from the other side, and not to shoot when they approached our lines.

Several times, the agents sent to the other side, if they were men, turned out to be officers of the general staff disguised. The women usually were dressed as Galician peasants, but on one occasion, when I was unable to transfer two of the agents to the other side and had to entertain them in the little village house where I was living, I found that both of these Galician women were very cultured and very capable actresses engaged in the secret service.

They imitated the speech and manners of Galician peasants most excellently, but when there was no necessity for it they were perfect ladies with a very real knowledge of literature and music. One of them had a beautiful singing voice, which was greatly enjoyed by myself and a few young officers of my battalion.

In June 1915, we were still in this section. I received an order to capture prisoners at any cost, as our high command suspected certain changes of the Austro-German armies in this location and was very anxious to know what divisions and regiments were in front of us. If the prisoners refused to talk, we could tell by their papers and uniforms what part of the Army they belonged to and what the number of their regiment and division was.

I set out at night with about thirty volunteers. I ordered my men not to wear any equipment not strictly necessary for this raid and to wrap their boots in soft rags so they could march with the least possible noise. The day preceding this expedition I had crawled forward through the grass and bushes as far as it was safe, trying to find out where the best spot would be to make a sudden attack on the Austrians.

While we were moving forward with all precautions, my advance patrols reported some sort of movement ahead of us. I spotted a small patrol of Austrians crawling along, which had almost passed right by us. Without a shot we jumped on them and captured eight men with no loss of life on either side. Our mission fulfilled, we returned with our prisoners.

One of the men was a Czechoslovakian, and from the Polish I knew, I understood that the Austrians were making a local advance, trying to cut off my three companies from the river with a sudden night attack, and the patrol we captured was a part of this advance.

As soon as I got back to my three companies I ordered every man to get ready. When we observed three battalions of Austrians maneuvering to cut us off from our little bridge, we opened fire on them, and without waiting for instructions we started to move to the eastern side of the river, over the bridge.

When we had all crossed the bridge, I saw that a few companies of Austrians had succeeded in crossing the river to the left and right of the bridge, and were already on the Russian side. There was a danger that they would cut us off, but I knew that a few of my men had already reached our lines and told the troops occupying our main position of the local advance. The only thing that concerned me, now that we were across, was that our main position might open fire before we all could reach it.

We raced for our positions and the race was a close one, with the Austrians on either side of us. As I was making my way through our barbed wire, I heard the Russian commanders giving orders to get ready to shoot . When I heard, "Safety off!" I screamed at the top of my voice to wait until we had all gotten through before they opened fire on the Austrians who were right behind us.

I got entangled in the barbed wire, and had a very hard time freeing myself. One of the noncomissioned officers from our main position ran forward at the risk of his life (the Austrians were already shooting at us at very close range) and, cutting the barbed wire with special clippers, helped me disentangle myself. I was badly scratched and my clothes were torn to pieces, but as soon as we fell into our trenches our lines opened a very heavy fire, and the Austrian attack was repulsed.

I got to the nearest field telephone and called up the headquarters of my regiment to tell them what had happened. Fortunately the prisoners we captured had already reached regimental headquarters and our high command had the information it needed.

From divisional headquarters came an order that this "U" bend of the river was so valuable that we had to take it back from the Austrians. As I knew every bush and hill of this particular section, the task was entrusted to me.The colonel of my regiment asked me over the phone what I needed to recapture the river bend. I asked for two battalions and eight machine guns. By daylight they had arrived and we started the counterattack on the Austrians. By a very swift advance we forced our way across the bridge and rapidly expanded on the other side. The resistance we met was feeble, and in about two hours we were occupying all that was necessary to hold the bend of the river.

When I established telephone communication and reported the complete

John Reed Sees the Russian Retreat

Although best remembered today for his reports on Pancho Villa and the Russian Revolution, the American journalist John Reed also covered the Russian front in World War I. In the spring and summer of 1915, *Metropolitan* magazine sent him to this little-known theater of the war. Reed passed through many of the same towns and cities as did Sergievsky, such as Rovno and Lemberg, and he witnessed the calamitous Russian retreat in Galicia, which Sergievsky describes on p. 67. Here are some excerpts from his reporting:

Ternopol station was a place of vast confusion. From a long military train poured running soldiers with tin teapots. . . . Officers shouted and cursed, beating with the flat of their swords. Engines whistled hysterically, bugles blared—calling the men back to their cars. . . . Around the hot-water tanks was a boiling, yelling mob. . . . Hundreds of peasant refugees—Poles, Moldavians, and Hungarians—squatted along the platform waiting stolid and bewildered among their bundles and rolls of bedding; for as they retreated the Russians were clearing the country of every living thing and destroying houses and crops. . . . The station-master waved futile hands in the centre of a bawling crowd of officers and civilians, all flourishing passes and demanding when their various trains departed. . . .

Half-way down the street we met a column of soldiers marching four abreast toward the railway station, bound for the front. Less than a third had rifles.

They came tramping along with the heavy, rolling pace of booted peasants, heads up, arms swinging—bearded giants of men with dull, brick-red hands and faces, dirty-brown belted blouses, blanket-rolls over their shoulders, intrenching-tools at their belts, and great wooden spoons stuck in their boot-tops. The earth shook under their tread. Row after row of strong, blank, incurious faces set westward toward unknown battles, for reasons incomprehensible to them. And as they marched, they sang. . . .[1]

No one knew when the train for Lemberg left. . . . So we plunged again into the frightful melee at the station, stacked our bags against the wall, and sat down to wait. Long files of stretchers bore groaning wounded to hospital-trains, running soldiers jostled each other, officers bawled hoarsely, sweating conductors made despairing gestures about their trains blocked interminably along the tracks. A fat colonel confronted the harassed station-master, pointing to his regiment drawn up along the freight platform as far as the eye could reach.

"Where the devil is my train?" he shouted. The station-master shrugged.

There were cavalry officers in green trousers, with broad sabres; subalterns of the automobile and aeroplane corps who carried blunt, ivory-handled daggers in place of swords; Cossack *atamans* from Ural and Kuban with pointed, turned-up boots, long caftans open in front and laced at the waist, tall fur hats barred on top with gold and red, belts bossed with precious metals and silver-mounted *yataghans*; generals of various degrees of generality. There were club-footed officers, near-sighted officers who couldn't see to read, one-armed and epileptic officers. Minor officials of the postal service and the railway went by dressed like field-marshals and carrying swords. Almost every one wore a uniform with gold or silver shoulder-straps; their number and variety were bewildering. Scarcely an officer whose breast was not decorated with the gold and silver badges of the Polytechnic or the Engineering School, the bright ribbons of the Orders of Vladimir, St.

success of the attack, which took only two hours at a cost of only ten wounded, they could hardly believe it. An officer of the general staff soon arrived at my headquarters to investigate the situation.

Our activities on the Golden Lipa were almost the same for over a month, being forced to withdraw to the other side of the river and then recapturing the bend again. Then, due to the situation on the other sections of the front, a withdrawal was ordered. We retreated at night, and to all appearances our retreat was unnoticed by the Austrians as we were not followed. When we stopped for a day, the Austrian scouting parties did not appear on the horizon until very late in the afternoon. Their major forces did not appear at all. That night we retreated another few miles without any interference, and we did this repeatedly for several nights.

This was the first retreat I had personally experienced since the beginning of the war. It was a very unpleasant feeling, depressing the mood and morale of everybody in the army. The strategic reasons forcing the retreat were explained to us, of course. Still, every foot of the conquered soil had been bought at such a dear cost that to give it up and retreat night after night, mile after mile, without firing a single shot and without the slightest pursuit from the enemy, was very disappointing and depressing.

It was with a certain relief that we received an order, finally, to stop at a position prepared and strongly fortified by the engineering divisions. The Austrians appeared only after two days, but made no attempt to attack. They started to dig in on the opposite range of hills.

In the autumn of the same year we were moved across to the Romanian border in Bessarabia. The soil of this province is famous for its fertility, but the black, liquid, sticky mud it makes during the autumn rains is unbelievable, and our progress on the roads slowed to one kilometer per hour. The artillery had the hardest time: its wagon trains were almost two weeks behind. I suppose the Austrians were experiencing the same difficulties, because during the rainy season no actual fighting was done. Some action started only when the frost made the roads more passable, and the artillery and ammunition could be transported better.

In December a night attack was ordered on the Austrian position. While advancing in complete darkness in front of my company, I fell into a mantrap about six meters deep, covered by dry branches and leaves. I knew that in such a trap, on the bottom, there might be a sharp stick or some other device to kill those who fell in it, so while falling, I concentrated all my attention on falling as straight down as possible without bending over.

I fell in a straight position, right beside a sharp post. By doing so I saved my life but I sprained my ankles and ripped the ligaments to such an extent that it was six weeks before I could stand up without crutches. I did not want to be evacuated with such a minor injury and, as a special privilege, asked to remain at the regimental headquarters. I told the colonel that to report to a hospital with a sprained ankle would be a disgrace.

War in the Air

During my stay at the regiment's headquarters with this injury, an order came asking for officers who would volunteer for aviation, as the aviation service was expanding. It was clear to me that the first period of the war, when the infantry was making interesting maneuvers and marching movements in the field, was over. We were dug in in dirty trenches, and the infantry warfare was becoming more and more monotonous and inactive. I was glad of the opportunity to take up aviation again, and applied for a transfer.

My request was granted and I was assigned to the Sevastopol Military Aviation School. Before going to school I was sent to the 25th Scouting Squadron for a short time as an observer, to get acquainted with the activities of military aviation under actual war conditions.

The 25th Scouting Squadron was equipped with French Voisin two-seater planes, powered by a pusher Salmson engine. Our tasks were scouting, photography, and correction of artillery fire. For our own protection we had one machine gun.

The Voisin was a slow machine and not very maneuverable, which was a big disadvantage in encounters with much faster and more maneuverable German planes. Most of our missions called for flights rather deep into enemy country, and we lost a considerable percentage of our planes in aerial fighting there.

In the spring of 1916 the squadron was located on the Western Front. (The Western Front on the Russian side was about the middle of the front from the Baltic Sea to the Rumanian border. The northern part was called the Northern Front, then came the Western Front, then the Southwestern Front, and then the Romanian Front.)

On one bright day [June 6, 1916] we received orders to go about one hundred kilometers back of the German lines to a certain railroad station and find out how many trains and railroad carriages were there, the formation of the trains, and which way the trains were headed, then how many trains were be-

11. Members of the 25th Scouting Squadron pose with a Voisin LA in June 1916. Sergievsky, wearing a mustache and binoculars, stands behind the unit's cook. The pilot in the Voisin is probably Lt. Khudiakov. *Courtesy of National Air and Space Museum.*

tween this particular station and the next station east and the next station west, and which way they were heading.

The mission called for several hours of flight behind the enemy lines, at a section of the front where we knew the Germans had fighter squadrons. When the assignment came, our squadron leader told us that he did not want to choose anybody for this mission because he considered it too dangerous.

He offered to draw lots. First the pilots drew, and a very good friend of mine, Lieutenant Khudiakov, drew the lot to go. Then he asked that the drawing of lots for an observer be stopped, and said that if Captain Sergievsky* was will-

---

* Sergievsky actually was still a lieutenant at the time.

ing to go with him he would not want another observer, because he felt better protected with me as his machine gunner and observer. Looking for an interesting experience, I was very glad to accept.

The interesting experience started as soon as as we crossed the line. We were attacked by a two-seater that wanted to bar our passage. My pilot told me to keep the plane away by machine gun fire, but he did not maneuver into fighting position. The two-seater landed after several attempts to stop our progress west, and we proceeded on our way.

After completing our mission and collecting all the information the staff wanted, we turned back. We were about half way home when we were met by two single-seater fighters, who simultaneously started repeated attacks on our Voisin. The

12. Standing on the rear seat without a belt or parachute, Sergievsky was firing at the German fighters when Lt. Khudiakov was wounded and lost control of their Voisin. Here a Voisin gunner, safely on the ground, demonstrates the firing position. *Courtesy of Thomas Darcey.*

Voisin, a pusher biplane, is very badly protected from the rear; the plane attacking us from behind and above could come to very close range and shoot at us, while it remained well protected from my fire by our own tail surfaces.

I saw the coverings on the wings ripped in many places by tracer bullets. The cockpit was also shot through in many places, sending splinters of wood flying around. I was shooting as best I could, and the pilot was flying in a straight line east, not having a chance in the slow and clumsy Voisin to give the single-seaters a real fight.

All of a sudden the pilot slumped down over the stick and our plane started to fall out of control. I stopped shooting and reached over the pilot to grab the stick. I had managed to straighten out the plane when the pilot came to. He was shot through both legs, high in the thigh. His right leg was badly fractured and he could not operate the rudder. From my position behind him, I could only partly help him operate the stick. He told me he would attempt to make a landing before he lost too much blood, if we could make it within a very few minutes.

Giving full throttle and at the same time pushing the nose down, we considerably increased our speed and crossed the lines at an altitude of only a few

13. Wounded Lt. Khudiakov is visited by his comrades after the June 6, 1916, air battle. Sergievsky, standing hatless behind him, had shaved his mustache since being photographed in front of the Voisin earlier in June. *Courtesy of Alan Durkota.*

hundred feet. All the Germans' ground fire, artillery and infantry, was concentrated on us. Fortunately neither my pilot nor I was wounded by this fire.

Close behind our lines I spotted the Red Cross hospital tents. Indicating them to my pilot, I asked him if he could land on the little lawn in front of the tents. He made a beautiful landing, but fainted immediately after it, and was taken out of the cockpit unconscious. Only the fact that we landed right in front of a field hospital, and that an operation was performed on the pilot within minutes after he was wounded, saved his fractured leg from amputation.

When I looked over the plane I found over sixty-five bullet holes in the cockpit and in the fabric of the wings.

I telephoned the information we gathered during the flight straight to corps headquarters, and then called our own squadron, telling them our location. Soon after, a car arrived with a reserve pilot to take the plane over to the squadron field.

When I arrived at the squadron's headquarters the squadron leader informed me that he would not send me out again for a period of at least ten days, so that my nerves could be steadied after such a terrible experience. But in two days we all had to fly again. The squadron was needed about 250 kilometers south of our location, in another section of the front where heavy fighting had started. That was the beginning of the Brusilov Offensive.

In our squadron we had a Cossack lieutenant, Shevirev. He was a splendid pilot, fearless as most Cossacks are, but he had one shortcoming. Though possessing flying technique in the highest degree, he never knew his location in the air. The moment he left our airfield he would turn back to the observer and ask, "Where are we?" We all knew this quirk of his and we always teased him about it.

The squadron was ordered to head south, but not to fly in formation. To hide our movement from the German observers along the front, the planes were to leave at ten-minute intervals.

Knowing of Lieutenant Shevirev's tendency to get lost, the squadron leader wanted to assign one of the more experienced observers to fly with him. But Lieutenant Shevirev insisted upon flying with his Cossack mechanic, who had been with him since the outbreak of the war. He insisted that he could not get lost flying along the front for such a short distance as 250 kilometers and, besides, he was going to prove that he knew where he was. The squadron leader gave in.

I was very good friends with Lieutenant Shevirev, and when he started his motor and got ready to go I climbed up to his cockpit to say good-bye to him.

As I was doing so he took off his helmet and made the sign of the cross over himself. He was a very religious man, and always did this before every flight.

When the squadron assembled at the new station, all the planes had arrived there safely with the exception of Lieutenant Shevirev's. He was missing. We all hoped that he had landed somewhere back of the lines and that we would get news from him in a few hours. Night came, and there was no news.

Two days passed, and a German plane dropped a little package attached to a small parachute right in the center of our field. The information in the package was that Lieutenant Shevirev had landed at a German airfield right opposite our new location. Sure that he had arrived at his destination, he shut off his engine and started to climb out. When he saw soldiers in German uniforms running toward him he climbed back into the cockpit and made several attempts to start the motor. As the motor did not start, he took his machine gun and kept the Germans away until all his ammunition was exhausted, then he drew his revolver and fought off the Germans to his last cartridge. In this exchange of shots he was slightly wounded, but he still made an attempt to burn his plane.

In their communication, the Germans praised Shevirev's bravery highly, reported that his wound had been treated, that he was comfortably resting in a prison camp, and added that we should not worry about his health or his condition.

Lieutenant Shevirev was captured in his Cossack uniform. We had the right, in the Air Force, to wear our former regimental uniforms; the only distinction was that on the epaulette we had to attach the black eagle as the insignia of military aviation. I suppose in his very picturesque Cossack uniform he made quite a sensation on the other side of the lines.

After the war was over, late in 1918, I met Lieutenant Shevirev in Kiev when he was on his way home to his native Don. He told me an additional detail about his capture. The Voisin plane that he was flying has four wheels. The two rear wheels are the main ones, carrying the weight of the plane on landing and taking off, while the two front wheels just prevent the plane from flipping over. The technique of taking off in a Voisin is slightly different from that of any other standard type. Instead of pushing the control stick forward, as in any other plane, in the Voisin you have to hold the stick slightly back, in order to make it run on the rear wheels. A German pilot who did not know that started to make a standard takeoff in the Voisin, and pushed the control stick way forward, forcing the plane to run on the weak front wheels. When he hit some uneven ground, the front wheels collapsed and the plane flipped over completely. The pilot was pinned down in the wreckage and instantly killed by the engine behind him.

By August of 1916 I had sufficient experience as an observer to get my training in the aviation school, and I proceeded to Sevastopol, which is in the Crimea, on the Black Sea.* During the few months that I spent there, I learned to fly all the types of military planes then in existence, trying to qualify for a single-seater fighter plane. Besides their standard training, pilots who wanted to get assigned to single-seater fighters had to go through special training in stunt flying and in aerial shooting and fighting.

I was lucky enough to get through all my training without a single accident to myself or to the equipment in the very short period of five months. After graduating, I was assigned to the Second Fighting Squadron, located at Radzivilov on the former Russian-Austrian border in Galicia.

I considered my assignment to the Second Fighting Squadron a very lucky one for me, as this squadron had a distinguished reputation, with many air victories to its credit.

The first commander and actual organizer of this squadron was Captain Kruten, whom I knew in Kiev before the war. He was a very young man, extremely energetic, conscientious, and one of the best pilots I ever met in my life. His flying and his aerial fighting technique were quite amazing. In the very short period in which Russia had had single-seater fighters for its Air Force, he already had seven aerial victories officially credited to him. He was sent to France and England to learn about their organization of fighter aviation. During his few weeks there, he took part in several aerial engagements on the Western Front.

We often heard complaints about the Russian Air Force, that it was unable to stop the German scouts, photographers, and bombers from crossing our lines on their tasks. People who were not well acquainted with the actual situation were always pointing out that on the French and English fronts, the Allies' air forces were capable of checking most of the attempts of the German planes to cross. These critics blamed Russian pilots for not being energetic enough, or for not having enough knowledge of how to use valuable equipment to accomplish what the Allied pilots had achieved on the Western Front.

---

* Sergievsky applied to the aviation school in August but did not go there until November 6, 1916.

 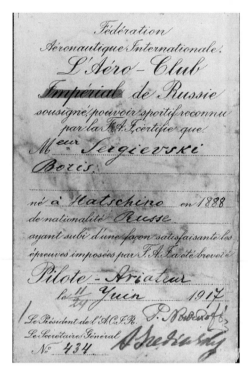

14. Sergievsky's FAI license as "Pilote-Aviateur," issued (in French and Russian) on June 11, 1917, when he was already flying combat missions. The word "Impérial" has been crossed out of the name of the Russian Aero-Club; Kerensky's Provisional Government had replaced the Imperial Government in April. *Courtesy of the editors.*

Captain Kruten made an exhaustive study of aviation forces on both the Western and Russian Fronts, and taking as a basis the number of fighter planes and the length of the front, he proved by calculation that, in order to maintain the same standard of service as on the Western Front, the Russian Air Force would need to have 272 times as many planes.

I was very glad to join the squadron of such a distinguished leader, but when I arrived at Radzivilov I found another officer in command of the squadron—Captain Baftalovsky. Captain Kruten had been promoted to group leader, his headquarters being situated some 150 kilometers south, and including six squadrons.

The work of the Second Fighting Squadron was very strenuous. At daybreak we had to be in the air, flying in pairs and forming a so-called "aerial barrage" on our section of the front, trying to prevent German scout planes and bombers from crossing. Those who remained on the ground had to be in full readiness right by their planes, and went up as soon as the crossing of German planes was reported by telephone from the trenches. The enemy's aerial activity on

The Air War in the East

Except for the months he spent as a gunner-observer in 1916 and in training, Boris Sergievsky's World War I service as an aviator came during the Eastern Front's final year of fighting, 1917.

For most of 1917, the front line in the east ran from near Riga, on the Baltic, south until it reached German-occupied Romania, and then curved east to the Black Sea. Most of the front was inside Russian Empire borders. But Sergievsky's fighter squadron was stationed at the edge of the one remaining slice of Austro-Hungarian territory still held by the Russians. Sergievsky had marched through this same area as an infantry officer in 1914. It was a multiethnic corner of Europe that was to change hands several more times in this century. The ground beneath the air battles Sergievsky fought became Polish territory between the wars, then part of the Soviet Union, and today lies in Ukraine.

With Russia increasingly in political turmoil, 1917 on the Eastern Front saw relatively little ground fighting. But the war in the air continued. Sergievsky's is one of the very few firsthand accounts of this fighting from the Russian side.

Throughout the war, Russia's air forces were far smaller than those of England, France, or Germany. At the outbreak of war, Russia had less than 300 military aircraft. By the end, despite huge losses, it had several times that number. Many planes were out of service, however, because of crippling shortages of fuel, skilled mechanics, and spare parts. When Sergievsky was flying fighter planes in mid-1917, there were an estimated 500 Russian pilots at the front.[1]

Supply problems bedeviled Russian fliers throughout the war. In 1915, for example, France sent aircraft and engines to its Russian ally. The shipment got as far as Greece, but the Allied failure to gain control of the Dardanelles made it impossible to send it further. So the planes were shipped back, around Europe, to the Arctic port of Arkhangelsk. But by the time they arrived, the harbor was ice-bound. When, after the spring thaw, the aircraft finally reached Russian aviators in mid-1916, they were far outclassed by the Germans' newer models. Other planes sent by Russia's Western allies were sometimes obsolete to begin with. Those built in Russia itself suffered from erratic workmanship in the factories, and some languished on the ground for months for lack of engines.[2]

Such difficulties led to a high death rate for Russian pilots, and to German air dominance over the Eastern Front for almost all of the war. Sometimes Russian ingenuity conquered problems, however: when Ensign Vasily Yanchenko was shot down behind enemy lines in 1915, he found the problem was a bullet through his gasoline tank. He plugged the hole with a pencil wrapped in insulating tape, pumped in fuel from his reserve tank, took off again, and completed his reconnaissance and bombing mission.[3]

Prewar Russia was home to several distinguished aeronautical pioneers, such as Igor Sikorsky, who was later to become Boris Sergievsky's employer in the United States. Sikorsky designed the world's first four-engined heavy bomber, which Russian forces flew throughout the war. In fighter aircraft, however, the Russians were more dependent on British and French help. Those planes not imported were often, like the Nieuport fighters Sergievsky flew, built in Russia under French licensing.

Russian fighters were organized into squadrons of nine or ten planes each; there were four squadrons in a fighter group. The officers in Sergievsky's squadron, where he reports only one pro-Bolshevik pilot, seem to have been unusually loyal monarchists; when the Russian Civil War began, roughly one third of all pilots joined the Reds.[4]

AH

this section of the front was intense; there was not a single day when we were not engaged in an aerial battle. We were flying an average of eight hours a day, which, in a single-seater fighter, is very tiring and nerve-wracking. The only days of rest we had were when it rained and no flying could be done.

For the first few days after my arrival, the squadron leader took me as his second. He instructed me not to take part in the fight, but to watch him and learn how to maneuver. The losses of the squadron were so heavy that young pilots from various flying schools were constantly arriving to replace those killed in action. Within about two weeks of my arrival at the squadron I was already considered a veteran, many younger and less experienced pilots having arrived after me.

I was soon allowed to go up on my own and I had several successful engagements with my German opponents; but because most of our activity was concentrated over the German lines, my first few victories could not be officially credited to me. To get official credit for a plane brought down you had to bring it down on our side of the lines.

The standard equipment of our squadron was the single-seater Nieuport fighter plane of French design, most built in Russia on a license, with a rotary Le Rhône engine. The Nieuports had a splendid climb and perfect maneuverability, but were not quite fast enough for the latest German planes.*

As I grew experienced in the tactics of aerial fighting, I developed my own technique of attack. My main principle was to be within range of the enemy's guns the least possible time, by making a series of consecutive short attacks from the direction of the enemy plane's blind spots. Our squadron leader was a pilot of an older school, and his tactics were quite different from mine. He tried always to attack from a higher altitude, diving straight at the enemy two-seater planes, ignoring the fire of the rear-seat machine gunner protecting it. Flying like this and quickly approaching to a very close range, he would turn

---

* Sergievsky's squadron flew several variants of the Nieuport 17 single-seater, which was the best fighter available to the Russian air force. But when Sergievsky arrived in June 1917, the squadron had on hand only five Nieuport 21s—basically N. 17s with an 80-horsepower Le Rhône engine in a horseshoe-shaped cowling instead of the N. 17's 110-horsepower engine. The Nieuport 17 had been a brilliant success over the Western Front in 1916, with many French, British, and American Escadrille Lafayette pilots scoring victories in it; but by 1917, both the Allies and the Germans on the Western Front were flying faster and better-armed fighters.

15. Sergievsky with his Nieuport 17, a French fighter license-built by the Russian Dux Company. This is No. 1438, which he flew in combat from September through November 1917. The bracing wire from the top of the rear strut to the landing-gear leg, a Dux addition, may have kept Sergievsky's top wing on when his Nieuport's V-strut was shattered by antiaircraft fire. *Courtesy of the editors.*

away only to avoid a direct collision, then climb again and repeat such a straight-on attack.

I followed the same tactics for the first few fights, but judging by the number of bullet holes my plane received during every engagement, I knew that I was taking too many chances and would have to develop a different system.

With some other pilots, I started to practice a stunt that became my favorite method of attack and was successfully adopted also by other members of my squadron. Instead of following the enemy plane from behind, I would try to meet him head-on, but higher. Due to the relatively great closing speed of the two planes, I considered my shooting unnecessary, and his shooting not dangerous to me. But I always noticed that when I approached enemy two-seaters this way, the enemy machine gunner would aim his gun straight ahead, trying to meet me with his fire.

When I was right above the German plane, I would make a rapid wingover and dive right on top of him, already flying in the same direction. While the gunner had to swing his machine gun all the way around before he could fire, I could shoot at the enemy plane at very close range. As soon as I saw that the machine gunner was ready to fire at me I would sideslip, fall below, and try to make a second attack from below the stabilizer, but would not expose myself to the enemy at a very close range.*

The execution of this maneuver required a very accurate judgment of the relative speeds of the two planes. The wingover on top of the enemy machine should not be executed too high, or the machine gunner could turn around and shoot before I could open fire at close range. But too close a wingover increased the danger of colliding in midair.

It was a much easier to fight a single-seater plane, which had no rear machine gunner and could shoot only forward with a fixed machine gun, just as I had. Then it was a question of who had the more maneuverable plane, and who was more skilled in manueuvering.

Sometimes, an enemy single-seater and I would find ourselves flying right alongside each other, trying to gain altitude, because in a fight between two single-seaters, the one who was higher up had all the advantage of attacking the other one from on top and behind, where a single-seater is quite unprotected.

I had a memorable fight against a German single-seater Roland. We met at the front and exchanged a few shots, then we both wanted to gain altitude. Flying right alongside at a very close range, I could even see the German flyer's face and his little moustache. We were both in a very steep climb. The Roland being slightly faster, he was afraid that if he went ahead of me I would have a better chance to shoot at him from behind. So in climbing he was trying to zigzag, in order not to overtake me. My only concern was to get higher; there was no danger of my overtaking him.

When I finally got a few feet above him I was able to start an attack. I fired

---

* U.S. Marine ace Joe Foss developed the same tactic over Guadalcanal in 1942: "I liked to get out in front and above and turn back toward them and do an absolute straight overhead—where you can come right straight down on them. . . . A gunner shooting at you doesn't have a chance to aim at you then."

a few shots at close range, but then I had to veer off to the side to avoid a collision. By doing so I got below him, and it was his turn to attack. We maneuvered this way, each time having a chance to take just a few shots at each other, and then we would find ourselves at the same altitude and start to climb again.

This competition lasted for almost half an hour. Then finally I got the chance to climb considerably higher. The German, seeing that he could not outclimb me, turned towards the German lines and tried to get away. That was my best chance. I dove after him. He started to dive too, but being higher, I could dive more steeply. He could not dive as steeply, because he would not reach his lines in so steep a descent.

This time, I was able to fire at least a hundred rounds from my machine gun. When his engine gave out a cloud of smoke, I realized that the fight was over, and I felt that I should not try to kill him. It was enough to know that his plane was damaged or destroyed and he was going to be forced to land. I could see that his engine had stopped and he was simply gliding westwards. When I realized that he might be able to glide as far as the German lines, very reluctantly I started to shoot at him again. By maneuvering around him I forced him to change his direction and shorten his glide.

He landed in front of the first line of our barbed wire, and I turned and flew immediately to our flying field, took a car, and drove right back with some of my friends to where I had left the enemy plane.

When I arrived, the infantry officers told me the pilot had climbed out of the cockpit and started to run towards the German lines. Our infantrymen climbed out of the trenches and ran after him. In his heavy flying uniform, he was unable to run fast. He took off his leather coat and threw it to the ground. His nearest pursuers stopped to investigate the pockets and gave him another head start again. He kept dropping pieces of his flying suit whenever his pursuers got too close. By the time he reached the German lines, he was running in his underwear, but the German soldiers realized what was happening and started to shoot at his pursuers, and they had to turn back.

The only trophies that we had of this victory were his helmet, his leather coat, and his flying uniform.*

---

* Many years later, in the United States, Sergievsky told this story at a gathering of veteran aviators from several countries. As he finished the tale, an astonished German-accented voice rang out from the back of the room: "I vas dat man!"

The Germans realized that the plane would be taken behind the Russian lines as soon as it got dark and started an intensive artillery fire which partly destroyed the plane.

This victory was the first one officially credited to me because I was able to produce a damaged engine and parts of the destroyed German plane as proof of my victory together with many affidavits of the infantrymen who witnessed the end of my fight—the moment when the German plane landed in front of our barbed wire.

Destroying German observation balloons became my favorite sport for a while. I would fly over the lines at about 4900 meters (16,000 feet) altitude and fly right above one of the balloons. The antiaircraft artillery would start firing at me, but at such an altitude I considered myself pretty safe, and I would remain circling above the balloon, waiting for one of the shells to burst close to my plane or right below it.

Right after such a close shot, I would pretend that my plane had been hit. I would make a falling leaf descent, finally going into a tailspin, but still trying to come as close as possible to the observation balloon. The Germans would cease firing, seeing that my plane was falling, and thinking that it was already shot down. When I was level with the observation balloon I would suddenly straighten out and fire incendiary bullets into the side of it. When I saw the balloon burst into flames, I would dive down to the ground and fly away across the lines very low, skimming the treetops so that those Germans who saw me would be already too late to fire.

I succeeded in shooting down three balloons using these tactics, but I must admit that it worked only once at every location where I tried it. On my second attempt in the same vicinity, the Germans did not stop firing as my plane was falling down, and when I saw that the descent was becoming very dangerous I had to straighten out and fly away without accomplishing my aim. Very probably, information about my tactics was forwarded to all sections of the front, because after my third balloon I never was able to approach them in the same way.

Our squadron headquarters was situated in a manor house near our field, and near the town of Radzivilov. It had been left by its proprietor with all the furniture—tables, beds, bed linen, kitchen utensils, and dishes—and the only thing we had to provide for our officers' mess in the way of equipment was the silverware, which had been either carried away or lost by the troops that first occupied the place. It was the most comfortable billet I ever experienced, and

16. Sergievsky, seated with his cap on his knee, poses with fellow officers of the Second Fighting Squadron and nurses from the Radzivilov field hospital— presumably "ladies of the best classes" rather than the "other elements" that Sergievsky disdained. *Courtesy of Alan Durkota.*

we were fortunate enough to have a cook who was formerly chef of a leading restaurant in Kiev. In summertime we had our dinner only at about 10 P.M., and that was the time we would discuss all our experiences of the day and make our plans for the next day's work. Naturally, there were only two topics of conversation: aerial fighting and beautiful women.

Once in a while we even had parties to which guests from other squadrons were invited, and also some officers from corps headquarters, and regiments that were in reserve in the same vicinity.

We were even able to accumulate quite a decent cellar of wines, our aviation pay being much higher than pay in any other branch of the service. But as a rule, when we had good flying weather, no drinks were served in the officers' mess, and as a reminder, a huge bottle of milk was put in the center of the table.

In the vicinity of Radzivilov were several big field hospitals, and the nurses of these hospitals provided the feminine touch at our parties. I must admit that when ladies visited our parties were much more dignified than when they were stag parties.

Many ladies of the best classes of Russian society joined the ranks of regular nurses in the field hospitals, wishing to be closer to their relatives and also out of a sense of duty to their country. Of course, there were also other elements that used nurse's uniforms to their own advantage. But it was very easy after exchanging a few words with them to find out who was who.

Due to the very convenient location of the squadron, the wives of some of our officers were frequent guests at our headquarters and stayed there for several months at a time. My wife spent about two months of the summer of 1917 at the front, but seeing aerial fighting every day in the skies to the west, and trying to recognize her husband's plane among those falling in flames and smoke was too much for her nerves, and I had to insist on her departure.

Soon after, I was given command of the squadron. This happened when my squadron leader, Captain Baftalovsky, was severely wounded in an aerial fight above the German lines. Following his usual tactics, he was flying straight towards a German two-seater, ignoring the machine gunner who was firing at him. In diving for the attack he was shot in the right shoulder, the bullet passing through the length of his body, coming out through the thigh of his right leg. He blacked out, but only for a few seconds. Being a very strong man he regained consciousness and control of his plane, but he felt such a rapid loss of blood that he realized he could not fly back to the squadron's field. He just reached the front lines and, landing right behind the Russian trenches in a hayfield, flipped over.

He was immediately pulled from his plane by our soldiers and carried to the nearest hospital. There he insisted on being transported to squadron headquarters. He wanted to personally transfer the command to his successor. Being the senior in rank in the squadron, I was to be that successor. Judging from the seriousness of his wounds, we realized that it would be a long time before he could return to duty.*

It was a difficult time to be in command, due to the tense political situation.

* Captain Baftalovsky, wounded on June 19, 1917, resumed command of the 2nd Fighter Squadron early in September, relieving Sergievsky and granting him a two-week leave. During this leave, Sergievsky attempted to requisition seventy-five liters of alcohol for the squadron mess, as described on page 94.

The front was still holding fast, but in the rear revolutionary propaganda was destroying discipline, and the position of those who had any responsibility was getting more and more difficult. I could not complain of any trouble in my own squadron; all our mechanics were loyal in spite of the fact that some of them had extreme socialistic ideas.

The most restless elements in the squadron were the men taking care of the supply wagons, but as all the fighting in the squadron was done by officers, we had no difficulties in fulfilling our duties at the front.

From our fellow officers in other branches of the service we knew already of cases when entire regiments would refuse to take their positions in the front lines. After receiving the orders to move forward they would hold meetings and discuss whether they should go or not, and was the order for them to go to the trenches justified, or should they remain in reserve? Naturally those who advocated remaining in reserve were more successful.

Kerensky appeared at our front at this time and by endless speeches tried to pursuade the soldiers to maintain discipline and go on with the war, but very often during the height of his eloquence there would be a loud voice from the crowd of soldiers, "If you want to make war, go to the trenches yourself!" The revolutionary propaganda was rapidly spreading and affecting more and more all the branches of the service.

Our own supply wagon men had a meeting, to which I was invited as a representative of the officers. They declared that they had taken care of the horses long enough, and now the officers should take care of the horses. After this resolution was passed, I took the stand and told them that the officers were perfectly willing to take care of the horses, provided that the supply wagon men would fly our planes; we would simply exchange duties.

A long silence followed my offer and then the resolution was changed, the leader of the revolutionary movement saying that it would be necessary to send some of the soldiers to the flying academy before they could take over the flying duties, and that temporarily they would carry on with their duties with the horses.

In the meantime German aviation was very active, trying to see what was going on behind the front infested by the revolutionaries. We had more flying and more dogfights than ever.

That summer a young second lieutenant named Shudnovsky arrived at the squadron, straight from flying school. He was just twenty years old and was probably more of a child than even his age suggested. He was most eager to

17. Lt. Shudnovsky, killed in August 1917, when he collided with a German two-seater he was attacking from above. *Courtesy of Alan Durkota.*

take part in aerial fighting, which he thought was the most thrilling and most interesting thing in the world.

At this time I was already the oldest and most experienced pilot in the squadron, all those who were there before me having been killed or wounded. So I assigned Lieutenant Shudnovsky to fly in a pair with me and not take part in the engagement, but just to look. But, whenever we had a dogfight, which was every day, he could not keep out of it and also would try to help me out. I took special care in teaching him my favorite maneuver of attack, but I noticed that his wingover on top of the German plane came a little too close to be safe. On several occasions I warned him to look out, but one beautiful day in August

The Other Side

World War I on the ground was, it could be said, the first of the modern wars, where millions of soldiers were blown to pieces by shells fired by distant men they never saw. But the war in the air was the last of the old-fashioned wars. Fighter pilots fought at close enough range to see each other's faces. They developed an etiquette, like dueling swordsmen of an earlier time. When Boris Sergievsky's fellow ace Capt. Evgraph Kruten (see p. 75) shot down one German plane, he discovered on the body of the dead pilot a photograph of the man with his wife and child. Kruten then dropped the photo over the enemy airfield with a note in German: "I am extremely sorry about the dead father, but war is war, and if I had not killed him, then he would have killed me."[1]

After the war, surviving airmen from both sides compared notes. On at least one occasion (see footnote p. 81), Boris Sergievsky later met a German flyer he had dueled with; he may well have met others.

A picture of life on the other side of the lines can be found in the recollections of Hans Schröder, a German aviator who wrote his memoirs after the war. During the summer of 1916, he and Sergievsky both flew over the same sector of the Galician front, where the Brusilov Offensive, the last great Russian advance of the war, was going on beneath them. They were both observer/machine gunners in two-man reconnaissance planes; it is possible that they exchanged bullets, for each took part in aerial battles during this campaign.

Schröder's description of life on the German side of the lines—the good food and drink, the courtly rituals of dropped messages—resembles Sergievsky's portrait of the same vanished world:

Lieutenant Lehmann . . . was not so lucky when he took off with Acting Officer Thiele . . . they were hit by a Russian shell, and had to land at once, although they were still far behind the Russian lines.

For two days we had no news of them; then on three successive days the Russians dropped us messages to announce that they were safe and unwounded. One of these messages was painted on a strip of paper fifteen meters long; then came a letter written by Lehmann himself. The third time we got a note from a Russian airman, who added humorously that they "expected a few more of us."

This sporting comradeship of opposing airmen is a fine thing. We dropped an acknowledgement to say that we had received their messages, for which we thanked them. As Lehmann's father was very ill, it was great relief to him to learn of his son's safety so quickly. . . .[2]

In addition to our interesting and satisfying duties in the air we had a glorious season of hunting in the Russian woods. It was not long before the section lived almost entirely upon our spoils of the chase. Partidges and pheasants, wild ducks and rabbits, wild boars and elks were all to be found in this game paradise, in which Bismarck is said to have hunted so often.

We generally returned home late from our hunting, but were ready to take off at 4 A.M. the next morning.[3]

AH

1917, when he was flying in a pair with me, we met three German planes flying in battle formation and attacked them. I saw him make a very close wingover over a German two-seater and collide with him in midair.

His plane actually cut the German's fuselage in two. The wings of Shudnovsky's plane were torn away by the impact. That was at an altitude of about 4,200 meters (14,000 feet) and some 15 kilometers behind the German lines.

In a few days a German plane flew low over our flying field and dropped a message, together with Lieutenant Shudnovsky's wallet and some photographs of his family. Also included were a detailed description of the place where he was buried, a map of the cemetery with an indication of his grave, and photographs of the funeral procession, the church service, the grave, and the monument.

There was also a request to acknowledge the receipt of this message and to inform them about the fate of their two pilots who were shot down on the previous day (shot down by me and both of them taken prisoner). They gave me the approximate hour when they would expect a return message and promised not to attack the messenger plane that would fly over their field at this hour.

I flew the message myself, and I must admit that they kept their promise, for although I flew very low, dropping the message on their field, and they had a few planes in full readiness, no one tried to take off and fight me. After the exchange of messages we resumed our everyday fighting again.

Very often our squadron was assigned to escort our slower two-seater observation and photographic planes, to protect them against aerial attacks. We would fly much higher, circling above them, and when they were attacked by German planes we would in turn attack them from above. If there were several planes together a regular dogfight would start. In some of these fights it was hard to tell who actually should be credited with victories over the enemy planes, because several of our planes were shooting at the same plane simultaneously. In such fights the heaviest losses were always among the slower observation planes. They could not maneuver fast enough to take better defensive positions.

With the advent of faster pursuit planes and more elaborate maneuvers in aerial attack, the importance of machine gun fire in aerial fighting was very great. We established our own firing range in our squadron and practiced machine gun shooting at moving targets practically every day.

The extreme cold and the lower pressure at higher altitudes made machine guns work a little differently up there, and troubles with machine guns were not unusual in an aerial fight. I remember one incident when we succeeded in catching a German plane on an observation flight about fifty kilometers behind our lines. With two pursuit planes it was a sure thing that we could down him. My partner was a very skillful fighter and we attacked the German plane simultaneously from both sides. The German machine gunner could not decide which of the two attackers was more dangerous to him and was wasting quite a lot of his shots not knowing which way to aim.

After the second attack my machine gun jammed. Knowing I would need a few minutes to fix it, I pretended my gun was all right and continued to dive at the German plane, trying to attract the gunner's attention as much as possible to give my partner a chance to bring the plane down.

I was surprised to see how close my partner went on every attack on the German who still flew on. My plane was already riddled with bullets and I was getting really angry. To my astonishment the German flew quite safely across the lines, and further pursuit became useless.

My partner and I landed together on our field. We both jumped out of our planes and ran to each other shaking our fists high in the air. I screamed at him that my machine gun had jammed, and I was making sham attacks to give him a chance to bring the plane down. He burst into laughter. His gun had also jammed, and he had been taking chances to give me the same opportunity!

Another time perhaps it would have been more fortunate if my machine gun had jammed entirely. I was after a slow German two-seater way back of our lines. From all evidence it was already damaged and was making its way very low towards the lines, quite apparently in trouble, with black smoke coming from its exhaust.

Almost behind our front lines was a town called Brody. In spite of the closeness of the front, life was still going on there. As the German plane staggered toward home, almost touching the treetops and the roofs of the little town, the market was open in the little square in the center of the city. I saw quite a few people there as I made my last dive at the German plane, still trying to bring him down over our lines. I opened fire, diving almost vertically, as the German plane passed over the marketplace.

I found out later that one of my bullets struck a civilian there. It hit the top of his head and went through the whole of his body vertically. The population of Brody was constantly under fire, and one more casualty was not even noticed, but I felt very bad about it.

It was always an unpleasant thought to me to kill or wound anyone in aerial fighting. The main objective was to bring the plane down and if possible to bring it down behind our lines so that we could use it. It would be very fine to take pilots as prisoners, weakening the Austro-German squadrons, but the idea of killing an airman always disgusted me. Fighting the elements was quite a sufficient danger, and a certain sportsmanship and fraternity among the airmen existed in spite of so many years of war.

The airplanes assigned to the fighter squadrons were much more up to date, much faster, and much more reliable than the airplanes in any other squadrons, therefore it was quite the usual thing that if there was some very important mission at Army headquarters that the Air Force had to do, the mission was assigned to one of the fighter squadrons.

It is hardly reasonable to expect that a pilot flying a single-seater plane, who has always to watch for a sudden attack from behind, would do a very thorough job of observing the ground. He might miss quite a lot of things. Consequently we made a rule that when such a task was assigned to our squadron, a least two and sometimes three planes would go out together. One of them would fly low, not paying the slightest attention to what was going on in the air, and the pilot would concentrate entirely on the maps and on the ground observations, making all the notes and actually leading the flight. The accompanying plane or planes would ignore what was going on on the ground, would not even know where the leading plane was conducting them. Their full attention would be devoted to protecting the plane making the scouting trip. They would have to look out for possible enemy planes and attack them at first sight.

I particularly liked such assignments because it was always very interesting to see what was going on behind the enemy lines. The sensation of crossing the enemy lines and going deep into their country was like visiting another world.

I quickly discovered that there were certain altitudes where ground fire was more dangerous. At high altitudes—say, above 3,000 meters [10,000 feet]—no rifle or machine gun could reach us. But the special "zenith batteries" which were installed in many important points along the front had a very high reach, and having measured triangular bases on the ground they were able to find out by observation and calculation not only the altitude but also the speed of our planes. Their first volley would often bracket a plane and do serious damage to it. Even great heights—up to 5,000 or 5,100 meters [16,000 or 17,000 feet]—would not help against them.

Respecting the zenith batteries, I worked out a scheme for managing to pass these danger zones. When approaching such a zone, I would fly perfectly straight, just waiting for the first shots of the battery. As they could not possibly guess the velocity of the wind at higher altitudes, I could expect that the very first shots would not be exact.

After the first shots were made, and I saw the smoke from their shells somewhere near the plane, I tried to visualize what was going on in the battery. Continuing my straight flight I was telling myself, "Now the officer commanding the battery is applying the correction for the wind." I would allow, say, fifteen seconds for his calculations. Then I would wait a few seconds for his new commands to the battery. After this I allowed a few seconds for the execution of the command. When I calculated that the order to fire had been given, and probably the shells were already on the way and it would be too late to apply the new correction for a change in my course, I would change my course from ten to twenty degrees.

In most cases I would see shells from the zenith battery burst exactly at the spot where I would have been if I had kept my course straight. Then I repeated the same tactic. I would again allow a certain time for the battery commander to make the new allowance for my change of course, and for his command to be executed, then change my course at some sudden angle, repeating this until I was out of the danger zone.

In applying such tactics, that is, in trying to imagine myself at the battery while it was shooting at me, I succeeded in passing the dangerous zones almost always without damage to the plane.

But on one occasion I probably made some sort of mistake in my calculations, or the officer commanding the battery waited longer for his next command and found out my new course, and I took a direct hit from one of his shells.

My lower left wing was very badly damaged, and the "V" strut of the Nieuport broke in two. The longer part of the "V" was entirely destroyed, and only the shorter strut leading to the rear spar of the upper wing was holding. That happened at an elevation of over 4,500 meters [15,000 feet]. The whole lower wing was moving as I looked at it, back and forth, up and down. I was expecting any second it would collapse; it was actually hanging only on the wires, and the strut had no rigidity whatever.

In those days we had no parachutes. I was afraid to glide in a straight line. I did not think that the wing could stand the stress of a straight flight. Shutting off my engine in order to eliminate all possible vibrations, I started to glide,

18. The pilot standing in front of French-built Nieuport 21 fighter No. 2176, on its back after a rough landing, may be Sergievsky, who flew this aircraft on at least one mission. The pilot's binoculars suggest that he was returning from a reconnaissance flight like those Sergievsky describes. *Courtesy of Alan Durkota.*

slipping on the right, healthy wing. That way the left wing was carrying the least possible load.

Continuing my awkward slip on the right wing, I crossed the lines and glided all the way to our own flying field. Only for the landing did I straighten the plane out. As the wheels touched, the left wing fell down on the ground, and I was left with the right wing only. That was one of my narrowest escapes.*

On many occasions the high command needed to know what sort of troops—Germans or Austrians—were occupying the trenches in front of us. It was harder and harder to get prisoners from behind reinforced positions and several lines of barbed wire. Communication through spies and through neutral countries was too slow, and on several occasions such a task was given to the Air Force.

At first it looked as if flying so low that you could actually see the color of the uniforms would be extremely dangerous; and so it would be if the flying had to be done only a few hundred meters above the ground. I found out by

* The lower wings of the Nieuport 17 were less than half the area of the upper wings, a design layout called a sesquiplane. This design was highly efficient aerodynamically, but the narrow, single-spar lower wings, originally designed to pivot as air brakes, were inadequately braced against twisting and thus prone to failure. Courtney Campbell of the Escadrille Lafayette was looping his Nieuport 17 when the lower left wing broke off; he too managed to glide to a safe landing. The German Albatros D III and D V fighters of 1917 adopted the Nieuport's wing layout and suffered the same failures.

experience, however, that if a fast plane flew very close to the ground, just a few meters up, jumping the trees and little hills, everybody who saw it would already be too late to shoot at it. It would be gone before one could grab a rifle.

I applied this kind of tactic very successfully myself, and I recommended it to other members of the squadron. I would fly very low, and could even fly along the trenches, seeing the soldiers jumping out of their dugouts to look at the plane; but it was already too late for them to do anything about it. I would be hidden by some unevenness of the ground or by a little forest or hill.

By knowing every contour of the countryside and studying photographic maps of the trenches in front of us, I could find out if there was a German regiment there simply by the color of their uniforms, and what part of the trench the Germans occupied and where the Austrian units would start again.

There were bullet holes in the wings after such an expedition, but they were very few and probably of an accidental nature. I do not think anybody could aim at us. Probably these bullets were simply the ones that we would ourselves find in the air.

Weather permitting, both sides flew every day. At daybreak, two of our planes would take off and fly along the front about a kilometer behind the German lines, trying to see any enemy aerial activity and also what was going on right behind the lines. The rest of the squadron would be in full readiness at the field. The many flying hours and very long days in summertime made most of the pilots so tired that they would lie down right on the grass in the shadow of their plane's wings and fall asleep.

No artillery or machine gun fire, no matter how close, would wake them up, for these sounds did not concern us. But the slightest hum of an engine would act on the subconscious of the pilot, and he would be immediately wide awake and in his cockpit in full readiness to take off and fight the aerial enemy.

There were so many dogfights, and they were so much like each other, that it would be rather tiresome to describe every one of them.

The officers in the Air Force, as in all the other branches of service, had a right to two weeks' leave. These were bright spots in our lives. All through the war, in my infantry regiment and later on in the squadron, I do not remember a single case when anybody was back late from such a leave, because they knew well that the next one in line was sitting on his suitcases waiting for his turn. No one would dare to rob his friend of even a few hours of leave, knowing how he would feel about it himself.

During one such leave I wanted to combine business with pleasure and went to the city of Smolensk, which was the distribution headquarters of pure alcohol for the Army. The sale of alcoholic drinks was prohibited in Russia during the war, and it took some doing to keep an adequate supply in the squadron's mess. We worked out our own technique of making rather good vodka from pure distilled alcohol.

The commandant of Smolensk had at his disposal huge distilleries, and it was up to him to authorize the distribution of alcohol to different Army units. In each case, an officer had to accompany the requisition and explain to the very severe general what the alcohol was needed for.

In our squadron office we made out a requisition for five pails (75 liters) of alcohol. With this requisition in hand I reported to the office of the commandant. There were at least twenty officers in the waiting room. Most of them were colonels and lieutenant colonels in charge of provisioning Army units—hospitals, veterinary units, and technical detachments.

The general came into the waiting room and everybody stood up. He moved from one officer to another, glancing at the requisition, and in a very terse way asked, "What for?" Everybody was frightened and gave different excuses and explanations, but in most cases the general knew that the alcohol was being requisitioned for drinking purposes, and he became more and more angry at the continual lies that he had to hear.

To one of the veterinary colonels who had a requisition for 400 liters he said, "Are you going to wash your horses in alcohol? Get out of here!"

When my turn came, I knew I hadn't a chance. I had no explanation ready for why I wanted the alcohol. The general looked at me. I was the lowest in rank there, and an aviator. "I suppose you will tell me that you have to wash your engines in alcohol." I knew that I had nothing to lose so I answered him, "Your Excellency, we are going to drink it." The general turned around to the rest of the throng. "Here is a brave young man, who was the first of all of you to tell me the truth. I am going to grant his request."

The remaining few days of my vacation I spent in Petrograd. I had a very good time there, going to theaters and seeing moving pictures, which were quite a novelty in Russia then.

Returning to the front, I found as usual quite a few of my old officers missing from the squadron, lost on the other side of the front or shot down in aerial battles on our side. There were again young men, almost children, who were sent as reinforcements from the flying schools. It always was a heavy feeling of responsibility to send these inexperienced boys over the lines, but I had no alternative. The losses in the Air Force were very high, and the schools hardly could keep up, sending newly made aviators to replace the losses at the front.

The location of my squadron was to the north of the town of Ternopol, where Minister of War and Prime Minister Kerensky was launching his big drive, trying for the first time in history to move an army, not by orders, but by force of eloquence and persuasion. The attempt to advance on Ternopol was disastrous, resulting in a considerable loss of life and a retreat of the Russian lines.

The supply base for my squadron was situated near Ternopol. I drove out there, together with my wife, who was visiting at that time, and with other officers, to get new propellers for some of our planes. Our trip coincided with the retreat around Ternopol.

On our way back, driving along the front, we saw disturbing signs of disorderly retreat, and the highway, which was supposed to be about twenty-five kilometers back of the lines, became rather dangerous. When we were climbing one of the steep hills on that highway, the engine overheated and stalled. No matter how hard we worked on it we could not start it again. Looking through my field glasses I saw the Austrians advancing towards the highway from the west. We had to leave the car right there on the road and make our way on foot. To Mrs. Sergievsky this was just a funny adventure. I was disgusted because I could not carry away the propellers that I needed so much.

In crossing through small meadows and bushy places we would find wildflowers and Mrs. Sergievsky would stop to pick them. We had quite an argument about these flowers, because if we kept stopping to pick flowers we would be taken prisoner. Still she managed to assemble quite a beautiful bouquet.

We walked all through the night. At daybreak we were picked up by a car driving along another highway a little deeper behind our lines. They gave us a lift to our squadron.

4

Revolution and Upheaval

While we were having our share of fun and troubles at the front, the revolution was making its own way in the rear, and its influence at the front was growing all the time. Cases of insubordination were now common in other branches of the service. We were luckier in aviation. Our mechanics were still loyal to us and we had no real problems in completing our tasks, including most of the fighting.

But in the autumn of 1917, after the Bolsheviks took power in Petrograd, there were orders to stop fighting. The Bolsheviks wanted peace at any price, and before they even had official peace negotiations started, they wanted local negotiations right there at the front. They hoped to destroy the morale of the Austrians and Germans, just as they had destroyed the morale and discipline of our own Army, if they could get in close touch with them in local negotiations. We disregarded such orders and were carrying on with our duties.

In November 1917, when all fighting was prohibited by order of the Revolutionary Committee of the Army, a German two-seater plane flew over and proceeded to carry out its observation work behind our lines. When I ordered my plane out of the hangar there was a certain hesitation among the mechanics, and the chief mechanic told me, "Captain, if you fly now and fight this German plane you will get in trouble with the Revolutionary Committee of the Army. Of course, our own committee will try to protect you, but they are getting quite angry out there, and you had better watch your step."

I did not stop to argue with him, I was in a hurry to get the German while he was still way behind our lines. I went up, fought, and brought the German plane down. That was my last plane brought down on the Russian front.

The news of my downing a German plane after the local armistice was declared immediately spread everywhere. There was a special meeting of the Army Revolutionary Committee which put me on trial. I was not called to tes-

Sergievsky: An Ace for the Tsar?

For decades Soviet and Western aviation writers[1] repeated Sergievsky's claim that he shot down eleven planes and three balloons. But researchers have always found it hard to verify pilots' wartime accounts of aerial victories, and Sergievsky is no exception. Though historians have tentatively linked Sergievsky's claims with several enemy losses, they have yet to find records that document most of these claims. But the fact that official documentation is missing after decades of war and upheaval does not mean that an event did not take place. For example, the pilots of the two planes he downed in August 1917 (p. 88) were captured, providing living evidence of his victories—but the surviving files do not include a report on this combat.

To date, only three of Sergievsky's claimed victories have been confirmed by other sources. His description of his final aerial victory of the war squares with the Austro-Hungarians' recorded loss of Hansa-Brandenburg C.I (U) No. 269/17 on December 1, 1917 (p. 97).[2] Sergievsky describes this combat as occurring in November, because Imperial Russia's Julian calendar lagged behind that of the west by thirteen days. (He also calls his opponent a German—an understandable error when all enemy planes wore the same black crosses.) The Russian *Army Herald* announced on June 6, 1917 (Julian calendar): "In the area of the city of Brody, Lt. Sergievsky fought with two enemy planes, one of which landed in enemy territory, evidently damaged."[3] This "damaged" plane may have been the German Roland D. II fighter whose pilot escaped across the front lines on foot by shedding his flying clothes, and confirmed Sergievsky's victory in New York years later (p. 81).

A Russian communiqué dated June 18, 1917, said that Sergievsky fought an enemy two-seater and a fighter near Brody, forcing them to withdraw after repeated attacks.[4] A German two-seater from Feldflieger Abteilung 27 crashed in the trenches that day, killing both the pilot and the observer.[5] Without prisoners or wreckage to support his claim, Sergievsky could not be officially credited with a victory.

Sergievsky's eleven claimed aerial victories may have included enemy planes shot down while he was flying as an observer/machine gunner in 1916. He later told interviewers that he had flown 155 combat missions. The summary of his flight logs he carefully saved and brought out of Russia shows 98 flights as a fighter pilot in 1917.[6] Incomplete records from his squadron of the previous year show him flying 15 observer/machine-gunner missions between April 27 and July 14, 1916.[7] Records covering the period from then until he left that squadron on October 24, 1916, have not been found, but if Sergievsky had continued flying roughly the same number of missions per month, he could easily have accumulated a grand total of 155 missions.

For nearly three-quarters of a century, no one in the West knew what sort of Russian military records survived from World War I. But in the 1990s, historians at last got access to previously closed archives in Moscow. An American scholar, Christine White, and a Russian one, Sergei Zhuravliev, were able to find dozens of documents mentioning Boris Sergievsky, including his military personnel file.[8] Unfortunately the crucial papers—the pilots' after-action flight reports from Sergievsky's squadrons—are incomplete. Of his 98 missions as a fighter pilot in 1917, after-action reports have been found for only 51, and no comparable reports have turned up on his flights as an observer/machine gunner in 1916.

The 1917 combat reports from the Moscow archives describe in cryptic military language the results of many aerial dogfights: an enemy bullet hole in Sergievsky's propeller blade, enemy planes chased back across the lines, "bullet holes in my left wing," and several occasions when an enemy plane "declined battle." Sergievsky is many times "fired on by enemy artillery" and once "fired on by our own artillery." But the only recorded victory is the Austro-

Hungarian aircraft downed on November 19, 1917 (Julian calendar). The report also mentions something omitted from his memoir: other pilots were flying with him that day. Here is how it reads: "Nov. 19. Military Pilot Staff-Captain Sergievsky in Nieuport 17 No. 1438. 1 hour 15 minutes. Pursuit of enemy aircraft. 3,500 meters [maximum altitude reached]. Radzivilov-Brody-Podkamen-Brody-Smolno-Radzivilov. Reached and attacked enemy plane 10 km from Radzivilov. Combined operation with pilots Lieutenants Ingaunis and Snigirev. Brought down the enemy plane, which fell on the barbed wire of the 2nd line of trenches 3 km from the town of Brody and was there completely destroyed by our artillery fire."

Without the missing records, researchers can only speculate about Sergievsky's other claims. As Sergievsky notes, he spent hours patrolling alone behind enemy lines, where victories could not be officially confirmed. It is also likely that some of his foes did not crash. Spinning down as though mortally stricken was a common means of evading a pursuer in World War I aerial combat. Sergievsky did this himself when attacking balloons. In the midst of dogfights, pilots seldom could watch a falling plane until it hit the ground. Sergievsky, flying alone or with a novice wingman, had to keep his attention focused on the living—friends and foes. Like thousands of other fighter pilots in this and other wars, he reported the facts as he saw them, knowing, as he says, "In some of these fights it was hard to tell who actually should be credited with victories."

AF

---

tify, but the Revolutionary Committee gave orders to the men of my own squadron to put an armed guard around the officers' mess and to declare all the officers under arrest. In the meantime they were deliberating about what should be done with me.

I realized that, when the Army started to be ruled by revolutionary committees, and when a strict fulfillment of our duty was a crime, that was actually the end of the war for us. I considered it useless to remain there and to pretend that we could do anything when it was already too late.

I called all the officers of the squadron together, and put the question before them straight and short. I told them, "I am leaving the front. I am going to Kiev where I know some of the organizations against the new regime are starting their work. I think I will be much more useful there than here, and I ask you, who wants to go with me and who wants to remain."

With the exception of one second lieutenant who had socialist ideas, every member of the squadron was willing to go with me. It was impossible for us to take along our planes or cars, because all the squadron equipment was already under armed guard. But I intended to move the squadron later on to a place where it could be employed in the coming civil war. It was clear to me that the civil war would start soon.

I instructed one of the older officers to remain with the squadron, and to report to me at a given address in Kiev about everything that was going on.

Then I had to work out some plan of getting away. In thinking over all possible ways to escape, I did not want to tell them even to the officers who were willing to follow me. I kept my project secret. I simply told everybody to pack their baggage and send it with their orderlies to the railroad station, from where a train left every night for Kiev. The orderlies were instructed to proceed to Kiev with the officers' baggage, not waiting for the officers themselves.

About ten o'clock that night, a very agitated mechanic of my squadron, who was a member of the Revolutionary Committee, knocked at my door. He was extremely excited, and told me that he had run all the way from the headquarters of the Committee, where a resolution had just been passed on my action of the previous day—the shooting down of the German plane.

For violating the orders of the Revolutionary Committee, for breaking the terms of the armistice which the Revolutionary Committee had made with the local commander of the Austro-Hungarians in front of us, for insubordination to the highest authority of the Army (which was now the Revolutionary Committee), I was sentenced to death.

My mechanic implored me to run away as fast as I could, because a detachment of the guards of the Revolutionary Committee was already on the way to arrest me and execute me at daybreak. I considered that my baggage was already on the train at the station, with that of the other officers. The guards around the officers' mess were all my own men, and when all the officers walked one by one through the door, the guards pretended that they did not see us.

We walked to a nearby field hospital that was our meeting point. I went to the chief surgeon, who was in charge of the hospital and the hospital transport. In a few words I told him about our situation and asked him to lend us two horse carts for a few hours. I did not tell him where I was going to go; I simply told him that I had to put some distance between me and the place where they would be looking for me. He was glad to oblige.

I knew all the roads in the vicinity of the front very well. Taking side roads and paths through the forest, I led our group on a wide arc, and by daybreak arrived at a small railroad station fully fifty kilometers east of the location of our squadron. We wore overcoats without rank badges on the shoulder straps, put over our flying uniforms.

The War Winds Down

"During the afternoon of March 13, 1917," writes Winston Churchill, "the Russian Embassy in London informed us that they were no longer in contact with Petrograd."[1] The Russian capital was swept by revolution. Rebels arrested the Tsar, and the country came under the rule of a Provisional Government headed by Alexander Kerensky.

Urged on desperately by Britain and France, Kerensky vowed to continue the war against the Central Powers—who were, after all, occupying much Russian territory. But this decision was his undoing. His country had been bled white by the war: food was short, soldiers mutinied, workers struck, ethnic minorities rebelled, peace demonstrators filled the streets.

In such conditions, it was hard to get the Russian Army to do battle. In July, a brief Russian advance into Galicia, near where Boris Sergievsky's air squadron was stationed, petered out, turned into a rout (see p. 95) before counterattacking Germans and Austro-Hungarians, and provoked more rebellions in the ranks. The embittered Russian troops were in no mood for additional sacrifice. There was little more ground fighting during 1917.

In the air, however, the battles continued almost the entire year. The Russian pilots were officers, far less affected than foot soldiers by food shortages, exhaustion or revolutionary fervor. Although the army on the ground beneath them seldom left its trenches, they continued fighting the Germans in an almost private war of their own.

"While the [Russian] infantry, cavalry and artillery soon disbanded themselves, the air forces fought on until the very last moment," writes Edgar Middleton in *The Great War in the Air*, "The Revolution broke, still they fought on; the armies disbanded in hopeless disorder, still they fought on."[2]

In November 1917, the Bolsheviks staged their coup d'état, ousting Kerensky and taking power. At the front lines, Russian soldiers were already fraternizing and bartering with troops in the enemy trenches, or were simply beginning to walk home. Understandably, they did not take kindly (p. 100) to officers like Sergievsky, who wanted to keep on fighting the war which had already taken millions of lives. In December, the Bolsheviks negotiated an armistice with the Germans at Brest Litovsk, and World War I on the Eastern Front was over. A new and equally painful phase of Russian history, in which Sergievsky was also to play a part, the Russian Civil War, was about to begin.

AH

We all boarded the train at different times and in different cars. The next day the squadron assembled in my apartment in Kiev. Everyone was safe. The baggage also arrived safely. Our orderlies reported that the night train from Radzivilov had been surrounded by the guards of the Revolutionary Committee and very thoroughly searched. The train was delayed over two hours. All the roads leading from the squadron's quarters to the railroad station were heavily patrolled, and all through the night a general search was made of all the possible places in Radzivilov for me and the officers of the squadron. The armed guards of the Revolutionary Committee accompanied the train to the next station. Then, being sure we were not on board and could not

escape by train, they left the train just before we boarded it. My trick had worked perfectly.

Kiev was full of activity. It was not yet under the power of the Bolsheviks, and various organizations were trying to form some sort of resistance to the Red troops moving on Kiev from the north. At this time we knew that in south Russia, on the Don River and in the vicinity of the northern Caucasus, General Kornilov was organizing a new volunteer army.

We considered that it would be useless to join the army of General Kornilov just as ordinary fighters, without our planes. We believed that we would be much more useful to the cause of the White movement if we could get our equipment first. Some of the other aerial squadrons already had arrived at Kiev from the front, realizing that the war was over. Thousands and thousands of soldiers were leaving the lines, filling all the trains to their fullest capacity and sitting on the roofs and hanging on the steps of the cars. The Army was leaving the front.

I was in constant correspondence with the officer I left as my representative and observer with the squadron. He reported to me that after our departure there was a general meeting of the squadron and the second lieutenant with the socialist ideas was elected squadron leader. Then in his next report, my observer informed me that the socialist lieutenant was acting suspiciously. He reported that there was already a sort of armistice existing on the front, that some of the Austro-German air force officers were visiting the squadron and were holding mysterious conferences with the new squadron leader behind locked doors. In my turn I wrote to my observer, asking him to watch closely all the actions of the new squadron leader. If he found anything suspicious about the lieutenant's actions, he was to immediately inform the corps area headquarters where the chief of staff was still an officer of the general staff, and the same one who was there when I was in command of the squadron.

Then came the news that the Revolutionary Committee had decided to evacuate all the planes and all the supplies of the squadron from the front because no more fighting was expected.

The next report informed me that the planes were loaded on railroad flatcars and gave the approximate time of the departure of the squadron from Radzivilov. By this time it was clear to me and my observer that the new squadron leader had some sort of treacherous plan in mind. When the day of the departure of the squadron was set, my observer arranged with the chief of staff of the corps area that a special guard should be sent to the station.

The chief of staff and our officer were also present. Just before the train was to leave Radzivilov a few Austrian officers arrived, and after they exchanged some papers with the new squadron leader, the latter gave the order for the train to move west instead of east. Immediately he was arrested, and on him was found 30,000 Austrian crowns, the price paid by the Austrian Air Force for the squadron equipment. It was all arranged that the whole material equipment of the squadron was to be transferred to the Austrian side of the lines, which was only about eight kilometers from Radzivilov.

The chief of staff of the corps area, after arresting the new squadron leader, put my loyal officer in charge of it, and he brought the squadron to Kiev. The new squadron leader was also transported to Kiev as a prisoner and put in the military prison there.

Later he was tried for treason and, as the war was officially still going on, he was sentenced to death. But political events were moving so fast that before his sentence was pronounced he was freed by the Bolsheviks, who made a local revolution in a part of Kiev and, as their first action, liberated all the prisoners from all the jails regardless of the crimes they had committed.

The Kiev airdrome, a few miles from town, had accumulated quite a massive amount of aviation equipment. Several air groups and quite a few squadrons from the front all assembled there. Some of the squadrons flew over to join the new army that was organized in the south of Russia, the others declared themselves the Ukrainian Air Force. I decided to temporarily keep my squadron in Kiev, because quite a substantial White organization had assembled there, and in case of any fighting this organization would need an air force.

In the spring of 1918, Kiev had already passed several times from the hands of the Whites to the hands of the Bolsheviks, then to the hands of the Ukrainians. There were local revolutions in the garrison in the suburbs of the city. Going to bed in the evening, nobody knew under what regime he was going to wake up in the morning.

Finally a more or less steady Ukrainian government was organized, headed by General Skoropadsky. He started to organize all branches of the service and we succeeded in getting a certain amount of gasoline, which was so necessary for squadron training and practicing by new pilots.

Skoropadsky had a considerable program, not only for the army, but for all the branches of government. But his rule was challenged by socialist sections of the Ukrainians, and a revolutionary movement against his regime started,

out in the country. The Ukrainian movement was strongly supported by the Bolsheviks, and the fighting went on around Kiev.

Our supply of gasoline was not of high quality. We were flying every day, deep into the country, trying to find out where the advancing forces were assembled. Some of our planes were forced to land due to bad gasoline. Almost on every flight the motor would sputter, stop for a while, and then start working again. That sort of flying was very nerve-wracking, especially as the pilots knew that if they were taken prisoner by the Russian or Ukrainian Bolsheviks they would be tortured and eventually killed. Civil war is a very cruel war. The Whites tended not to take prisoners if they were known to be communists, and consequently the Bolsheviks were killing outright all the officers that they managed to take as prisoners.

Kiev was getting short of food supplies. I made a special flight to the province of Batavo, where the estate of my father-in-law was situated, to bring some flour by plane for the needs of my family. I knew that his estate was in a rather quiet part of the country, but in going there and coming back I don't know how many lines of different fronts I had to cross. The Whites were fighting the Reds, the Ukrainian Bolsheviks were fighting the Russian Bolsheviks, and the Ukrainian and Russian Bolsheviks were fighting the government of General Skoropadsky. The Greens, who were more or less just organized bandits, 30,000 strong, led by a man named Makhno, were fighting everybody, if they only could get something out of the fighting.

When I landed on a lawn in front of my father-in-law's estate, I was not sure what forces occupied it, but fortunately there was nobody there but my father-in-law and his servants. I flew back with a heavy sack of white flour, which brought great joy to my family in Kiev.

In the autumn of 1918 the circle of enemy forces tightened around Kiev, and it became apparent that the advancing Ukrainians, headed by Petliura, would overpower the defending forces. There were posters all over the town which stated, "You Don't Have to be a Hero, But You Ought to Join the Volunteers." The boys from the high schools, the students from the polytechnic college, all the officers who happened to be on leave in Kiev, the government employees, were joining the ranks of the defenders. My younger brother, Roman, who was then a first lieutenant of artillery, joined the ranks of the volunteers as a private in the infantry and was fighting somewhere on the outskirts of town.

I happened to catch the Spanish fever [flu] at this time, but we were so short

The Russian Civil War

Civil wars are cruel, and the Russian Civil War was one of the cruelest of them all. Both the victorious Bolsheviks and their opponents massacred prisoners and civilians. Medical supplies were short. The fighting extended to almost every corner of a vast country. No accurate casualty figures exist, but the death toll is estimated in the millions. Harvests were disrupted, refugees clogged the roads, and in 1921, just as the fighting ended, millions more people died in a famine.

The Civil War began in earnest in 1918, as opponents of the previous year's Bolshevik coup d'état took up arms. For most of the next three years the Bolsheviks were fighting the Whites: widely scattered armies led by former tsarist generals. Some of these commanders aimed at restoring the monarchy; some mainly sought power for themselves; a few talked vaguely of constitutions and reform. Their funds came mainly from the privileged classes, and from the other major countries of Europe, which did not want Bolshevism to spread.

Germany, Britain, France, Italy, the United States, Canada, and Japan all sent troops to support the Whites. Though they were reluctant to get drawn into actual combat, many of these countries also funneled arms and supplies to the various White armies. Yet another set of troops sometimes joined the chaotic fighting as well: armies of various ethnic groups, such as the Finns, Poles, and Ukrainians, who were trying to escape from centuries of Russian rule.

The first Russian Civil War campaign that Boris Sergievsky fought in (pp. 103–8) was that waged by Pavlo Skoropadsky. Skoropadsky was a large landowner and one of the wealthiest men in the Ukraine. He ruled much of that territory in the second half of 1918. An unscrupulous despot, he censored the press and restored property to the wealthy. Skoropadsky talked of bringing back the glories of Imperial Russia, but was basically installed by the Germans. They wanted a puppet regime in charge while their troops occupied the Ukraine and shipped its grain back to a hunger-ridden Germany. What fighting Skoropadsky's forces engaged in was less against the Bolsheviks than against Ukrainian nationalists. When they toppled him from power at the end of 1918, he took refuge with his patrons in Berlin.[1]

The next campaign Sergievsky joined (pp. 109–12) was a major turning point of the Civil War. In the summer and fall of 1919, an expeditionary force under the White general Nikolai Yudenich was armed and supplied mostly by the British. The force established itself at Narva, in today's Estonia. Yudenich aimed at making a quick, decisive march on the old Russian capital, Petrograd, just over one hundred miles away. If he had succeeded, it would have been an enormous symbolic and strategic blow.[2]

Yudenich almost made it. Sergievsky was with the vanguard of the army, which reached Pulkovo Heights, the suburban hillside site of a famous observatory. From there the Whites could even see trains pulling out of one of Petrograd's stations. An officer offered a general a look through his binoculars, the story goes, but the general declined, saying that the next day he would be walking on his beloved Nevsky Prospekt.

One of Yudenich's commanders, however, too eager to be the first to reach the city, had neglected orders to veer aside and cut the Moscow-Petrograd railway. As a result, the Bolsheviks were able to send in supplies and their top military commander, Leon Trotsky, in his famous armored train. As often in the Russian Civil War, his oratory and brilliant leadership proved decisive. Trotsky's troops fought a battle with the Whites at Pulkovo on the night of October 21, 1919, and forced Yudenich's army to retreat. The Bolsheviks won a major battle in southern Russia the same day and another in Siberia two weeks later. Never again were the Whites able to threaten Moscow or Petrograd.

Although the war dragged on and Sergievsky fought briefly on yet another front (pp. 115–17) the following year, there was no hope of a White victory after the battle at Pulkovo Heights.

AH

of fighting pilots that in spite of a high fever I was flying every day. Coming back after the flight, I usually was so weak that I could not climb out of the cockpit and had to be lifted out of it by my mechanics. Finally my condition became so serious that I had to stay in bed, and due to the strain of flying with the high fever, I almost died. The doctor who was attending me told my wife that I was the first human being in his whole practice who had lived through such a high fever—42.5 degrees Celsius [108.5 degrees Fahrenheit].

When I was recovering from my sickness and was still very weak, the conditions on the Kiev front grew worse than ever. We expected that the city would be taken any day. The defenders of the city were retreating under pressure of the advancing enemy, and fighting was already going on in the streets of the suburbs. The artillery had already taken positions on the city streets and squares. Every minute, the windows were shaking and trembling and breaking from the explosions of our own fire and from the shells of the enemy.

One of the shells hit the roof of our house, and went right through the roof and ceiling. Part of the ceiling and the chandelier fell right on the table of our dining room, where dinner was about to be served. Very luckily nobody had taken his place at the table yet. We were just entering the room.

In early November 1918, I found out that in a few hours the airdrome would be occupied by the enemy, and there was no place that we could fly away to. I did not want to leave my powerful fighting plane in the hands of the enemy and went to the aerodrome to destroy my plane. That was the day when I was saved by one of my former infantry soldiers, as related in the previous chapter.

Our squadron now had no planes, and the situation was desperate. The few remaining defenders of the city decided to try to make their way out and perhaps join some other White forces somewhere, we did not know where. But we decided to assemble in the center of the city, in the museum. Each officer had to carry a rifle and a sufficient amount of ammunition.

Over 2,000 officers had assembled in the museum when the victorious army of Petliura entered the city. The museum was immediately surrounded by the Petliura forces. Field artillery guns were set up along all the streets leading to the museum, and also a great many machine guns were installed, not only on the streets but also on top of most of the buildings surrounding the museum.

We were only 2,000 and had only rifles and a limited amount of ammunition. The senior officer of our group started negotiations with the Petliura forces, offering certain conditions under which they would let us through, with our arms, unharmed.

While negotiations were going on all communications with the outside world were cut. We had no food, the water supply was cut, and we had to agree to the terms of the Ukrainians. They promised to let us out if we would surrender all our rifles in the hall of the museum.

As soon as our rifles were surrendered, the Ukrainians declared that they would set us free, not all together, but individually. After everyone had been tried, and if we were not guilty, we would be released. The date of the trial was never mentioned.

The water supply was reestablished, but for the first few days we were given no food. Then our relatives were allowed to bring food. Our wives and mothers and sisters waited in line outside the museum, insulted by the Red guards, waiting for their turn to transmit the food packages. Those who had no relatives did not receive any food. Naturally those who received any food distributed it among their less fortunate companions. The amount of food that my wife was bringing in was sufficient to feed almost all the officers of my squadron.

We were packed in the rooms of the museum to such an extent there was not enough room to lie down on our backs. The whole floor was taken up, and we all lay on our right sides. If one man on the end of the room turned over, everyone would have to turn over with him, onto his left side.

In the meantime, our fate was decided in some revolutionary tribunals of the Ukrainian socialists. The museum was naturally not adapted for holding 2,000 prisoners. The plumbing facilities were quite inadequate. There were no bathrooms. We were not allowed to go outside for exercise, and because there was insufficient room inside to move around, we had to all sit or lie down almost on the same spot. There were no brooms to sweep the floors. Dirt was rapidly accumulating, and the quantity of lice was getting unbearable.

One night I was sitting on the window sill, with almost no clothes on, trying to eliminate the invasion of lice from my clothes, when a terrible explosion shook the whole building. The center part of the roof of the museum, which was a glass dome, fell in, one of the walls collapsed, and the sound of the explosion was followed by terrible shrieks of people wounded by the falling glass and stones from the wall.

As we found out later, a faction of the Ukrainian Bolsheviks decided to get rid of all the prisoners by blowing the museum up with dynamite. The dynamite was probably not of very good quality or not properly placed, because the destruction of the museum was only partial. Only the dome and one wall were destroyed, but it gave us a good chance for escape.

Immediately after the explosion we heard the rattle of machine guns on the streets. The Ukrainians were trying to shoot down those who were running from the museum onto the streets. But I did not try to escape through the street. Leaping through the opening in the wall, I ran through the backyards. Jumping over several fences, running in a very wide circle, and avoiding the guarded area around the museum, I went home.

When my wife rushed to meet me with outstretched arms I told her, "Don't touch me, I am too dirty and full of lice. Quickly, prepare a hot bath and start a good fire in the stove to burn my clothes." I enjoyed that bath the most of any I ever had in my life.

After a good meal we started to discuss what had to be done. I knew that in a few hours the Ukrainians would try to re-arrest me. Soon other officers of the squadron arrived and we had a hasty conference with them. It was decided that we could not stay in Kiev, it would be suicide. I went to my mother's apartment and asked her to take care of my boy, who was then six years old. My brother refused to leave the city, saying that someone had to stay with mother to protect her and help her under these critical circumstances. I could not take my boy along because we had to walk out of the city and maybe fight our way out. He was too small to go along, but my wife was ready to start. We could take with us only such possessions as we could carry ourselves.

When I said good-bye to Mother I did not know that I would not see her and my son for ten years, and that I would never see my brother again.

It was about two o'clock in the morning when we set out from Kiev on foot. We had a very long and difficult walk before we were able to board a train, way out in the country, which was carrying some of the German soldiers being evacuated from the Ukraine.

The train went very slowly, and the cars were overcrowded. The train would be stopped at some little station, or even out in the country, and shooting would start from both sides of the train, the bullets passing through the walls of the cars. The women would lie on the floor of the car and the men would shoot through the windows until the train could again move forward.

It took us ten days to reach the German border. As soon as we crossed the border the train moved faster, and before long we arrived at Berlin.

After cleaning up in one of the Berlin hotels, I reported to the office of the representatives of the White Russian organizations and was assigned to the Interallied Commission for Re-evacuation of Prisoners of War, at a camp in Ulm on the Danube River. The senior officer was an American, Captain Marshall. There were other members of the commission representing England and France, and several members representing Russia, because the camp at Ulm was mainly filled with Russian prisoners of war.

The prisoners in the camp numbered almost 10,000, and most of them were already very strongly under the influence of the Bolshevik propaganda. They had their own meetings and committees and were discussing complicated political problems. They did not want to be repatriated immediately, being afraid that they would be drafted into some army and compelled to fight again. The whole situation disgusted me.

I got in touch with the Allied Mission in Berlin, and obtained permission to leave for England in order to join the Royal Air Force. Together with Major Sakhnovsky, whom I knew during the German War in Russia, I organized a group of about twenty aviation officers who happened to be in Germany and we moved as a group to England.

The British War Ministry was maintaining a camp for Russians near New Market. Our air group was first sent there, but we were able to get an assignment to one of the flying schools for examination. After a flight test I was sent to an instructors' flying school at Feltwell, Norfolk, where I remained for only a few days, getting aquainted with the newest types of British planes. Then I got an assignment as a flight instructor in the Royal Air Force, with the rank of captain, at the Netheravon Flying School, situated on the Salisbury Plain.

Among the pupils assigned to my group at this school were twelve of the officers of the air group organized by us in Berlin. Some of them were from my old squadron.

The easy, orderly life in the school, after the strain of the war, was a great relief to me. The few months that I remained there as an instructor were like a wonderful vacation. But when we learned that Russian White armies fighting on various fronts were in great need of trained aviators, I resigned from the British service and got an appointment as squadron leader in the White army commanded by General Yudenich. This army, called the Northwestern Army, was fighting on the territory of Estonia and Pskov province, heading for Petrograd.

The sea trip to Narva, where our transport was disembarked, was uneventful. In October of 1919, I was again on Russian soil.

At this time, the Northwestern Army was about 10,000 men strong. It is quite amazing how this army was organized and how it grew almost from nothing. First, there were only about 500 volunteers, officers and men, who started the movement. As they marched toward Petrograd, entering little villages and liberating them from the Bolsheviks, the peasants and reservists would join them. Then they would encounter a Bolshevik regiment, and some of the companies would surrender and go over to the Whites. In a very few months, the army grew from 500 to 10,000 men.

It had no ammunition supply. If a regimental commander reported that he needed some ammunition, the usual answer from headquarters would be, "Take it from the Reds."

England had sent over some of her most obsolete old planes, with which we had to organize the air force of the new army. I received an R.E.8 airplane, which I saw only in museums in England. It had an air-cooled [V-12] engine; the front cylinders were always too cold, the rear ones always too hot.

The first flight I made in it almost ended in disaster. I had orders to find out what reinforcements were being rushed to Petrograd from Moscow by the main Moscow-Petrograd railroad. For this purpose I had to fly far inland and along the railroad

19. Sergievsky during his service in England as a flying instructor in the Royal Air Force during 1919. As always, he is wearing his Order of St. George; its cross hangs below his RAF pilot's wings. He also is wearing his Russian Military Pilot's Badge on his right breast pocket. *Courtesy of the editors.*

line. When I was on my way back, over the center of Petrograd, I gained considerable altitude, not trusting my engine very much, and I was quite right. With a sound of an explosion the engine stopped. It actually flew to pieces in the air. Looking forward I saw only some of the cylinders standing there, the others were completely missing.

By this time the Bolsheviks had established a rule for treating army officers that they took prisoner. Into every star on the shoulder straps they would drive a nail several inches long. Having a staff captain's shoulder straps with four stars on each strap I considered it a rather upleasant situation. In my mind's eye I counted eight long nails, and I thought that I had better try to glide to our lines.

Very fortunately a strong east wind was blowing, but I did not know the exact location of the lines, because they were swiftly moving all the time. I suppose that in all my aviation career I never made a more efficient and longer glide. When I was over Narva, which I knew for sure was in our possession, I still had 1,300 meters of altitude. I made a good landing on the Narva field, and felt myself the happiest man in this world, being surrounded by my friends inquiring from where I had come so noiselessly. I suppose that I could win a glider contest with this R.E.8.

Our aviation equipment in the Northwestern Army was so inadequate that we really were unable to do any useful work, so once in a while we would volunteer to go with the infantry and fight in the ranks, because against every man in the White Army there were at least twenty-five or thirty Reds. And still in every encounter with the enemy, the Northwestern Army was always victorious.

We were moving swiftly forward, and soon we were actually at the gates of Petrograd. We could see

A Letter of Recommendation

In the fall of 1919, Sergievsky was restless. Though he was enjoying his stint as an RAF flying instructor, the struggle for Russia was still in doubt, and he could not stand apart from it. But he wanted to return as a pilot, not a foot soldier. The following letter of recommendation, originally handwritten,[1] doubtless enhanced his reputation as a leader of pilots.

B Squadron
Netheravon Flying School
Royal Air Force

Captain Sergievsky
Russian Forces

The above named Russian officer has been serving in my squadron as a flying instructor. He is a very able pilot who flies all types of single and two seater machines excellently and with real accuracy. He is a capital instructor who can explain and teach with success, and seems to fill his pupils with an excellent morale and enthusiasm. He is keenness itself, conscientious to a degree, and a tireless worker for the advancement and improvement of his pupils. He is a most popular officer both with English and Russian colleagues, and a natural leader. I think he would be an ideal flight commander, possessing as he does a thorough sense of discipline and command, energy, initiative, and resource.

RH Peck, Squadron Leader
B Squadron

Netheravon
22.9.19

AF

the tops of the churches and the bright dome of the Cathedral of St. Isaac. But our advance was too swift, the lines of our communication grew too long, the front too extended for our number. The quicker we moved forward the deeper we were plunged into the midst of the Bolshevik armies which were rushed from every direction to save the capital. At the gates of Petrograd we found ourselves entirely surrounded and had to fight our way back.

With our usual success we fought our way back, not leaving any prisoners, carrying away our dead and wounded. We crossed the border of Estonia. Our army was disarmed by the Estonians and part of it put in internment camps.

During our advance on Petrograd, entire companies of the Red Army would surrender to us. During our retreat, some of those companies surrendered back to the Reds. We had to work out some sort of a trick in order to keep those who had already joined our ranks.

Whenever a company of the Red Army surrendered to us, we would line them up and say, "All the communists and commissars, two steps forward." As they were very much hated by the rest of the Red Army, if they did not step forward they would be pushed forward from the ranks. There were usually only a few of them in each company, maybe two or three. Then we would take their names and also take the names of the rest of the company, and make out a statement saying, "Company so and so of the Red Army delivered their communists and commissars—names so and so—and themselves executed them." This statement would be put in an envelope, taken in an airplane and dropped over the Red front.

That was a certain guarantee that there was no way back to the Reds for this company. They would not surrender now, being afraid of persecution for what they had done to their communists. Maybe the system was cruel, but we found out it was the only way to keep the Reds who were volunteering to serve with the Whites.

The air force of the Northwestern Army was not put in an internment camp. We were free to go wherever we wanted and to do whatever we liked. Only our planes were confiscated by the Estonians. There was also a search for arms in our quarters and we had to surrender even our personal revolvers and automatics. The Estonian officer in charge of the search party seemed overly careful and took as an arm also a small, decorative sword which was a part of the flying uniform of the officers in Russia.

As this sword was in itself a decoration, had the Emperor's initials on it, and an inscription "For Bravery," the loss of it was painful to me. I went to the commandant of Tallinn and asked him to return the little sword to me. He was doubtful, said that the order was to disarm the Northwestern Army, and that the sword was considered an arm. Then I asked that he order the sword brought to his office and take a look at it. When it was brought in and put in front of him on his desk, I told him, "If you consider that this sword is dangerous to the independence of the Estonian Republic you can keep it. If not, give it to me, because it is valuable only to me, and not for fighting purposes." He took the matter up with the War Minister of Estonia; finally I got my sword, and I still have it.

Estonia is a very small country and it was in its first year of independence. To obtain any sort of employment was very hard for a foreigner. Most of the men and officers of the Northwestern Army had to make their living working in lumber camps in the forests. That work was very hard and very poorly paid.

Among the officers of the Northwestern Army and their families who ran away from Russia were quite a few representatives of different sorts of art— singers, actors, artists, dancers. They tried to get together and organize some sort of a theatrical company which would help to make a living for themselves and would also help Estonia, which was rather poor in native talent.

A small company of singers was organized and they started rehearsals of the Offenbach operetta, *La Belle Hélène*, in one of the theaters in Tallinn. Mrs. Sergievsky was chosen for the part of Hélène. The part of Paris was assigned to a prominent tenor from the Theater of Musical Drama in Petrograd. They went on with rehearsals every day.

Having nothing better to do I was present at most of the rehearsals, taking Mrs. Sergievsky to the theater and back after the rehearsals. Two days before the opening night, the leading tenor fell sick with a severe case of typhus. There was a regular panic among the members of the company. The show was already sold out and some of the money already spent. It was impossible to do the show without the leading tenor and just as impossible to pay the money back. Somebody suggested that I try to sing the part, because they had heard me singing bits of it in the intermissions during the rehearsal.

As I had never tried or intended to be a professional singer, at first I flatly refused. But every member of the company implored me to try, and perhaps save the situation. I had to work night and day to study the part. It was my first appearance on the stage.

I suppose I was completely lacking in artistic temperament because I did not get excited or nervous at all. The main thing for me was to save the money which the company needed so much. I knew that whether I sang well or badly nobody could claim their money back, because it was announced that the part of Paris, due to the sudden sickness of the leading tenor, would be sung by an amateur singer.

I still believe that I did not deserve the acclaim which followed my performance, but the success was such that the manager of the theater immediately after the performance came to my dressing room and offered me a year's contract at a very good salary. Planning to go on fighting on some other front, I declined his offer. I said that I would sing in performances that would not exceed the limitations of my voice, as long as I was in Tallinn, but I could not guarantee how long I would stay there.

After *La Belle Hélène* I sang in several other Italian and Russian operas, including *Traviata, Rigoletto,* and *Lakmé.* Our company traveled through all the main cities of Estonia with continuing success.

Such performances were possible for me because while I was still in college, I took some singing lessons from my aunt, who was a prominent singer in Italian and Russian opera companies. But I did it just for fun, liking music. I never took it seriously and never studied to become a singer. In later years I was present often during the rehearsals of the opera class of the conservatory of Kiev, where my wife was studying. Sometimes the opera class would assemble in our apartment, which was large enough and convenient for such meetings, and often, if one of the singers who was needed for an ensemble was missing or late, the other singers would ask me to sing the part. It was easy for me to learn a part quickly because I had an unusually good musical memory. But never before did I think of appearing on the stage to sing in public. This "side gift" of mine actually saved us from starving in Estonia.

While traveling with the theatrical company around Estonia, I was in constant communication with the White Russian organizations still fighting on other fronts, and was waiting only to collect enough money to make the journey to south Russia or to Siberia where fighting was still in progress.

Finally a transport was organized, and with some men of my own squadron I was able to sail from Tallinn to Gdansk, which was the new seaport of Poland, assigned to it by the Versailles treaty. From Gdansk we had to take a train and proceed through Poland. Arriving at Warsaw, I reported to the military representative of the White Russians attached to the Polish high command. From him I found out that I had a commission to organize the air force of the Third Army of General Wrangel, who was then fighting with his two armies in southern Russia.

His Russian Third Army was fighting on the Polish front, facing east. At this time the Poles were at war with the Bolsheviks and they considered the Third Army of General Wrangel as their ally. Several civil organizations were helping to supply the Third Army in Poland. The most important of these organizations was headed by the famous revolutionary leader Savinkov. Formerly he had belonged to the terrorist group of the revolutionaries, and was one of the organizers of the assassination of Grand Duke Sergei, who was the governor general of Moscow. Savinkov was also responsible for many terrorist acts during the old regime in Russia, but he occupied high official positions in the Kerensky government.

With the advent of the Bolsheviks he became an emigrant, and with the energy which was so typical of him he joined the White organizations. All his life, Savinkov was a conspirator and a terrorist. He always wanted to be active, always wanted to play a larger part in politics.

After the White movement failed, he was unable to wait in idleness, he wanted to do something. He went incognito to Russia, but was arrested as soon as he crossed the border. In a few days there was a report in the Bolshevik newspapers that Savinkov had committed suicide, throwing himself out of a window of the prison. It remains an open question whether he threw himself out or was thrown out.

While Savinkov was in Poland he obtained considerable help from Marshal Pilsudski. They were pals from their school days and were connected by personal friendship and common revolutionary activity for many years before the war. Due to the "pull" that Savinkov had in high Polish circles, it was possible to get sufficient supplies for the Russian Third Army, which actually had no base of its own and no territory to operate from.

A very young general, only twenty-eight years old, General Permikim, was in command of the Third Army. He joined the Bulgarian Army in the War of 1912 as a private, and so distinguished himself in that war that he rose to the rank of colonel. When the war against Germany started in 1914, he joined the Russian Army as a private again, and got promotion to the rank of captain. He was one of the original organizers of the Northwestern Army, and due to his unusual bravery and exceptional gifts in the methods of civil warfare, he was promoted to the rank of general.

The soldiers had real adoration for him, and some of his exploits were told from man to man like fairy tales. His assignment to command of the Third Army was met by unanimous approval.

In organizing the air force of his army I had to report personally to him. I succeeded in obtaining several two-seater fighter and observation planes and started to train the flying personnel in the proper use of them, with our base at the flying field of Mokotovo near Warsaw. I had all possible assistance and co-operation from our allies, the Polish Air Force.

There was a very difficult situation on the Polish front at this time, and the French General Weygand arrived at Warsaw. General Permikim was called to Warsaw for a war conference with General Weygand in November of 1920.

While the conferences were going on, we received a message that the Third Army had advanced too far east and was apparently cut off and surrounded by the Reds. Immediately General Permikim decided to join his army in distress. There was only one way to get to it—by plane. I was assigned to fly him over the front and find the army, wherever it was. We knew only the general direction. It was a difficult task as we did not even know whether there would be a landing field available anywhere near the army.

Our flight had to start the next morning at daybreak. When we arrived at Mokotovo, a heavy fog was hanging low over the airfield. Technically speaking, there was no ceiling and no visibility. In front of our hangar stood our best plane, the latest type of German two-seater fighter, a Halberstadt.

I informed the general that we would have to wait for more favorable weather conditions. The general replied that his army was in trouble and that he wanted to be with it, no matter what chances we had to take. We had to fly.

The plane was not equipped with instruments for blind flying as they did not exist then. I rose above the fog and flew toward the sun in the general easterly direction of the army. There was not even a compass in the plane, and soon the skies were overcast by heavy clouds. I lost sight of the sun, and there was no way to tell which way was east, west, north, or south.

I tried to find some sort of an opening below to see the ground and identify some landmarks in order to ascertain our position. After about two hours of flying I finally succeeded in descending through the fog and found a railroad line which I could identify by the bridges as the one going east, approximately in the direction we had to take.

We flew on for a considerable length of time, until the weather became so heavy that a continuation of the flight became impossible. I was actually flying through a dense fog, very low, trying to follow the railroad line. Obstacles like railroad stations, water towers, and high trees near the line would rise right in front of me and I had to jump them like obstacles in a steeplechase. As the fog thickened it became more and more dangerous, and an immediate landing was imperative.

Near one of the railroad stations I found a flat piece of ground which looked to me like a possible landing place. I tried to make a good three-point landing on it, but the moment the wheels touched the ground they sunk to the axles. It was a marsh. Slowly the plane turned upside down. I had a slight cut on my forehead from hitting the instrument panel, and the general had a slight injury to his neck.

When we climbed out from under the plane we did not know where we were, whether the district was occupied by the Polish Army, or by the White or the Red Army. If it was the Reds, we decided to fight until we were killed, because certain death after terrible torture would be our lot if we became prisoners.

Fortunately, the station was located in the Polish zone. We were immediately taken to a Polish hospital and treated with the utmost courtesy. From the Polish officers we found out that the Third Army was nearby, and that it had disentangled itself from the difficult situation of the previous day. The general was able to proceed to his headquarters on horseback. I was ordered to take the train back to Warsaw and go on with the organization of our air force.

A few days later Poland signed an armistice with the Soviets and the Third Army was left to itself. The Polish Army was not our ally any more, but it was not our enemy. The armistice signed by the Poles did not concern the Third Army.

An army of about 10,000 men could not expect to fight successfully against the Red Army of Russia. Eventually we had to retreat and crossed the border of Poland on the River Zbruch. The Polish authorities, according to international law, had to disarm and intern their former allies. At our base at Mokotovo our airplanes had to be confiscated. It was the end of the civil war as far as we were concerned.

Just as in Estonia, we were left to our fate in a foreign country, with nothing but what we had on our persons. Mrs. Sergievsky and I again had to call on our musical talents and, organizing a small opera company, we toured several towns in Poland, making a decent living for ourselves.

In the meantime the rest of the army was put in internment camps, and their fate was not to be envied. I heard of the very successful activities of the American and English Y.M.C.A., especially their prisoner of war departments.

20. Sergievsky, in the center wearing black pants, sits amid a group of interned Russian prisoners, who are whiling away their time doing bodybuilding in a YMCA camp, probably at Toren, Poland, in 1921. *Courtesy of the editors.*

They had a considerable amount of money left from their war work in western Europe, and their representatives arrived in Poland to organize relief in the prison and internment camps for Russian and Ukrainian armies.

Thinking that through the medium of the Y.M.C.A. I could be useful to my fellow countrymen in trouble, I applied for work with the American Y.M.C.A. My knowledge of English and other qualifications made it possible for me to get an assignment as an attaché of the American Y.M.C.A. to one of the largest internment camps, in the fortress at Toren. Later I was transferred to the greater Poznań area.

During my work with the American Y.M.C.A., I got to know the secretary who was in charge of the Toren camp. His name was Evald Kvam. He was from a small town in North Dakota and was of Norwegian descent.

If ever on this earth there lived a real Christian soul, that was Mr. Evald Kvam. I never could image such devotion as his to the task that he undertook, of helping the unfortunate prisoners. He labored day and night. All the money at his disposal, which was quite considerable, was not sufficient to fill all the relief work. Out of his modest salary he was helping the prisoners to the extent of almost starving himself. He gave away his personal belongings. If he saw one of the prisoners wearing a very poor pair of shoes and his own shoes would fit the prisoner, he would give away his own shoes. Finally he had only one change of clothes, two changes of underwear, and one pair of shoes from a rather big wardrobe that he brought along with him.

Without knowing the language of the prisoners, he understood the soul of the Russian people better than many Russians do, and he loved with all his heart those whom he was helping. The prisoners simply adored him, but some of them would take advantage of his generosity.

I tried to protect his interests and save him from extreme exploitation of his generosity. But most of his personal help was done so secretly that no matter how closely I would try to watch him, he would quickly dispose of all his salary and his belongings before I could do anything about it.

There came a change in the personnel of the Y.M.C.A., and Evald Kvam received an order to turn over his camp to another secretary and go back to America. But his life already was so entangled in the needs and lives of the prisoners that he felt he could not leave them in this difficult period. He went to Warsaw and appealed for permission to stay, even without salary. But the head of the Y.M.C.A. would not change his mind, and the order for Evald Kvam to depart was repeated.

The train in which Mr. Kvam had to leave from Toren was going at midnight. At the close of office hours in our little Y.M.C.A. office, when he turned over to me all the Y business of the camp so that I could turn it over later to the new secretary, we said good-bye.

I told him that I would go and see him off at the train. With a very strange smile he told me, "Of course you can go to the station, but perhaps you won't find me." Not understanding the meaning of this sentence I asked him, "Are you not going away?" He smiled again and told me "Oh, yes, I am going away tonight." He left me quite puzzled.

Quite a few of us went to the station. The train arrived and departed. Mr. Kvam was not there. I thought that he had simply postponed his departure, but wondered why he did not let us know about it, knowing that we would get up and walk over a mile to the station at midnight.

The following morning the new secretary, Mr. H. D. Anderson, arrived. We had to turn over to him the stock in the Y warehouse, which was located in an old German barracks not far from the camp. With the new secretary we went to the warehouse. It was locked from the inside, and I could not open it with my key. We had to get a locksmith to force the lock.

When we entered the warehouse we found the body of Evald Kvam hanging behind a blanket in one of the closets. There were quite a few letters on him, some addressed to me, some addressed to his friends.

Mr. Kvam was always very fond of our religious services in the Russian Orthodox Church, and although officially a Lutheran, he attended our camp church every Sunday. In one of his letters he asked to be buried by the Russian priest who was his personal friend and with the rites of the Russian Orthodox Church.

It is amazing how thoughtful Mr. Kvam was about every detail that would follow the discovery of his body. He wanted to make it as easy for us as possible. Knowing the effects of death by hanging, like the falling out of the tongue, he had put one bandage over his mouth, another one under his chin, closed his eyes, and put a third bandage on his eyes so that we would not even have to bother with closing his eyes. When we removed the bandages his face was perfectly peaceful and did not show any signs of the kind of death he had inflicted on himself.

The funeral of Mr. Kvam was quite an event in the prison camp. Hundreds of war veterans who could not be moved by anything in life or death were weeping like children. The chorus hardly could sing because every member was a friend of the dead man, and a friend who owed something to Mr. Kvam. The Polish authorities of the camp and quite a few Americans from Warsaw, including most of the personnel of the headquarters of the Y.M.C.A., arrived for the funeral.

Mr. Anderson, the secretary replacing Mr. Kvam, asked me with perfect franknesss to tell him what I thought was the best policy to take. Should he resign or try to carry on the work Mr. Kvam was doing? Being frank as he wanted me to be, I told him that to carry on the work the same way Mr. Kvam had done was impossible for any human being, but if he would keep it as his supreme aim in his work, he would be very useful in remaining on the job.

I had the pleasure of working with Mr. Anderson for over a year. After the death of Mr. Kvam, he really did a wonderful job, not only in the Toren camp,

but also when he was assigned to be the head of the large Poznań area with several camps in it.

While working with the American Y.M.C.A. I was waiting all the time for something to start again on one of the borders of Russia where we could take up our arms again. But almost two years went by and nothing was happening. The main event was the crossing of the Polish border by the famous bandit, the leader of the Greens, Makhno, who was made prisoner, together with his wife and his staff, in the same camp where my office was located.

Besides the American Y.M.C.A. there was a mission of the British Relief Committee working in our camp. Their splendid work, mostly among the families of the interned prisoners, was outstanding, and our Prisoner of War Department fully cooperated with the British Relief Committee.

5

On to New Worlds

In 1923 I saw no more hope of getting back to Russia. I concluded that it would be much better for me to choose some other country for permanent residence and try to start life all over again. From what I heard from my friends and read in books, magazines, and newspapers, the only country on earth that could become my new adopted country was the United States of America. Although I had no relatives there and did not know a single soul, I decided we would go there on our own and started to save the necessary money for a passage for myself and Mrs. Sergievsky.

In August of 1923, I secured two third-class tickets on the Royal Mail liner *Orduna* and we sailed from Cherbourg, France, to the United States. When we landed in New York our capital was $60 and a lot of ambition.

I went to the employment bureau of the Y.M.C.A. on 23rd Street and secured a letter of recommendation which stated that I was a civil engineer and an aviator. With this letter I started to go from one office to the other asking for some sort of employment. Very quickly I found out that nothing could be done in the field of aviation. There was a tremendous over-supply of wartime aviators in America, as in every other country. Civil aviation did not exist.

The $60 was shrinking rapidly. I went to the office of the company that was building the Holland Tunnel at that time, and presented my credentials. The engineer who interviewed me said that it was customary in America to start from the bottom and although I was an engineer, would I be willing to take a pick and shovel and go to work as a laborer in the construction of the tunnel?

Every time I drive through the Holland Tunnel I feel proud that I actually built part of it with my own hands. From my school days, all through the years of college and military service, I was very fond of sports and always kept myself physically fit, so the heavy manual labor on the tunnel construction was not too hard for me. I felt fine, and even though we often worked overtime, loading and unloading barges of cement and carrying heavy sacks of it on our

Sikorsky II: Starting Afresh in America

Warned by a loyal worker that the Bolsheviks were coming for him, Igor Sikorsky escaped from Russia in February 1918. Making his way to Paris, he designed a large bomber for the French Air Service, and the government approved a construction contract—only to cancel it when World War I ended. Sikorsky, thirty years old, with a remarkable ten years of accomplishment in aviation behind him, faced unemployment and poverty. He decided to pursue a new aviation career in America.[1]

Arriving in New York in March 1919, Sikorsky found few opportunities. To the public, aviation meant daredevil barnstormers in war surplus Jennies. Sikorsky's first two attempts to start airplane companies quickly collapsed for lack of funds. His designs for bombers for the U.S. Air Service netted him only $1,500; there was no money to build them. To survive, he taught night courses in mathematics and astronomy to other Russian émigrés—and married a fellow teacher, Elizabeth Semion, in 1924.

In 1923, Sikorsky and a group of Russian financial backers launched the Sikorsky Aero Engineering Corporation. The émigré community also provided the workers and the site for an alfresco factory—a chicken farm in Mineola, Long Island, owned by Victor Utgoff, a former Imperial Russian naval flier. The Sikorskys and the Utgoffs lived in the farmhouse. Other Russians came whenever they could to work on the company's first project—a twin-engined, fourteen-passenger biplane transport.

Boris Sergievsky was among these grease-stained regulars, "calling each other Baron, Count, or General, like inmates of an asylum, and making tools of anything handy," according to the *New Yorker*.[2] They made the airplane's fuselage of angle iron cut from war surplus cots found in a nearby junkyard. Surplus navy turnbuckles and cable braced the structure, used Hispano-Suiza motors provided marginal power, even the tires were secondhand. Sikorsky's friend, the composer Sergei Rachmaninoff, contributed $5,000 to complete the plane in a rented hangar at nearby Roosevelt Field.

On May 4, 1924, the Sikorsky S-29-A (for America) staggered into the air, lost power in one of its two worn engines, and crash-landed on a golf course. But it was soon repaired and, with 400-horsepower Liberty engines, proceeded to impress the American aviation world with its capabilities. Over 400 air-minded passengers went for a ride in the S-29-A's spacious cabin in 1924, and publicity stunts like toting two baby grand pianos to Washington in the S-29-A demonstrated its ability to carry large freight loads.

None of these demonstrations led to orders for more S-29-As, and in 1926 the company leased the one and only S-29-A to the colorful racing pilot Roscoe Turner.[3] But this junkyard airplane, created by a dedicated band of émigrés on a chicken farm, had already launched Igor Sikorsky's second career in aviation. And in February 1925, the federal government authorized the Post Office Department to award airmail service contracts to private airlines for three to five years with guaranteed subsidies for each mile they flew. New airlines needed new airliners, and Sikorsky was ready to provide them.

AF

necks, I managed to gain about twelve pounds [5.4 kilograms] in three weeks at work in the tunnel.

On Saturday afternoons I would go out to one of the airfields on Long Island, to watch the airplanes and try to get aquainted with the pilots and the mechanics. I simply could not stay away from the aviation game. I soon found out that Mr. Igor Sikorsky was building a large plane on a farm on Long Island, the first of his planes in America. I visited him there and renewed my acquaintance with him, which had started in Russia in our college days. The plane was not ready yet, and due to lack of funds it was hard to tell when it was going to be ready.

At Roosevelt Field I found a young pilot who was just learning to fly, and who had a little Jenny of his own. I offered to give him instruction in the plane for the right to fly it myself. We started to carry paying passengers for five dollars a trip, splitting the income. I found my wings again, but that was only on weekends.

Working on the tunnel, and later in the National Biscuit Company factory during the long week, I was constantly thinking of the few hours Saturday afternoon and all of Sunday which I would spend at the airfield. I was so eager to fly as much as possible during these few hours that I did not allow any time for meals and would have my first real meal only after sunset.

In 1924 the work of the Sikorsky Aero Engineering Corporation had advanced to such an extent that it was possible for me to join them. I started to work as a draftsman, and also did the stress analysis of the planes. When the first plane since my employment by the Sikorsky Corporation was completed (the S-31), I was assigned to test it. Mr. Sikorsky remarked that it was logical that the man who did the stress analysis should test the plane (and be the first to face the consequences if there were any mistakes in the stress calculations).

The S-31 was sold to Argentina through the Fairchild Company. Powered by a Wright Whirlwind engine, the S-31 was quite a successful design, with very high performance for its power. Unfortunately only one plane of this type was ever built.

The S-32 was a much larger plane, powered by a 420-horsepower Liberty engine. It was an open-cockpit plane with three separate cockpits. The two front cockpits each held two passengers, and the pilot was in the rear cockpit. There was ample room for baggage also. The plane was ordered by the Andian National Corporation for work in South America. It was designed as a landplane, but with provision to substitute pontoons for the wheels.

The tests of the S-32 were successfully completed, and demonstration flights were made for the representatives of the purchaser. During those flights I per-

21. Sergievsky, third from left, and his fellow Russian émigré workers in front of the Sikorsky S-29-A that they have nearly completed, in the spring of 1924. *Courtesy of Igor I. Sikorsky Historical Archives, Inc.*

formed different stunts with the plane and even looped it to demonstrate its strength.

The Andian National Corporation already had a pilot for their South American work, but apparently they were not sure that he would stay long enough in South America. During one of the demonstration flights, a representative of the company asked me if I would be willing to go to South America and fly the S-32 for them, if it turned out that their pilot could not stay in South America. I told them that it all depended on the amount of money I could make there, that I was flying not for fun, but to make my living, and I would fly where I could make that living best.

22. The sole S-32 being serviced at the factory before it was shipped to Colombia, where it bore the name "Ancol" on its nose, large company identification letters "A-2" on the fuselage side and an "A" on the rudder. National license numbers were not yet mandatory even in the United States in 1926, and the S-32 never carried any. *Courtesy of Igor I. Sikorsky Historical Archives, Inc.*

I had forgotten all about this conversation when, about two months after the plane was shipped to South America, I received a telegram offering me the job. At that particular time the Sikorsky Corporation had no orders on hand. There was only one plane being built. That was the S-35 three-motored transatlantic plane built for a flight from New York to Paris for the famous French ace, René Fonck. The calculations for this plane were already completed, and I felt that at the time it would not be a blow to the Sikorsky Corporation if I accepted the South America offer. I had a very friendly conference with Mr. Sikorsky and his assistants. We all agreed that I might do better for the Corporation if I accepted this new job and perhaps could get some business from South America. We all agreed also that our parting was only temporary.

ON TO NEW WORLDS

Russian Contributions to American Aviation

"The greatest danger of early aviation was starvation," Igor Sikorsky said later; "The only time you got a good meal was when you were asked to give an after-dinner speech."[1] Nonetheless, booming post–World War I America was a magnet for foreign aircraft designers. Giuseppe Bellanca came from Italy to build some of the most efficient airplanes of the 1920s; Dutchman Antony Fokker followed in 1924 to build his famous trimotor transports for America's new airlines.[2] Bavarian-born, self-taught engineer Edgar Schmued came from Brazil to join Fokker's U.S. branch, which became North American Aviation in the mid-1930s. By 1940, Schmued was design supervisor on the team that created the legendary P-51 Mustang design in just 102 days.[3] Albert Gassner designed fighters for Aviatik in Austria in 1916, came to America after the war, and worked his way up to chief engineer for Tony Fokker in New Jersey. (In 1938, he and another American, W. K. Evers, took a freelance trip to Germany, where they designed the Junkers 88 twin-engined bomber, a Luftwaffe mainstay in World War II.)[4] Frenchman Armand Thieblot, invited to the United States by aviation entrepreneur Charles Levine in 1927 to design a long-range monoplane, went on to design Fairchild's PT-19, C-82, and C119.[5]

As these Western Europeans were making their way to the United States, the Russian Revolution was driving hundreds of talented Russian engineers and designers into exile. Many of these exiles established new careers in New York, Connecticut, and New Jersey, where substantial Russian émigré communities had sprung up. A few, like Sikorsky and de Seversky, became famous; others are little known despite their accomplishments.

Michael Stroukoff typifies the Russian émigré designers whose creations are better known than they are. A contemporary of Sergievsky and Sikorsky at Kiev Polytechnic, by 1945 Stroukoff was founder, president, and chief engineer of Chase Aircraft in West Trenton, New Jersey, designing large, all-metal cargo gliders for the Army Air Force. His XCG-20 of 1947, the largest glider ever built in America, pioneered the high-wing, rear-loading cargo carrier layout that has been standard ever since. When the U.S. Air Force lost interest in gliders, Stroukoff hung two radial engines under his glider's wings in 1949, creating the XC-123—first of a new class of assault transports that could land with the airborne troops on rough fields, bringing heavy equipment. Chase could not produce quantities of aircraft; Fairchild won the contract and turned out 300 C-123Bs and other improved versions, including one with retractable skis.

Meanwhile, Stroukoff had borrowed two B-47 jet pods from the Air Force and hung them from the wings of another XG-20, transforming it into America's first jet transport, the XC-123A, which first flew in 1951. Stroukoff's efficient wing design could handle the higher speeds, but there was little room in the fuselage for anything but jet fuel. Stroukoff then developed the YC-123D, a pioneering experiment in boundary layer control using suction slots in the upper wing surfaces. His final transformation was the YC-123E of 1955, called the "Pantobase" because its retractable wheels and sturdy boat hull let it operate from snow, ice, water, sand, and rough fields. None of Stroukoff's experimental variants entered production. Fairchild C-123Bs served the Air Force well as a combat transport in Vietnam, but their Russian-American designer remains little known, despite his amazing variations on a single airframe design.[6]

Alexander P. de Seversky, by contrast, became famous early. Returning from his first combat sortie as an Imperial Russian Navy aviator in 1915, he lost his left leg below the knee when a hung-up bomb destroyed his plane on landing. Undaunted, he returned to combat flying a year later and had claimed thirteen victories when his right leg was shattered in a motorcycle crash. His government sent the personable young hero to Washington as air attaché in

1917. When the Bolsheviks seized the Russian government, he stayed on, changing his surname from Prokofiev-Seversky to de Seversky. His test-piloting skills earned him a commission as a major in the U.S. Air Service a few years later, even though he had not yet become an American citizen.[7]

By 1930 de Seversky was a well-known test pilot—one of ten certified to fly Sikorsky aircraft by the builder's insurance company, along with Sergievsky, Lindbergh, and racing pilot Frank Hawks. He was trying to start his own company, and wrote Sergievsky from Palm Beach that he was delighted by Sergievsky's record-breaking flights: "People keep congratulating me on them, and it helps my promotion. Keep it up."[8] De Seversky soon began breaking records himself and Sergievsky often received congratulations for them. The two pilots joked about the confusion when they got together in New York City or the Adirondacks, but they spent more time singing Russian songs while de Seversky's brother accompanied them on the guitar.

In 1931, de Seversky launched his own aircraft company, producing a beautifully streamlined, all-metal monoplane, the SEV-3. The SEV-3 was designed by another émigré from the Russian Empire, Alexander "Sasha" Kartveli (born Kartvelichvili), who had come to the United States from France in 1927 with Armand Thieblot.[9] (Though de Seversky was full of creative ideas, he needed an experienced designer to put them into practice.) Making the most of his meager resources, de Seversky modified this aircraft several times to meet the needs of various customers. The U.S. Army Air Corps bought the two-place version as the BT-8 trainer in 1935, and a later, more powerful single-seater variant as the P-35 fighter in 1936. These were the first all-metal, cantilever monoplane trainers and fighters purchased by the Air Corps .

De Seversky was looking for more orders in Europe early in 1939 when his company's board of directors fired him, citing his reckless spending. (According to a 1939 employee,[10] de Seversky had outraged Army Air Corps leaders by selling twenty export fighters in South America, complete with engines and instruments provided and paid for by the U.S. government, and the Air Corps generals demanded his ouster.)

World War II was coming and the United States needed Kartveli's promising designs produced, but not with de Seversky at the company's helm. The company, renamed Republic Aircraft, produced 15,000 of Kartveli's P-47 Thunderbolt fighters in World War II and his later fighter designs, the F-84 and F-105, served the Air Force well for the next thirty years.

De Seversky found a new career, writing and lecturing on the need for a powerful air arm. His best-selling 1942 book *Victory Through Air Power* and an animated film version he made with Disney persuaded millions of Americans that air superiority was the key to victory. He won the prestigious Harmon Trophy in 1939 for his advanced aircraft designs, and won it again in 1947 for his tireless promotion of air power.

Igor Sikorsky also relied on a team of fellow Russians from the start.[11] Michael Gluhareff, born to wealth in Russia, had experimented with gliders and airfoils before World War I. His GS-1 airfoil (for Gluhareff-Sikorsky) and his wing designs contributed to the record-breaking performance of the Sikorsky flying boats. Boris Labensky, previously an engineer on a tsarist destroyer, designed the Sikorskys' engine mounts and kept the whole production process moving. Nicholas Glad, another destroyer officer, designed the interiors of the flying boats. Jimmy Viner, Sikorsky's nephew, worked on the S-29-A as a teenager and grew up to become a test pilot of his uncle's helicopters. At least one Russian prince worked as a Sikorsky mechanic, and a dozen other survivors of the revolution contributed to Sikorsky's success in America. Yet from this team of talented people, only Sikorsky and Sergievsky became recognized public figures.

AF

On March 31, 1926, accompanied by Mrs. Sergievsky, I sailed from New York on one of the liners of the White Fleet, the United Fruit Company boat bound for Cartagena, in South America.

Born in the north of Russia and living most of my life in northern latitudes, I was afraid that I would not be as able to stand the equatorial heat in South America as people of southern origin. Before sailing I had to undergo a strict medical examination to find out how I would adapt to the tropical life. When I told the doctor about my doubts, he told me that one's state of health was much more important than one's place of birth or even race, and that I would adapt easily to the tropical conditions.

We had to undergo a lot of different vaccinations, and were provided with quite a file of health certificates.

The first stop of the boat on the way south was in Kingston, Jamaica. While the boat was lying there, we rode in a taxi through the streets of Kingston and out into the country as far as time permitted. It was my first glimpse of the tropics, and I found it fascinating.

The next stop was the Panama Canal, and we were much impressed by this great achievement of engineering science. Then, fourteen days after our departure from New York, we landed in Cartagena, Colombia, a city that claims to be one of the first, if not the first, built by whites in America. It boasts a history of well over three hundred years, and was originally built by the Spaniards as a fortress where they could accumulate gold from various parts of the Americas, awaiting the arrival of the Spanish fleet to protect the shipments from pirates on the way to Spain.

There are many books and novels written about this period of history, and getting acquainted with the history of the place where I was to live for a few years, I read quite a lot of them. I learned that pirates would attack the city and try to sieze the gold before the arrival of the Spanish fleet. When the pirates succeeded, they would kill off the entire population and leave the city in ruins.

After three hundred years one can still see traces of these struggles in the city. The old part of Cartagena is surrounded by a wall so thick that the taxis ride around on it, showing the city to the tourists. Two cars can easily pass each other on top of the wall. There are quite a few old forts around the city and bay, and the entire place looks very romantic and picturesque.

But the heat there is perfectly unbearable. The first few weeks after our arrival we had to stay in a hotel which had none of the familiar comforts of American and European hotels. In the meantime a house was being completed for us by the Andian National Corporation. Their settlement was outside the city on a lovely beach, and the heat was much less oppressive there. Built with all the modern accommodations, the houses for the employees were quite roomy and comfortable.

I had to start my flying duties on the second day after my arrival. The Andian National Corporation was building a pipeline and pumping the oil along this line, from a place in the mountains about 800 kilometers [500 miles] up the Magdalena River. There were no railroads or automobile roads between the coast of Colombia and the interior. The only means of transportation were the river boats, which were antiquated and very slow, with a single paddle wheel behind. They could not carry any substantial amount of cargo. Although the interior of Colombia is very rich in minerals and oil, the greatest task was not to get this wealth, but to transport it to a seaport.

Fast and reliable communication between various points and pump stations was necessary during both construction and operation of the pipeline. The S-32 was used for inspection trips by the higher officers of the corporation, for carrying payrolls, for carrying small spare parts up to the pump stations if they had any trouble with their machinery, and for maintaining communication along the whole pipeline.

Once in a while officials of the company had to go on business to the capital of Colombia, Bogotá. The city itself had no place to land a seaplane, but its port, called Girardot, was situated on the upper Magdalena River.

My first assignment was to fly the assistant manager of the company to Girardot. During this flight I saw what the general flying conditions in Colombia were.

It is advisable to fly very early in the morning there, on account of the heat, but early in the morning you may encounter a dense fog over the river. Then along the upper part of the Magdalena River, there are several high ranges of mountains that have to be crossed. Some of these mountains, having no vegetation on them, are simply huge rocks that are heated by the equatorial sun. They heat the air around them, and make it so much less buoyant that a plane has difficulty in maintaining altitude.

The Magdalena winds its way through the mountains like a snake and has many rapids. It requires great skill to land a seaplane on it. The landing place in Girardot is a very short straight stretch of the winding river. You must come down between high cliffs of rocky mountains and then land on a very narrow and swift

The Problems of Flying in Colombia

In the April 11, 1927, issue of *Aviation* magazine, Boris Sergievsky published an article entitled, "The Problems of Flying in Colombia." He described the tortuous, week-long passage from Cartagena up the Magdalena River by boat and train to Bogotá, making it clear why the Andian National Corporation had established its own air service to maintain its eight pumping stations and over 400 miles of pipeline along the river. Then he described the difficulties of flying over this tropical terrain:

Although the climate of Colombia may be described as endless summer, there are two distinct seasons, the dry season starting at the end of November and the rainy season starting at the end of April. During the dry season a mist which never turns to rain obscures the sun and causes very poor visibility. The pilot, having no horizon, must fly seeing only directly below. A very thorough knowledge of the country is required under these conditions. Flying is often done at an altitude of thirty feet, and sometimes right over the surface of the water just skimming it. In such visibility it is impossible to fly overland to the river from Cartagena, and the pilot must follow the sea all around through Puerto Colombia and Barranquilla.

During the rainy season, however, the visibility is much better allowing one to rise as high as 7,000–8,000 ft. with an average of from 2,000 to 5,000 ft. This permits of making the short cut from Cartagena to the river, a saving of 1 hr. 20 min., and further saving along the river, very considerably reducing the time. Flying in the rainy season has other hardships. Every day it is raining somewhere and while cruising several hundred miles along the river one is absolutely sure to encounter a heavy rain somewhere. I will not dwell on the uncomfortable feeling of the pilot when floods of rain strike him in the face while traveling at over 100 mph. The torrential rains completely close the visibility, soak goggles and windshield and sometimes force the plane down. During the past year, however, the *Ancol* was forced down only once on account of rain, even though the *Ancol* flies even when the aerial traffic of the air mail is stoppped on account of bad weather.

Another hardship of the rainy season is the heavy heat storm, especially in the mountainous region where the high rocky mountains approach the sides of the river at Dorada, growing higher and bigger to the south. The heat storms occur usually in the afternoon when the rocky sides of the mountains are overheated by the vertical rays of the equatorial sun. From some of the valleys the hot air rises with terrific force, throwing the plane up a couple of thousand feet, while, a moment later the plane runs into a descending stream of cold air rushing in to replace the hot and the machine drops down rapidly only to be shot up again. After flying through several such storms inspection showed that the stresses which the plane had to undergo were much greater than theoretically calculated.

The landing place at Girardot gives some thrill too, even when the weather is smooth. The river here runs very fast between walls of rock over 200 ft. high. The straight section is very short, so that the landing is made following the curve of the river. Each landing is a stunt. The take-off is even harder for the space is very limited by curves of the river and the high banks. Thus each take-off from Girardot must be made by flying under the railway bridge and crossing the river into the short straight-way. Under normal conditions in the United States or Europe such a take-off would collect a good crowd of spectators to see a very unusual stunt. But the fliers in Colombia consider it just a part of their daily work.

AF

mountain river. While making that first trip up the Magdalena River to Girardot I realized why the pilot who first had the job there did not want to stay.

Along the river were eight pumping stations, which were necessary to maintain the pressure in the pipeline and to overcome the elevation of ground between certain points where the oil could not flow by gravity through the pipeline. We arranged a landing place in front of each of the eight stations on the river, and trained a small ground crew of natives at each place to handle the plane when it came in after landing and get it to the shore.

The water in the Magdalena River, as in most tropical rivers, is muddy, of a grayish-yellow color; it rises very high during the rainy season, and drops very low during the dry season. There are always plenty of floating pieces of driftwood in it, and coming to a landing the pilots have to be very careful.

A German company named SCADTA had been operating between the seashore and the interior for several years before our arrival, and they cooperated fully with us. We worked out a code of signals, so that if I saw a SCADTA plane in distress on the river I would know whether he wanted me to land alongside of him, or to proceed and inform his company about his position.*

My contract with the Andian National Corporation was for two years. During the first month of my work I had a friendly conversation with the local manager, Mr. M. M. Stuckey. During our talk he found out that I was very anxious to get my mother and son out of Russia, and that I was saving most of my salary in order to get the necessary amount for their release and transportation.

He asked me how much more money, beyond what I had already saved, would be necessary to bring them out immediately. I told him, "Oh, about $1,000 more." Without saying another word, he pressed a button on his desk. When the chief accountant appeared he told him, "Please advance $1,000 to the Captain, and make with him whatever arrangement he wants to cover that advance."

---

* SCADTA (Sociedad Colombo-Alemana de Transportos Aéreos), the Colombo-German Aerial Transport Company, started scheduled airmail and passenger service in Colombia in 1921. Founded by Austrian aristocrat Peter Paul von Bauer and staffed with German veterans of World War I, the airline quickly became a money-maker and the pride of Colombia. Von Bauer's goal was to extend SCADTA around the Caribbean—but Juan Trippe had the same goal for his fledgling Pan American Airways, started in 1927. Trippe stirred U.S. government fears of German pilots flying over the Panama Canal, thus blocking SCADTA's progress northward. After further devious negotiations, Trippe bought control of SCADTA in 1930, but he did not fulfill his promise to "de-Germanize" SCADTA until Germany and the U.S. went to war in December, 1941. Trippe visited Sergievsky in the Adirondacks during the 1950s, on one of his few recorded trips that seemingly had no business purposes.

Mr. Stuckey's generosity made it possible for me to purchase steamer tickets immediately and to wire enough money to Russia to enable my mother and son to emigrate.

After I left Russia in 1918, I tried constantly to find out about their fate, and for several years I wrote letters in vain. These never reached their destination. When I was able to locate my mother and son, and to find out anything about them, it was through the Hoover Relief Administration in 1922. At about this time also, mail communication between us was re-established, and I learned what they had gone through since I had left them at our house in Kiev.

I found out about the tragic death of my youngest brother, Roman, and about the terrible persecution that started soon after my departure, when my mother and little son were held responsible for my activities in the White Army.

Several trucks arrived one day at the house, and everything was taken out—all the furniture and all the personal belongings. The walls were simply left bare, and my mother was thrown into prison. There she was told that she should write to me and ask me to stop my anti-Soviet activity, otherwise she and my son would be killed.

My mother replied that I was doing what I considered my duty to my country, and that she knew me well enough to know that nothing could stop me from doing my duty. Such a letter would only make my duty more difficult and she was the last person in this world who would do anything to make it more difficult for her son. If they thought it necessary, they could kill her and the boy immediately and be done with it.

Being in very ill health, she almost died in prison. After several months she was let out with no place to go to and with only those belongings that were on her person.

She managed to get a small room for herself and the boy, and earned their living by giving French lessons to children. Payment for the lessons was made in black bread. It was a year of famine in Russia, and the quality of the black bread was awful. It was mixed partly with dried-out peas and partly with sawdust. It was hardly edible.

For almost a year they did not have a single meal that consisted of more than this half-rotten bread and hot water, having no sugar, tea, or coffee. They were actually dying from starvation when the workers of Herbert Hoover's American Relief Administration found them and gave them help.

After I got in touch with them I started to send food parcels regularly through the Relief Administration, and also some money, and their condition improved substantially.

It was one of the happiest days in my life when I got a telegram from the other side of the Russian border that they were out. The Soviet authorities raised innumerable obstacles before granting them passports and permission to leave the country, and only by bribery could it be accomplished. Their escape from Russia took practically all my savings from the few previous years, plus the $1,000 advance that I had to repay during the coming year.

They made a stop in Paris, where my mother made all sorts of efforts to find out the fate of my second brother, Gleb, from whom we had not heard since 1918. At the outbreak of the war he was employed by one of the government factories doing metallurgical work. He was not supposed to join the fighting forces, his work being necessary for the defense of the country. But he joined the navy as a volunteer and, after passing the examination of the navy engineering college, he was assigned to a submarine in the Baltic Sea.

When the revolution started there was an almost wholesale massacre of the officers of the fleet, but being at that moment out at sea in his submarine, he escaped the fate of most of the officers. When he came ashore he got a transfer to the Caspian Sea, to the naval aviation school there.

We were able to trace him escaping from the Caspian Fleet after the Bolshevik revolution and joining the British Navy in the Caspian Sea. Then all traces of him were lost. Mother stayed in Paris almost three weeks, and finally located some of his former fellow officers who knew his fate.

Gleb had returned from the British Navy, joined the White organization in Petrovsk on the Caspian Sea, and served as an officer there on one of the gunboats. During a Bolshevik mutiny in Petrovsk he was thrown overboard, as were the rest of the officers, and his body was washed ashore a few days later. It was found by his fellow officers ashore and buried in Petrovsk.

After getting this sad news, Mother had no more reason to stay in Paris and took a French ship (the *Île-de-France*) which, after eighteen days of travel, arrived at Cartagena.

I was constantly in touch with the office of the French Line in town and knew the progress of the ship exactly. The conditions of the bay in Cartagena make it impossible to enter the harbor after dark. The French ship arrived on the 15th of May, 1927, at about midnight, and dropped anchor outside of Cartagena harbor.

I saw the lights of the ship from the porch of my house, and I knew that there

High Life at the Sergievskys' Villa

Boris Sergievsky's mother and his son, Orest, soon recovered from their years of near-starvation in Russia and began to enjoy the good life in Cartagena. Although "the caste system was strongly in evidence" in local society circles, Orest wrote, the Sergievskys rose above it. He described the scene in his memoirs:

> Somehow, to be at the Sergievskys'—the pilot's villa—was like being on special, neutral ground. Our social soirées were a mixture of all nationalities, all kinds of personalities. I remember Father's mechanic, a small Scotch-Irish fellow, telling a risqué joke to a French countess; a Hungarian engineer courting a Spanish heiress, under the watchful eyes of a *duenna*, who sat fanning herself quickly; a handsome Viennese being wooed by a young American secretary.
>
> Among the company of a few Russians and other Europeans, Alexandra found several people who could sing. This resulted in concerts, at which selections from opera were sung. Father was called upon to perform. During their stay in Paris before sailing to America, Alexandra and Father used to sing in the Russian cabaret/night clubs to earn extra money, and the singing at musical evenings in Russia had proven very useful. Now, to bring some cultural life and artistic interest to the rather provincial existence of the calm, lazy days and nights in Cartagena, musical evenings and events were welcome.
>
> I was called upon to help with the make-shift scenery and costumes. There was a great deal to do and worry about, especially with Father, who was never one to enjoy dressing up in "silly" opera outfits. I remember many times having to use all my persuasive abilities to make Father change costumes. This was especially difficult when he had to sing two roles in the same opera, which he did in *Rigoletto* and *Traviata*. Father's voice had a good range. He could sing a love duet as Alfredo with Violetta, then break Violetta's heart in the next scene as Germont, the father. He sang the father, Rigoletto, with Gilda in one scene, and in the next was the amorous Duke. I remember holding up the curtain while making Father change his trousers on stage before letting him sing a different character. He occasionally had trouble remembering the lyrics, so at times I had to arrange prompt cards on the back of a chair somewhere on the stage, with the words to be sung, just in case.
>
> Father and his wife became familiar characters in Cartagena, Father because he was a well-known test pilot working for an American oil company, and Alexandra because she was a well-known opera singer and gracious hostess who loved to give parties and entertain at musical soirées. When Father drove through the city streets or suburbs, police would catch up to him, after some pursuit, and beg him to remember that he was not in the air, but on the ground in the city of slow traffic and siesta-loving people. Somehow they were too polite to give him a traffic ticket.[1]

AF

were my mother and my boy, and that they were probably looking at the lights on the shore, thinking of me and trying to imagine me in one of these houses on the beach.

We had been separated for almost ten years, and how many things had happened during those ten years! They were more than a lifetime's worth. I could not go to bed the whole night.

At daybreak, I drove out to the pier and was standing there when the ship docked. From a distance I could recognize my mother. The years and her sufferings had changed her greatly. When I left her in 1918 she was still so young-looking that everybody took her for my sister. Now an old, gray-haired woman was standing on the deck, her eyes full of tears, this time tears of joy, the first tears of joy in ten years.

When I left my boy he was a small fellow, almost six years old; now beside my mother stood a young man of sixteen, taller than myself. I did not recognize him as my son, Orest.

The day of their arrival and the reuniting of the remaining members of our family was our happiest day since the beginning of the Russian Revolution.

Orest and his grandmother were still underfed and rather weak, although since they had crossed the Soviet border, while living in Paris and on the boat, they had recovered part of their strength. After a very short rest, Orest started to work hard on studying English, and in about a year I was able to send him to Balboa High School in the Canal Zone.

During my work in Colombia I had to fly through terrific tropical rainstorms. You could hardly tell it was raining, it felt more like being under a waterfall. All visibility was blocked, the engine started to sputter, and eventually stopped. I had several forced landings, simply due to the rain, in spite of the fact that the engines were supposed to be perfectly watertight.

While visiting various pumping stations up the river, I hunted wild animals of the jungles, but had no real desire to kill them. The only animals I would kill with pleasure were the huge and very disgusting-looking alligators that were simply swarming in the Magdalena River. Sometimes, when flying low over the river, I counted hundreds of them on one sandbar. I succeeded in killing quite a few of them, the largest being twenty-two feet long.

On several occasions, high officials of the Colombian government or of the Catholic Church, which has great influence on political life in Colombia, requested the use of our plane to get from the seaport to the interior. I had several trips with different ministers of the government, and also with the Papal Ambassador assigned to Colombia.

During one of these courtesy trips, when I had as passengers the Minister of Industry and his wife, something happened to my oil lines and suddenly the oil stopped circulating. Before I could do anything the engine actually burst into pieces.

I was high enough to glide safely to the river and make a landing right in midstream, but the plane started to drift out of control. I couldn't do anything to bring it nearer to the shore. We drifted for miles before we sighted a little native village on the shore.

23. Sergievsky in Colombia, 1928.
Courtesy of the editors.

THE MEMOIRS

The natives had some canoes in front of their huts, and I asked our Spanish-speaking passengers to shout to the natives to bring out a long rope with which they could beach the plane.

When they successfully brought the plane to the beach in front of the native settlement, we found out that the nearest Andian station was about five miles upstream. I knew that there would be a motorboat there, which could take care of the passengers and also tow the plane, but there was only one way to get there, and that was by canoe.

Usually the native help is paid approximately twenty cents a day there. Three men are necessary to paddle the canoe. As it would take no more than two hours to make the five miles upstream in the canoe, I offered a dollar apiece to the natives to take us to the station, thinking that would be quite a good payment.

The natives had a conference among themselves, and flatly declared that they could not make the trip unless we paid them $27! The Minister of Industry was indignant. He preached to the natives about the virtue of helping those in distress and tried to impress on them his own importance as the minister of their country, the person next to the president. Nothing would help. They simply told us that this was their only chance to make some money, that a plane would never land in front of their village again, probably, as long as they lived, and they did not want to miss the chance. They knew that we would not be able to get away unless they took us in their canoe.

No argument could help. There was no telegraph or telephone, or any other way of communicating with the outside world. The next river boat might go by in a week or so, and if it went by at night we would miss it. We had to accept the outrageous terms.

I asked them why they picked the ridiculous figure of $27, and they said there were three of them, and they figured out that they could not make it for less than $9 for each.*

Naturally after we arrived at the station we got a motorboat to tow our plane, and also used our own telephone line, which led from station to station and to Cartagena. We were able to get a reserve plane to take care of our passengers. A spare engine was shipped from Cartagena in a motorboat, but it took almost two weeks to reach the station, going upstream.

During the two weeks of waiting for the new motor I read all the books at

* In 1927, $27 represented a substantial amount of money—about $550 in today's dollars.

the station twice and all the old newspapers that were accumulating there. It was a spot in the jungle with no place where you could go, even for exercise. Right at the river where the station was situated, the jungle was so thick that if anybody wanted to go hunting or to inspect the pipeline they would have to cut their path with machetes.

The dampness of the air on the river and the extreme heat weakened the fabric covering of the plane's wings and tail surfaces so much that it was necessary to change it every few months. Also, our first set of wooden pontoons was destroyed by microorganisms living in the tropical water. In the amazingly short time of two months of service, I could put my finger through the wooden pontoon. We had to order replacements from the United States—metal pontoons and new wing coverings. We also decided to get a new plane, and I made several short trips back and forth to the United States to get all our supplies and test our new equipment.

The second plane we received for our work in Colombia was a Sikorsky S-36, a small, open-cockpit flying boat, powered with two Wright Whirlwind engines. When Colonel Charles A. Lindbergh arrived in his *Spirit of Saint Louis* at Cartagena, he stayed there a couple of days and flew with me in our S-36.*

According to my contract, I had the right to four months' vacation after two years of service. My vacation was due in May of 1928, but we could not get a pilot to replace me. I managed to get away only in September of 1928, when a relief pilot finally arrived from the United States.

With the relief pilot came our third plane for Colombian work, a Hamilton monoplane on floats. I flew it once up the river with the new pilot showing him all the places and local tricks.

On my way to the States I stopped to see my mother and son in Panama, and we agreed that after I arrived in the United States, I would try to get permission for them to enter the States.

Before my vacation ended, the Hamilton Metalplane Company in Milwaukee, Wisconsin, asked me to come out there to test their new seaplane. I stayed in Milwaukee almost two months, putting the new seaplane through

* Charles Lindbergh's solo transatlantic flight in April 1927 transformed him into an international hero, "The Lone Eagle," and Sergievsky was not immune to his spell. After Sergievsky's death decades later, his son found and gave to the National Air and Space Museum nine of Sergievsky's World Record certificates and the menu of the Cartagena dinner honoring Lindbergh on Jan. 26, 1928; Lindbergh had autographed it for Sergievsky.

Sergievsky, Lindbergh, and the Sikorsky S-36

The Sikorsky S-36 amphibian established the design layout that brought the Sikorsky company its greatest sales successes from 1928 to 1934.[1] The S-36, prefigured by the experimental S-34, looked old-fashioned even in 1927. Its design echoed the Curtiss NC-4 that had flown the Atlantic in stages, back in 1919.[2] The tailplane with its twin rudders was attached to the long upper wing by a thin boom, while the boatlike hull hung from the wing on a web of struts. The twin engines, attached to the underside of the upper wing, were strut-braced, too. The stubby lower wing, mounted on the fuselage midline, looked barely large enough to support the twin stabilizing floats (the S-36 was a sesquiplane, not a true biplane). The landing gear hung out in the breeze whether it was up for water landings or down for runways. Nonetheless, the S-36 cruised at 100 miles an hour; few landplane contemporaries did much better.

The first S-36, which Sergievsky flew in Colombia for the Andian National Corporation, even had open cockpits like those on the NC-4. The S-36 sat low in the water and takeoffs must have given the occupants a good soaking if the water was rough. Charles Lindbergh, making a circuit of the Caribbean in his famous monoplane, the *Spirit of Saint Louis*,[3] can hardly have been impressed by the old-fashioned look of the S-36 when Boris Sergievsky gave him a ride in it during Lindbergh's January 1928 visit to Cartagena. But Sergievsky, good salesman that he was, may have pointed out the S-36's virtues to Lindbergh. The structure was strong and light. The strut-braced upper wing, which carried most of the load, was longer, thinner, and lighter than a cantilever wing of similar area could be. As a result, the S-36 and its descendants combined substantial range and carrying capacity with relatively modest power requirements.

As Lindbergh was completing his 7,000-mile circuit of the Caribbean, stirring hero worship and aviation fever everywhere along what was quickly named "The Lindbergh Circle," Pan American Airways leased an S-36B and sent it over Lindbergh's route to spearhead a commercial conquest: The establishment of Pan Am as the dominant airline to Central and South America from the United States.

Only six S-36s were built. The Andian National plane flown by Sergievsky was the only one with open cockpits; the S-36B models that followed featured enclosed cabins that seated eight. The U.S. Navy bought one S-36B for testing as a patrol plane and designated it the XPS-1. Frances Grayson, a wealthy realtor from Long Island, New York, bought an S-36B, christened it the *Dawn*, and set off with her pilot and two crew members on December 23, 1927, to cross the Atlantic. They were never seen again.

AF

its paces. Then I got a request from Andian National to report for work, not in Cartagena, but as supervisor of the construction of their new plane being built by the Sikorsky Cooporation at their College Point factory in New York. Andian National had ordered the new plane, an S-38 amphibian, to replace the S-36, which really was too underpowered, and could not carry out their work.

At this time also I got an offer from the Sikorsky company to join them again, as they were getting a big list of orders for the S-38, and a lot of test work had to be done. I wrote a letter to the manager of the Andian National Corporation

24. This S-36, leased by Pan American Airways in December 1927 to survey potential Caribbean routes, was the first of many Sikorsky amphibians and flying boats used by Pan Am to build its international system in the next ten years. The S-36 flown by Sergievsky in Colombia had open cockpits rather than this version's drier cabin. *Courtesy of Igor I. Sikorsky Historical Archives, Inc.*

explaining the situation to him, telling him of the Sikorsky Corporation's offer to me. I said that I wanted to resign from the service of Andian National, but in a way that would not inconvenience them. I would be perfectly willing to go on supervising the construction of their plane, fly it from New York to Cartagena, stay with it in Colombia for as long as it took for Andian National to find another pilot, and then to train him in flying this particular type of plane there in the tropics. I also listed in this letter of resignation several pilots I knew who would do well at such a job.

In reply I got a rather angry cable saying that my resignation was accepted at once and that they did not need my advice as to what pilot they should employ in my place. As a result of this telegram I automatically became again a member of the Sikorsky organization.

The pilot chosen to replace me in Colombia soon reported to the factory. It was my duty to take him up in the plane that he was supposed to take over from us, to show him how to operate it, and to check him out. During my first flight with him I realized that he was not qualified to fly this type of plane and especially not qualified to work under the handicaps of tropical conditions.

I reported this problem to the president of our company, who had a conver-sation with the head of Andian National about it. The head of Andian told our president in effect to mind his own business.

After a few practice flights, the new Andian National pilot started from New York to Cartagena. The first intermediate stop on the way down was at Norfolk, Virginia. During the takeoff in Norfolk, the plane was wrecked and sunk. The occupants of the plane miraculously escaped death and injury by being picked up by a Navy motorboat.

During the trial in the Bridgeport courts a few years later, when the insur-ance company tried to recover some of the money paid for the lost plane, I had the moral satisfaction of going over our correspondence and conversations with the officials of the Andian National Corporation, which showed that I had the full right to say, "I told you so."

6

Flying for Sikorsky over Two Continents

One of the first S-38s out of the factory was assigned to Colonel Robert McCormick, owner of the *Chicago Tribune*. I had to deliver it to Chicago. I flew from College Point, New York, against a very strong west wind, and when I was over Cleveland, I realized that I had been so much delayed by the high wind that I would have to land in Cleveland for gasoline.

At this time, good strip maps showing the locations of the airports were not yet available, and the Cleveland airport was not shown on my map at all. I had no idea whether it was east, west, or south of the city. It could not be north, because the lake was to the north.

I started a wide circle, flying around the city, widening the circles, looking down all the time, trying to find the airport, looking for an arrow or sign on any of the prominent buildings in Cleveland to indicate the general direction of the airport. In some other cities such signs were already painted on roofs or tops of gas tanks. There were none in Cleveland.

While I was making my fifth or sixth circle, one of the engines stopped from lack of fuel. I landed right in front of the Coast Guard station in the lake. From the Coast Guard men I found out the direction and the distance to the Cleveland airport. They also gave me a few cans of gasoline, sufficient to fly to the airport.

To the newspapermen who interviewed me the same night in my hotel, I told them what I thought of Cleveland not marking the direction of their airport on any of the buildings. I have flown to Cleveland many times since then, and on the roofs of all of the prominent buildings are arrows indicating not only the direction, but also the distance to the airport.

Upon arriving at Chicago I had to take Colonel McCormick, his friends, and people from the newspaper on several flights. It is interesting to follow the fate of this plane and of Bob Guest, the pilot who took it over from me. The next year, Bob set out to fly this S-38 to Berlin by way of Labrador, Greenland, and Iceland. He reached one of the bays in Iceland and anchored the plane there, but that night a strong wind drove a lot of floating icebergs into the bay, and the plane was crushed by the ice and sunk. Nobody was on board. Bob Guest and his crew stood helplessly onshore, watching the destruction of their airplane. That spring [1934], Bob Guest disappeared while flying a similiar plane in China; he was caught by fog while flying over the China Sea.

Approximately two S-38s were turned out by the factory every week. Besides testing every one of them, I also had delivery flights to make, and demonstrations. I could not deliver them all myself, and I had a few pilots to help me in this work. I was promoted to Chief Test Pilot of the Sikorsky Corporation and Head of the Flying Department.

In addition to several flights to Florida delivering S-38's to Pan American Airways, I had one S-38 flight to Hollywood. Part of the flight I made at night, flying over the roughest part of the country, the Rocky Mountains. There was no real need to make a night flight, but I wanted to see how the lighted airways operated. It was a beautiful night, and ahead of me I could see four or five airway beacons at a time. When I approached one of the intermediate fields, and its sound detectors picked up my plane overhead, all the boundary lines of the field would be outlined in lights, as would be the exact outline of the landing area. As I passed over, not attempting to land, the lights would snap out again. This lighted airport system is a great credit to the Aeronautical Branch of the Department of Commerce, which constructed it and is maintaining it.

Flying high over the deserts and mountains and valleys on the way to California gave me a real thrill even though flying is an everyday job to me.

The S-38 had been purchased by Howard Hughes, the young man who made several of the flying pictures in Hollywood—*Wings* and *Hell's Angels.* He wanted the plane to commute from the yacht he had recently bought to the shore. As I found out, Hughes inherited a huge fortune and, while carrying on the business of his father, he also produced moving pictures as a hobby.

On the day I arrived at his hotel in New York to get final instructions from him about the delivery flight, I was much impressed by this millionaire's methods of saving money. If this is the way millonaires are making their millions, I could never be a millonaire!

The Sikorsky S-38

The Sikorsky S-38 amphibian, introduced in 1928, saved the company from extinction. Some of the earlier Sikorsky designs, the S-29-A through the S-37, had shown promise, but the company had built a total of fifteen planes and not all of those had been sold.[1] With the S-38, Sikorsky finally had a plane that matched the needs of a new and expanding market. An 11-seat, twin-engined amphibian flying boat, the S-38 was ideally suited for the fast-growing Pan American Airways' routes around the Caribbean, where airports were scarce but sheltered harbors were plentiful.[2]

André Priester, Pan American's conservative Dutch chief engineer, preferred seaplanes because "A seaplane carries its own airport on its bottom," and so he gave his blessing to the boat-hulled S-38.[3] Priester was doubtless further reassured to learn that the S-38 was the first twin-engined plane able to maintain level flight on one engine, even at its gross weight. Other airlines and corporations and several rich sportsmen also ordered the versatile S-38, and a total of 111 were built in the next few years.

The S-38's design followed the pattern set by the S-36, but it looked even more antique. The two engines now were strut-braced below the top wing, and two booms carried the twin fins and rudders and the tailplane. The stabilizing floats extended below the small lower wing on more struts. Critics described it as the spare parts of a Sikorsky flying in formation.[4] But like its predecessor, it was sturdy and efficient, and its two 425-horsepower Pratt and Whitney Wasp engines gave it a range and cruising speed that matched most contemporary landplanes of its size.

Boris Sergievsky tested every one of the 111 S-38s built. He set four world records in one S-38 and flew others across three continents. Loyally, he does not mention the S-38's biggest flaw, which became evident on water takeoffs. Until the plane built up speed, the windshield, set well back on the hull behind the propeller arcs, was drenched with water and spray and the pilot could see nothing. Visibility returned only when the wing lifted the hull out of the water and "onto the step," skimming over the surface, just before takeoff.[5]

The S-38's other flaw resulted from its unusual fuselage stucture, which employed heavy aluminum outer plates screwed to a wooden inner framework. Electrolytic corrosion between the screws and plates required regular attention and repairs, especially when operating from salt water. Most S-38 owners considered this upkeep a small price to pay for such a reliable and efficient craft, and kept their S-38s in service for years.[6]

AF

25. The Sikorsky S-38 sold to Chile for the Prince of Wales's visit, photographed by Igor Sikorsky in Costa Rica during Sergievsky's delivery flight. Like most Sikorsky designs, the S-38 presented a surprisingly lean frame to the airflow, in contrast to its "flying forest" of struts when seen from the side. *Courtesy of Igor I. Sikorsky Historical Archives, Inc.*

I arrived early in the morning, at the appointed hour, while Mr. Hughes was having his breakfast. On the tray with his breakfast was the bill, which he had to sign. Mr. Hughes was very much in a hurry. Every minute of his time was precious. So he told me, and that was the reason why he could not receive me at any other time but during his breakfast. Still, he spent many of those precious minutes (I looked at my watch) in revising his breakfast bill before he signed it.

He made allowances and reductions from his breakfast bill for a certain amount of Puffed Rice that he did not eat. He ate about half of it, so he struck out the price, and put down just half. He ate only one egg out of the two that were brought to him, and so he struck the other out. As his breakfast was rather elaborate, and as he estimated the price of only what he actually ate of each item, revising the bill took almost twenty-five minutes.

When the question of the price of the delivery flight came up, I felt myself in a rather difficult position, because my bargaining ability was far below that of Mr. Hughes. He asked me to take less money than I usually get for such flights, on the grounds that he had just had an operation on his ear, and his doctor bill was so big that he would not have much money left for his expenses in New York, and please would I accept a little less money than usual?

In spite of the fact that I was very poorly paid for the trip, I enjoyed the transcontinental trip very much. To the credit of Mr. Hughes, he arranged for me, through his office in Hollywood, to meet several interesting people there, and to visit the studio while pictures were being made.

I visited the Paramount studio when Mae West's picture *She Done Him Wrong* was being made. They were filming the barroom scene; it was interesting to see the perfect coordination of work in that studio, how the crowds of extras were handled, how the sound effects were produced, and so on.

I also saw the making of a picture with Carole Lombard and Clark Gable. Gable had to walk in the door of a cabin in the forest, and Lombard, who was on the other side of the wall in the cabin, almost entirely undressed, had to say, "Just a minute," put some sort of a wrap around her, and open the door. Then they would start a conversation. While I was in the studio, that scene was repeated at least fifteen times—the same motions, same words, same expressions on their faces. I realized what hard work it is making pictures, how dull and tiresome it must be.

I also met Wynne Gibson, and was even photographed with her.

After a very interesting day in Hollywood, I flew back as a passenger on the American Airways plane, and in twenty-four hours I was back in New York.

The high performance of the Sikorsky planes made me think it would be worthwhile to try to break various seaplane world records, which were held mostly by France and Germany. The United States lagged far behind in the number of world's records credited to it. I made a study of what could be done on the basis of the actual performance of our planes, and submitted a memorandum to the management, indicating that the S-38 was capable of setting four world's records in the seaplane class, if we replaced the Wasp engines with more powerful Hornets, cleaned up some of the lines, and removed the landing gear to make it eligible for the seaplane class.

Four world's records were actually set in March of 1930. The first record I attempted was for altitude with a payload of 2,000 kilograms [4,500 pounds]. I was to take off from the North Beach ramp in Astoria, Long Island. Representatives from all the newspapers of New York City were there in great force. There were also trucks from Pathé, Fox, Paramount, and Universal moving picture companies.

The morning was not favorable for an altitude flight. The skies were overcast, and the temperature was low enough that I could expect ice to form on the wings.

The plane was all ready, the sealed barometer installed in it, the engines warmed up. I was standing on the ramp waiting for a change in the weather that would make the flight possible. Several of the newspapermen got annoyed at the delay, and told me that if I took off immediately I would have swell publicity, but if I postponed the flight nothing could induce them to come again to North Beach and freeze there waiting for the flight to take place.

I told them that I was not making the flight for publicity purposes, and if they were not interested they might just as well go home right then. The president of our company, Mr. Arnold Dickinson, who was there at the time, told me that the company did not expect me to take any chances, that it was entirely up to me whether to fly right away or to postpone the flight, that they believed in my judgment, and that I was not going to get orders from anybody about when and how to fly. I was very thankful for his moral support.

I believe that the disaster that happened to our S-35, when René Fonck crashed it while attempting to take off on his transatlantic flight, occurred because the presence of newspapermen, too much advance publicity, and everybody's expectations made him attempt a takeoff when the weather conditions were unfavorable. As a result, the plane was completely destroyed, and two men were killed.

After waiting for a few hours and not seeing any improvement in the weather, I postponed the flight until the next day, to the great disgust of some of the newspapermen and spectators.

The next morning, flying conditions were ideal. The flight was made and the record established. In the few days following, I set a second world's record for altitude with a payload of 1,000 kilograms [2,200 pounds] and speed on a closed course of 100 kilometers [62 miles]. I then established a third record for altitude with a payload of 500 kilograms [1,100 pounds].

The altitude attempts with the lighter loads of 1,000 and 500 kilograms necessitated the use of oxygen. We borrowed the oxygen equipment from the Navy Department. It consisted of a big cylinder, a tube, a regulating mechanism, and the mouthpiece.

I wanted to know how high I could go without using oxygen. I had all the apparatus for oxygen ready, but climbed as high as I could without taking it. At an altitude of 16,000 feet I started to feel that in order to get the necessary amount of oxygen in my lungs, I had to breathe much more quickly, but still it was not uncomfortable. At 18,000 feet it became a little uncomfortable, but it was still possible not only to sit still, but also to move in the plane without feeling a great fatigue. At approximately 20,000 feet I realized how much our senses depend on the amount of oxygen our systems are getting.

I knew for instance, that the day was a very bright one, with a wonderful sun, and not a single cloud in the skies, and still above 20,000 feet it seemed to me that the light was gradually fading away, that it was becoming darker and darker.

I knew also that my engines were wide open, and were producing a lot of noise with their open exhausts. That sound was quite deafening at lower altitudes. Up there where the air is less dense, naturally the volume of the sound drops, but still I knew that the engines were wide open, and that they would produce a substantial amount of sound. Above 20,000 feet that sound, to my ears, faded to almost nothing.

There was also a change in my entire mental attitude. When I started the flight I was full of "pep," and the importance of the flight was clear to me. I was very anxious and very eager to make the record. But together with the fading of the light and the sound, my desire to successfully accomplish the flight was also fading. It did not matter whether I made the flight or not, it even did not matter whether I lived or died. The only and urgent desire that I started to feel was to rest, to close my eyes and go to sleep, go to sleep for a while, even if it might cost me my life.

These were my feelings, but no matter how slowly my brain was working at this time, I realized that that was not the real and proper attitude, that this was just the change of my exterior feelings due to the lack of oxygen.

When I was on the verge of fainting, the altitude was over 21,000 feet. At this moment I decided to take the oxygen. I had to make a tremendous effort of will to reach for the oxygen tube which was right at my hand within easy reach. It seemed to me that it was a tremendous, almost superhuman effort to lift the end of this tube just a few inches to my mouth, and that motion almost entirely exhausted me.

But the moment I inhaled oxygen for the first time, the reaction was instantaneous. Just as if one turned on the light in a dark room, with the first touch of the tube to my mouth the day was bright again, the engines started their terrific roar, the desire to accomplish the flight, and the desire for and the joy of life came back to me simultaneously. Everything in life was again fine and important, and I was happy to live and to fly.

The maximum altitude shown on my instruments was 30,000 feet, but having the necessary amount of oxygen, it did not make any difference to me. The only discomfort I felt at these higher altitudes was from the very low temperature, which reached almost 30 below zero.

The next and fourth record I attempted to set was speed for a distance of 500 kilometers [310 miles]. We had a certified speed course 50 kilometers [31 miles] long, running from Execution Rock to a point off Fairfield Beach, Connecticut. In order to make 500 kilometers I had to circle that course five times.

I made several attempts to set that particular record. On the first attempt the engines started to overheat; I had to abandon the flight during the third lap. Additional oil coolers were installed. On the second attempt, part of an engine cowling worked loose and started to break and vibrate. The cowling had to be reinforced. On the third attempt, the airspeed indicator broke, and I could not even guess what my speed was, which was most important for a speed record.

Everything was going fine during the fourth attempt. I completed four laps and had just made the vertical turn at Fairfield Beach, starting my last lap. By the elapsed time I knew that I was bettering the world's record by over 30 miles an hour, and I was feeling very happy.

All of a sudden I saw a streak of solid white flame behind my right engine. Such flame could only mean high-grade gasoline burning. The amount of flame was increasing every second; I had to do something immediately. On a speed run you always fly very low. Before attempting to land I had to kill some of my forward speed, which was close to 150 miles an hour. I throttled the engines down, made a vertical bank, returning to Fairfield Beach, and landed the plane right in front of a row of cottages.

My intentions at first were to run the plane aground on the beach and try to escape before it blew up. Then, remembering the amount of gasoline still in the tanks, I thought that a fire would start on the beach and destroy the cottages and cause not only loss of property but perhaps also loss of life.

I turned the plane away from the beach, taxied a safe distance out in the sound, then made an attempt to extinguish the fire. I shut off the gasoline, cut the switch, and turned the fire extinguisher on the side of the burning engine, but nothing would stop the blazing gasoline. When I saw the flames reaching the big tank in the wing, I realized that it might explode any second.

I had no time to take off my heavy suit or even my gloves and helmet. I jumped through the window head first and started to swim to the shore. It was a frigid March day and the water was stinging cold. It was also very hard to swim in the leather, fur-lined flying suit.

I was making a great effort to keep my nose above the surface, swimming to the shore, and I had almost reached it when a canoe approached me. At

26. Boris Sergievsky hugs the cowled Hornet engine of the special S-38 seaplane in which he established three world records during 1930. He was seeking a fourth record on March 17, 1930, when this Hornet caught fire. He nearly drowned while swimming away from the burning S-38 in his fleece-lined coat, which weighed him down but did not protect him from the cold water. *Courtesy of National Air and Space Museum.*

first I was afraid that the man in the canoe would be too close to the burning plane. Feeling that I still could swim, I shouted to him to keep away and wait until I was further from the plane. After a while I waved to him to come to me, and when he reached me I was so exhausted that I could not climb into the canoe. I got hold of the end of the canoe and asked him to tow me to the shore. I remained in the water altogether for about fifteen minutes.

When I got to shore and looked at the place where I thought the plane would be burning, the surface of the water was perfectly unbroken, nothing was there. I did not see when it happened, but the man in the canoe told me that a few seconds after I left the plane, it disappeared in a huge burst of flame. It was not an actual explosion, but an almost instantaneous burning of the gasoline.

I was so exhausted when I reached the shore that I could not walk, and collapsed on the beach. William Wallace, my rescuer, and a friend helped me to get to the nearest cottage, where a very kind-looking woman was already standing on the porch with a big glass of whisky in her hand. She may have been breaking the law, but she certainly saved my life with that whisky.*

A few minutes later a doctor arrived and then officials of the company. The doctor could not find anything wrong with me, he simply told me to go to bed and try to get warm.

While my clothes were drying and people were coming in and out of the cottage, somebody took possession of my wallet, which had approximately $315 in cash, most of it belonging to the company, as I had to take care of the expenses of the crew at North Beach. The company later refunded that money to me.

It is very strange coincidence but this actually happened. While the plane was burning and I was struggling in the water trying to get to the shore, my wife, who was sitting in the car at North Beach waiting for me, had a vision of me swimming in a flying suit in the water. It was such a real vision that she jumped out of the car and went to inquire about what had happened. She was met halfway by a man rushing from the telephone booth at North Beach, shouting to her that the plane had caught fire, but I was all right.

After resting for a while in a hospitable cottage on Fairfield Beach, I was taken to the house of our Vice President and General Manager, Mr. W. A. Berry

---

* The woman who gave Sergievsky a glass of whisky was breaking the Prohibition laws, which were not repealed until 1933 but were almost totally ineffectual by the time of Sergievsky's crash on March 17, 1930.

in Stratford, where I got extra treatment against the cold in quite a variety of drinks, most of which consisted of straight Russian vodka. It warmed me up substantially, but did not affect me the way drinks normally do.

The house was actually surrounded by reporters. We had to admit them and give them a statement about what had happened and what we intended to do in the future. Of course our intention was to assign another plane and set the record.

Another plane for completing our program of world's records was ready in the summer of the same year, 1930. Instead of Hornet engines, supercharged Wasps were installed in it. It was important for us to find out what motors would give our plane its best performance.

I repeated all three of my altitude records and bettered every one of them substantially. We found out that for speed, the Hornet engine would give a better performance than the supercharged Wasps. We changed the Wasps for the Hornets again, and in the winter of 1930 made one more attempt at the 500-kilometer speed record.

But it seems that there was some kind of a jinx connected with this particular record, because on the takeoff I struck a floating cake of ice with my left side float and damaged it to such an extent that I had to get back to the ramp in a hurry, because there was a danger that the plane would turn over.

In the meantime, our company was completing negotiations with the Chilean Government about sending a plane to Chile to carry the Prince of Wales and his party. The Prince was due in Chile on his way to the British Empire Exposition, which he was to open in Buenos Aires.

Chile has few railroads, and its roads are not in good repair. The Prince of Wales wanted to visit quite a few cities in Chile, and the only way for him to do everything he wanted to do in the short time allowed for this would be in an airplane. He was traveling on a British cruiser, and he had to visit quite a few cities in the interior and on the seaboard. The airports in Chile were all inland, so the Chilean Air Force could not carry the Prince in one of their landplanes to his cruiser or to any of the seaports. The only logical solution of this problem was an amphibian.

A deluxe interior arrangement was made in the amphibian type S-38 which was assigned for the job.

[The May 1931 issue of *Sportsman Pilot* featured an article about this trip written by Boris Sergievsky, and his memoir says to insert this article here. An abridged version follows.]

The Prince of Wales is an ardent flier. He is perennially hopping hither and yon about Europe. It was not illogical, therefore, that during his recent visit to South America the Government of Chile was anxious to place a plane under his personal orders. The Prince was to visit Chile during the second half of February. Coincidentally, the Chilean Government had on order a Sikorsky amphibion,* which was to be assigned to the Prince's use.

It was my task to fly the ship to Chile and to train two Chilean pilots in flying and handling the ship, in case the Prince should accept the government's offer and use the Sikorsky during his stay in Chile.

The flight started at 8:00 A.M. January 26th from the Bridgeport, Connecticut, airport. It was a very cold winter morning. The ice floating on the Housatonic River made the use of our factory ramp and a water takeoff impossible. We had to take the ship to the Bridgeport airport across the road from the factory. The second pilot in the cockpit was Mr. Igor I. Sikorsky. In the cabin were our friends Mr. Gibson Paine and the charming Miss Dorothy Paine; Professor John Ostromyslensky, the well-known scientist; and George Grebenstchikoff, a prominent Russian writer. The crew consisted of two selected flight mechanics.

In spite of the bad condition of the field, the takeoff was smooth. I laid the ship on a straight course—Bridgeport to Norfolk, Virginia. In an hour and twenty minutes we passed Atlantic City on our left. The weather got better and warmer with every hour of our southward flight.

After four hours we landed at the Naval Air Station at Hampton Roads, Norfolk, Virginia. The sun was shining brightly, and there was a smell of spring in the air. In an hour, we again started south, leaving at Norfolk Mr. Grebenstchikoff, who took the train back to New York. This little cross-country flight was quite an experience for him. It enthused him so greatly he feels inspired with ideas for a book about aviation.

Between Norfolk, Virginia, and Morehead City, North Carolina, our course was overland. Forests, marshes, lakes, lagoons and very few villages or roads. Plenty of space and scarce population. South off Morehead City, we flew over the ocean, at times losing sight of the shore.

---

* Igor Sikorsky coined the word "amphibion" for amphibious airplanes, to distinguish them from frogs and other non-flying amphibians. Boris Sergievsky loyally used the amphibion spelling in his *Sportsman Pilot* article, but the term did not catch on.

At 5:30 P.M. we were over the Charleston, South Carolina, Naval Air Station. And there we landed for our first overnight stop.

The next morning at nine o'clock we took our seats in the plane. The course between Charleston and Miami is partly over water and partly along the coast. Daytona Beach, where so many automobile speed records have been established, is a most remarkable place when seen from an airplane. Flying along the coast of Florida one is surprised at the enormous marsh areas, partly covered by water. One sees an unusual amount of traffic on the few automobile roads extending north and south. Much less traffic is seen on the railroad lines.

In Florida it was quite warm. We easily forgot that we were there in midwinter and that only the day before we had been shivering at Bridgeport.

The cities of Palm Beach and West Palm Beach are very noticeable for their size and the prominence of their buildings. After we left Palm Beach, we saw Miami ahead, with its bridges to Miami Beach. There was a blimp flying west of the city.

Directly on our course was the Pan American airfield. Its wide white coral-covered runways stood out clearly from a great distance. The terminal building on this airport is an excellent example of beauty and comfort—an airport terminal as it should be.* At this airport we were met by courteous and efficient Pan American employees. In short order, clearances for the ship and passengers were arranged so that we might start for Havana the next morning. A telegram from Secretary of State Stimson was awaiting me at the airport with the good news that the governments of all the countries over which I was to pass had granted me permission to fly over, and if necessary to land in, their respective countries.

Next morning we started on a direct course to Havana, Cuba. Our takeoff was about five minutes ahead of that of the regular passenger-mail Pan American Fokker F-10. This plane slowly overtook us after we passed the Florida Keys.

After a little over two hours' flying through scattered clouds and occasional rain showers, we saw the Havana lighthouse right on our bow. A few minutes later we landed at the Havana airport and were met by customs officials and Mr. Paine's friends Mr. and Mrs. Terry Smith. The Terry Smiths have a lovely home in the vicinity of Havana, and I was glad to accept their kind invitation to stay with them, together with Mr. and Miss Paine.

* Though Pan Am and its Dinner Key Seaplane Base are long gone, the beautiful terminal building that Sergievsky admired lives on; it now serves as Miami City Hall.

27. The Chilean S-38, about to depart from Pan Am's Miami base on January 27, 1931. Sergievsky, grinning wolfishly, stands hip to hip with "the charming Miss Paine," while her father looks at the photographer (Igor Sikorsky), Prof. Ostromyslensky puffs on his pipe, and one of the Sikorsky mechanics gazes dubiously at the heavy load of baggage. *Courtesy of Igor I. Sikorsky Historical Archives, Inc.*

Since ahead of us was the hardest part of the trip, with long over-water flights and hotter climates, I decided to stay in Havana two days, in order to give my mechanics ample time to go over the ship and motors. This stay in Havana was really a complete rest, for the hospitality and comfort we found at the home of the Terry Smiths and the wonderful swimming at the Havana Yacht Club were indeed refreshing.

Havana was the final destination of all our passengers except Mr. Sikorsky, who intended to fly as far as Panama. From Bridgeport to Panama he was in the cockpit with me all the time. Mr. Sikorsky, one of the first to fly in the early days of aviation, was delighted to give me a hand at the controls. Every time after a takeoff was made, the ship set on its proper course, and correction for the wind drift estimated and incorporated, I turned the controls over to Mr. Sikorsky. He would keep the ship on the correct course for hours, giving me opportunity to take care of my maps, to relax, and even to snatch a little nap once in a while.

At 7:00 A.M. January 30th, we set out for the first long over-water jump from Havana to Belize, British Honduras. On this leg of the trip, we flew in formation with the Pan American plane, another Sikorsky S-38, as far as Cozumel Island. I proceeded on to Belize in order to have the ramp there clear for the mail plane so that we could start for Tela, Honduras, together.

My reason for flying in company with the mail plane was that we had no radio installation in our ship. In case of a forced landing at sea, we could not have given our position. As it was, messages could have been sent by the wireless operator of the mail plane, who was instructed to watch us all the time.

All the way from Havana to Belize, for five hours, we had good weather with moderate wind. At Belize, however, it was raining. Just before landing, we had to pass through several showers.

Belize looked very pretty from the air with its red-roofed white buildings surrounded by palm trees. But it is a hot place. I had just enough time to fix the ship's papers and take on some gas when the mail plane arrived. After it had unloaded the mail, we took off together on the course to Tela, Honduras.

The pilot of the mail plane, Mr. Culbertson, a very quiet man and an excellent pilot, led the way. I followed very closely, for we had information that at Tela the weather was quite bad. I knew that the flying field at Tela had no special marks and that in bad weather it would be hard to find for the first time, should I lose sight of the leading plane.

We encountered low clouds, sometimes fog, and heavy tropical rain, which at times was like a waterfall. First skimming the surface of the ocean, then rising over the palms on the shore and just clearing the trees of the hills, we went inland. I had one eye on Culbertson's plane's tail and the other eye on the tree-tops to avoid collision with the highest of them. I don't know how Culbertson found the field, but he got there. We came in right over a narrow little field, very uneven and soft. That was the Tela airport. We landed in a most terrific tropical rainstorm.

According to schedule we were to continue right over to San Salvador on the Pacific side. But ahead of us were mountains 7,000 feet high, which, together with the heavy rain, low ceiling and obscured visibility, made the flight impossible. We decided to stay overnight in Tela and see what luck we would have the following morning. Through the courtesy of the local manager of the United Fruit Company, we had a wonderful dinner and a pleasant place to sleep in the company's guest house, situated right on the ocean beach. After a night's rest and a good breakfast in the United Fruit dining hall, we started out to the field. The weather was a bit better. From San Salvador the report was favorable, ceiling and visibility being unlimited.

So off we went—first out to sea to be sure to avoid any unexpected contact with a mountainside. Then we started to climb until we were above the clouds at an altitude of 12,000 feet with a rich blue sky above and a sea of vapors below. We could see some little clearings between the clouds. Occasionally we caught glimpses of mountaintops and valleys below. After two and one-half hours, we were over San Salvador airport, all the bad weather behind us.

San Salvador is the last point to which the PAA Sikorsky planes fly on this run, the mail and passengers being transferred to trimotored Fords. Culbertson, with his ship, had to turn back; I said good-bye to him and sincerely thanked him for the tremendous help he had given me in locating the airports of Tela and San Salvador.

Because the trimotored Ford is faster than the Sikorsky amphibion, we had to fly alone from San Salvador to Panama. After refueling, we took off and flew through almost perfect weather at an altitude between 5,000 and 6,000 feet, in sight of the Pacific Ocean, but inland somewhat to be on the correct course to our next refueling stop at Puntarenas, Costa Rica. While flying over the wilds of Nicaragua, I thought what would happen to us if we should have a forced landing in the area controlled by our good friend Sandino.

In Puntarenas we stopped just long enough to get some gas and immediately started for David, Panama, encountering on our way several light rain squalls. At David we arrived after 6:00 P.M., just at dusk. We went to the Pan American Airways quarters, had an excellent dinner and a very restful night's sleep.

Next morning at daybreak we started for Panama. Flying along the Pacific side of the canal, we saw Panama City and Balboa and then flew the length of the canal to France Field on the Atlantic side.

At France field we stopped just about two hours. On the starting line was another Sikorsky S-38 of the Pan American-Grace Line waiting to take mail which had been delayed at Honduras by bad weather. The pilot of this ship was Mr. Claude. We agreed to fly in close formation southward, for there was a six-hour hop over water to Buenaventura, Colombia. Knowing local conditions, he advised flying very low over the water because, on the second half of the run to Buenaventura, we would encounter heavy rainstorms. It is better to fly low through them and keep one eye on the compass and one on the water through the side window. There is no forward visibility under such conditions.

I was really sorry to leave Mr. Sikorsky in Panama. Besides being very pleasant company on the trip, he was extremely helpful as a relief pilot on the long runs. From Panama southward, I had two mechanics for company. But although they were extremely useful and efficient on the ground, they could not be of much help in the air. I had to stick to the wheel for many long hours without relief.

A few minutes after leaving Panama, we lost sight of the shore, and for six hours it was the endless Pacific. Only occasional rain showers broke the monotony of that flight. The navigation was perfect; after six hours we sighted the Buenaventura lighthouse right on our bow. In a few minutes we landed in the bay and taxied to a floating raft to get some gas for the next leg to Tumaco, Colombia, where we would stay overnight.

On the following morning, February 2nd, both ships started together at daybreak. But Claude took the course to Guayaquil, Ecuador, and I to Saint Elena, the difference being about ten degrees. By calculating time and distance flown and by observing prominent landmarks on the shoreline, I knew exactly when we crossed the Equator. It was 8:15 A.M. February 2nd. It was too bad we could not go through the traditional ceremony when crossing the Equator for the first time.

After four hours of flight, we spotted Saint Elena, right on our course. Saint Elena is not in a closed bay, and the swell of the Pacific was very great. I had to make a crosswind landing on top and along one of the swells. Then we lowered the wheels and cautiously approached the Panagra Airways ramp on the shore. It takes skill to hit the ramp, taxiing crosswind on huge swells, because the ramp consists of two individual ramps, one for each wheel. When between two waves, each of them much higher than the ship, we could see neither the ramp nor the shore.

The crosswind takeoff, with the comparatively light load of two mechanics and baggage, was easy. I set the ship on the course to Talara, Peru.

Talara is one of the centers of the Imperial Oil Company. After a good night's rest there, we flew to Lima, Peru, in six hours, thirty-five minutes. It was necessary to make an intermediate stop for gas at Pimenta. Arriving over the place indicated on the map as an airport, I saw a series of low hills with deep creeks between them. I made two approaches for a landing, trying to find out which hill it would be easiest to land on and finally gently put the ship down.

At Lima we were met by officials of the Panagra and by the personnel and students of the Peruvian Military Flying School. Ours was the first Sikorsky to land at Lima. Its unusual shape and dimensions created quite a little interest.

Flying along the Pacific coast, I made the following observations: (1) There is a constant south-southwest wind blowing at sea level and low altitudes, and a strong north or northwest wind blowing at altitudes above 8,000 feet. (2) In this climate, there are much greater possibilities and advantages in using the altitude adjustments on the motors, even at low altitudes, than in the States. Flying at higher altitudes, over 10,000 feet average, and using the altitude adjustment to a limit, I succeeded in cutting gas consumption to seventeen gallons per hour per motor.

The jump from Lima to Arica, Chile, a distance of 700 miles, was more that I could expect to make nonstop. But there were no good fields where I could stop for refueling. I carried fourteen five-gallon cans in the ship, and after about two hours of flying along the coast, made a water landing in a well-protected bay of such size that we were able to stay away from shore while putting the gas in the tanks.

Arica is the port of entrance to Chile. The airport here is a few miles from the sea behind the hills and could not be seen from the sea. Later I learned that this was the case all the length of Chile.

The airport commander in Arica, a very polite young officer, informed me that the Chief of the Chilean Air Force, Commander Merino, and several companions had been missing for several days while on a flight in the south of Chile. I decided to rush to Santiago to help in the search with our Sikorsky, which would be an ideal plane for such a purpose.

Having about 1,200 miles ahead of me, I decided to take off from Arica at night so that my next landing for gas at Antofagasta would be made early the next morning. At 4:00 A.M. we took off with our landing lights on. For two hours we flew in complete darkness. At six the sun rose over the Cordilleras Mountains. I don't believe I have ever seen a more beautiful sunrise.

At ten o'clock we landed at Antofagasta, filled our tank hurriedly and rushed on our way south. We then laid our course straight to Santiago. We landed there at 5:15 P.M. February 5th, completing our journey from Bridgeport in sixty-eight flying hours.

We learned from the airport commandant that Commander Merino and his party had been found. His pilot on this trip was Lieutenant Felipe Latorre, who was the first pilot to receive instructions on the Sikorsky which was to fly the Prince of Wales.

Lieutenant Latorre proved to be a very capable young pilot. After a couple of hours of instruction, I was able to transfer him to the left seat of the pilot's cockpit so that he could take off and land.

On February 14th, I was asked to fly the President of the Chilean Republic, General Don Carlos Ibanes del Campo. We made a cross-country flight of over two hours to a town called Linares. Landing there was quite difficult, but we brought the ship down successfully. The President was very much pleased by the flight and the ship's performance.

In accordance with our contract, the ship was turned over to the Chilean government on the 20th of February. On the same day, the ship left for Antofagasta with Lieutenants Latorre and Olmedo at the controls to meet the two British Princes. Two Ford trimotors and several Fairchilds and Falcons were flown there as escorts. On the trip from Antofagasta to Santiago, our ship was used by the government as a baggage carrier, being loaded to capacity with the personal baggage of the Princes. Both Princes on this leg of their trip flew in the trimotor Ford.

The unusual shape of the amphibion attracted the attention of the Prince of Wales, who expressed a desire to be flown in it to Valparaiso. The trip to Valparaiso had been originally scheduled by train, and all the arrangements for meeting the Princes and the receptions and speeches on the way had been officially planned ahead of time. But the authorities had to change the whole program to comply with the directly expressed wish of the Prince.

The trip of the Prince of Wales and Prince George, with their party, from Santiago to Valparaiso was made in thirty-five minutes. It pleased the Prince to such an extent that he requested that the official program be broken once more so he might fly back to Santiago in our plane. Commending the ship, the Prince actually said, "We have nothing like that in England."

[In an interview with Geoffrey Hellman published in the *New Yorker* on November 9, 1940, Sergievsky claimed a larger role in piloting for the princes. He told Hellman that the Chilean government, embarassed because no Chilean was able to pilot the plane, dressed Sergievsky in a Chilean uniform; he flew Edward around for two weeks, "pretending to understand no English and looking as Chilean as possible."]

28. Sergievsky was piloting an S-41 like this when it was struck by a tidal wave off the coast of Chile. The Sikorsky S-41, introduced in 1931, was an enlarged version of the S-38. A monoplane—it lacked the S-38's small lower wing—the S-41 could carry a substantially greater load over a longer range. In the depths of the Depression, only six were sold—one to Chile, three to the Navy, and two to Pan Am, including the prototype, shown here. *Courtesy of Igor I. Sikorsky Historical Archives, Inc.*

After finally turning over the plane to the Chilean Air Force, I took a train from Santiago to Valparaiso, and boarded a Royal Mail Liner, *Orbita,* bound for England. I would have to change to another boat in Havana because the *Orbita* was not calling at any North American ports. The trip on the *Orbita* was very restful after the strain of flying in Chile. The trip took eighteen days from Valparaiso to Havana. There was a very interesting and carefree crowd of passengers, and I enjoyed myself very much.

When I reported back to the factory, our president, Mr. Frederick W. Neilson, greeted me with the news that I had to get ready to start for Chile in the newly constructed S-41, a much larger plane with two Hornet engines, which had been ordered by cable from Chile while I was on my way back. Mr. Neilson also informed me that the Chilean government had specified that it wanted me to bring that plane to them.

I only had five days at home and then started again, and in those five days I was kept busy in testing out the S-41.

This time our party included the Vice President of the Westchester Publishing Corporation, Mr. Robertson, and a former Russian Naval officer, Lieutenant Sovinsky, from the National Geographic Society. We also had a photographer on board whose task was to take pictures of the spots indicated by Lieutenant Sovinsky, using a special Fairchild aerial camera. As my course was over places that were partly uncharted, this photography would cover the blind spots on the maps of South America.

I also had two mechanics with me.

Our first landing was in Jacksonville, Florida, completing a nonstop flight of 914 miles in eight hours under very good weather conditions. We stayed in Jacksonville overnight.

When we woke up the next morning we found that it was raining, and fog was lying very low. The airport officials informed me that even the air mail was stopped by the weather, both ways, and also that the diesel engine endurance flight which was in progress over Jacksonville had to be stopped on account of bad weather.

But I was very eager to demonstrate the advantage of an amphibian, which could fly really low through thick weather over the water when flying over the ground is impossible, and started for Miami over the protests of the airport officials.

The fog got so thick that the only thing I could see, flying a few feet off the water, was the white surf on the beach as I followed the shore line of Florida. Only after we passed Palm Beach did the conditions improve slightly, and over Miami the visibility was fair.

We made a short stop in Miami, for clearance from the United States, and the same day hopped to Havana, Cuba. After an overnight stop there, we were joined by a Chilean flying officer, Lieutenant Silva, who acted as my copilot for the rest of the trip.

From Havana I laid my course to Belize, British Honduras. When I was about halfway to Belize I realized that I had a very strong side wind, against which I had to allow over twenty degrees of course for the drift. The same wind that was delaying me on my way to Belize would be almost a tailwind for the next stop, Tela, Honduras. Swiftly making a comparison of distance and necessary amounts of gasoline, I realized that with such a wind I could make Tela easily if I changed my course and missed Belize altogether.

Here it was a great advantage to have a skilful navigator in the person of Lieutenant Sovinsky. The engines were roaring so loudly that I could hardly talk to him, so I wrote him a note on a scrap of paper. "Decided to change course for Tela. Give me our present position and the new course."

I knew that I could make these calculations myself, but it would not be so accurate, because I had to fly the plane at the same time and would have to make them out on my knees, holding the steering wheel as I did them.

In not more than four minutes I got a note from Sovinsky: "New course is xx xx 'xx'" I laid the plane on this new course and in three hours the airport of Tela showed up right on the bow of the plane. All this was done entirely out of sight of land, when we were flying over the Gulf of Mexico.

We stayed overnight in Tela, where we were asked to dinner by the very hospitable manager of the United Fruit concession there.

At daybreak the next morning we made the long hop from Tela to France Field, Panama. The visibility approaching Panama was very poor. Part of the way I had to fly blind. I was not dead sure I was going to hit Panama right on the nose, because it was an eight and one-half hour flight, with no landmarks whatever to check the course.

After about six hours of flying, when according to my calculations we were approximately two hours off Panama, I sighted a steamer ahead, going in the same direction we were. I flew very low over it and saw that it was a Japanese steamer. It was a pretty safe guess that the Japanese ship was going to Panama in order to go into the Pacific, so I made a circle and flew once more right on the course being steered by the Japanese, and in this way checked my own course. A seagoing ship has much better facilities to steer an accurate course and can more accurately ascertain its position than an airplane can.

When in two hours we sighted the shore, it was exactly the entrance to the Panama Canal. It is hard to describe the feeling of satisfaction a pilot has on such occasions. It really is a great joy when, after many hours of suspense and flight through thick weather, you see that you are exactly on your course, and that the goal is straight ahead of you.

I will not go into a detailed description of the celebration which we allowed ourselves in Panama!

The next morning we started for Buena Ventura, Colombia. As soon as we left Panama we lost sight of the coastline. It was misty and soon it began to rain. The rain became more and more heavy, and although once in a while it stopped, we were passing from one rain squall to another, and we arrived in Buena Ventura in the midst of a heavy tropical downpour. We stopped in Buena Ventura only long enough to get some gasoline, and proceeded right away to Santa Elena, Ecuador, where we stayed overnight.

The landing place in Santa Elena is not protected from the heavy Pacific swell, which is running constantly, and once again it was quite a trick to land on it. The plane has to be landed along the swell, on the crest of one of the huge waves, and then has to be kept there by swiftly working the rudder and the throttle to drop down before the plane is hit by another wave.

From Santa Elena we made the long hop of over ten hours to Lima, Peru. Arriving at Lima, we found ourselves in the midst of one of the endless revolutions. Machine guns were rattling in the streets, and I felt myself quite at home. It was just like Russia. It was the day when one of the political parties in Lima had imprisoned their former President, and the new government was still establishing itself by force of arms. But this did not concern us much. We found a comfortable hotel and had a good rest.

The next hop from Lima was to Arica, port of entry for Chile. Part of the time I had to fly blind, and part of the time I had to skim the huge waves of the Pacific Ocean, due to the very low fog. While flying low we saw a tremendous number of sharks, thousands of them, including many hammerheads, swimming around in the water. I pointed these sharks out to my passengers, and asked them how they would like to have a crash around here. It seemed that nobody enjoyed my joke.

In Arica we took on enough gasoline to reach another Chilean airdrome, at Antofagasta, where we did not stop overnight, but just took on enough gas to reach our final goal, Santiago, the capital of Chile.

Between Antofagasta and Santiago are several high mountain ranges. When we were approximately 100 miles from our final destination, crossing one of these mountain ranges at an altitude of 18,000 feet, I noticed that the gas line leading to the right engine had broken from the vibration and that gasoline was leaking out freely. The engine started to cough.

The plane was capable of flying on one engine, but not at an altitude of 18,000 feet. To lose altitude over these rough, snow-covered mountains would be deadly dangerous. I immediately decided to fly to the sea, away from the mountains, and managed to glide to the Chilean naval air base at Quintero, sixteen miles south of Valparaiso.

There our broken gasoline line was replaced, and we flew to Santiago, where we were met by high officials of the Chilean Air Force and representatives of the press.

The Chileans were eagerly awaiting the arrival of this plane. They were very much in a hurry to accept it and I had to make some demonstration flights the day of my arrival there, in spite of the fact that I had covered 7,000 miles in seven days, and was pretty tired after such a feat.

An extensive program of acceptance tests was scheduled for the next morning. We started with speed trials, flying on a measured speed course, and got a substantially better speed than the one specified in the contract. Our altitude flights with full load were also made very successfully the same morning.

Only one test remained to be done before the final acceptance of the plane. That was to demonstrate the seaworthiness of the plane. That test was to be made at the Quintero naval base, where I had landed the previous day for repairs.

After lunch we flew to Quintero. In addition to the officials I brought along with me from Santiago, including the chief of the Chilean Air Force and a few of his aides and the agent of the United Aircraft Export Company, we also took several officers of the naval air base along. When we started for the open-sea tests there were eleven in the plane, including myself and one mechanic.

We made several maneuvers on the water, takeoffs, and landings, to the full satisfaction of the commission, and then proceeded for the final demonstration, a landing and takeoff from the open sea. I was not worried about this test, because on my way to Chile, at Santa Elena, the sea was much heavier than on this particular day, and still the landing and takeoff were accomplished without the slightest difficulty.

I made the landing about six miles offshore at the spot which the chief of the Chilean Air Force indicated to me. There was the usual Pacific ground swell, and the landing was executed in fine style.

As the plane was slowing down but still running on the step, I saw in front of me a huge wave rising without the slightest warning. (Later on I found out that it was a tidal wave.) At this moment I did not know what it was, I only knew that a crash was imminent. I had already lost my flying speed, and could not get away from it. But still I had far too much speed to have a collision with a solid, almost vertical wall of water rising above me approximately forty feet high. The only thing I had time to do was to switch off the engines.

The next moment we were entirely submerged. When the plane appeared from under the water it was a complete wreck. The wing collapsed and fell on the boat. The propellers of the engines, still turning by inertia, cut the boat in two a few inches in front of my legs. The plane was rapidly sinking nose first.

The forward compartment in which I was sitting with the Chilean pilot was already underwater. We had to get to the cabin, which was still out of the water, by breaking the window separating the pilots' compartment from the cabin.

The nine people in the cabin were naturally in a state of panic, and all rushed to the rear door. The only man who knew how to open that door was my mechanic, but for the moment he was knocked out by the shock of the impact of the wave and was sprawling on the floor. The remaining passengers all tried to open the door and only jammed it. I shook my mechanic by the shoulders. He came to and we made our way together to the door and opened it, and then helped all the passengers one by one out of the plane. We had fourteen life jackets in the plane. As soon as we were free of the wreck we started to distribute the life jackets among the passengers, fastening the back straps on those who were not good swimmers. When all nine passengers were provided with life jackets we started to look for the other jackets for ourselves, but there were no more. They had all been caught in the wreckage and sunk.

I looked in every direction. There was nothing left on the surface except one side float of the plane, which by chance had detached itself from the wreck and was floating some distance away, carried farther and farther from us by the breeze. I made pretty good speed in reaching that side float and pushing it back to the group of men in the water.

My mechanic, Vladimir Skory, was a great help to me all through the accident, and did not even think of procuring a life belt for himself until all the passengers had been provided for. He was swimming beside me in overalls, and like every mechanic on earth, every pocket of his overalls was filled with instruments and tools. He would take them out one by one, showing each of them to me, and say, "Captain, isn't it a pity that I have to throw that away."

I also tried to make swimming easier for myself, and finding that my coat was hampering my movements, I took it off and threw it away. I was very much aware that in the breast pocket of this coat were over $2,200 in traveler's checks and cash, expense money for the trip for myself and the crew. But the value of this loss was so infinitely small at that time of deadly danger that even if it had been a million, I would have thrown it away.

It was winter in Chile, and the water, which even in summer was cold from the Humboldt Current touching the western shores of South America, was now bitterly cold. The only consolation was that we were safe from sharks. When Skory inquired about sharks, I told him, "Don't you worry about that, there is a good side to everything. This water is too cold for sharks."

The first half hour we were rather cheerful. We were holding on to the slowly sinking side float, which was damaged and filling up; but we knew that at the naval base in Quintero they would realize that we were overdue and start a search for us.

After about half an hour of swimming, we heard the roar of the big engines of a Dornier Whale flying boat, which was stationed at Quintero. In a few seconds the boat appeared almost over our heads and went west, disappearing from our sight, then reappearing about ten miles south of our location before retuning to the Quintero base. Apparently the crew of the boat were looking for a big white plane in distress and in the growing dark they could not see our few heads sticking out of the water.

We realized that the next search for us could not be started until morning, which would be in about twelve hours or more. We realized also that our strength was almost gone, and that perhaps we could last a few minutes, but not a few hours in this cold water. Any attempt to swim six miles to shore in the rough sea was useless.

Then to our discomfort was added another thing. We had approximately 500 gallons of gasoline in the plane when it sunk. Now the gas tank had burst, far below us, and the gas had come up to the surface. We were actually swimming in a big pool of gasoline, and inhaling it. Two of the men were already sick from the fumes.

Still feeling myself in charge of the party, the Captain of the sunken ship, I ordered everybody to swim into the wind to get out of the pool of gasoline. After working hard for a few minutes and losing part of our strength in this effort, at last we were out of the gasoline, and that was a small relief.

I already heard voices saying that they could not stand the cold any more, it was unbearable, and that it was better to let ourselves go and sink now that there was no hope, no way to last until it got light. By this time it was already completely dark.

If at this moment anybody had offered me a bet on my life I would not have put a penny against a million dollars. I considered myself and the rest of our party one hundred percent dead, without the slightest hope. I have been in dangerous spots during my career; I had several close shaves during my flying days and at the front, I had been in great danger many times, but there was always some sort of hope that the circumstances might turn out finally in a favorable way, and that the danger would be over.

This time there was no hope. I was counting my life in minutes only. We all have heard stories of what a dying man thinks about, what he experiences in that very short time. I must say that I had no visions and it did not occur to me to pray to God. It is true that I remembered some events in my life. But I did not think of any sufferings that I had in life—the wounds that I had received during the war or the troubles or sorrows that are in the lot of every man. All that I remembered were the good things that had happened to me in my life, and my general feeling was, "Well, this and that and that were really excellent. I enjoyed it, I was happy, and I had my share of life. Now it is over, and good-bye, everybody."

I had thoughts of my family, but I did not think long about them, because worrying about what they would do, how they would act, and how they would accept my passing did not help much under the circumstances.

When almost one and one-half hours of such agony had passed and most of us were entirely at the end of our strength and our endurance, I saw all of a sudden a dark object coming close to us. It was a small rowboat with two fishermen. From the shore, they had seen the plane crashing through the tidal wave, they saw it sinking, and they started immediately to row in our direction, but it took them an hour and a half to reach us.

Immediately we started to climb into the rowboat. Those who were older and weaker went in first. The rowboat was so small that there was no room for all of us. When eight of our men were in it, it was filled to its capacity and almost swamped.

Three of us had to wait in the water, because the fishermen said that a second rowboat was closely following them. As the members of the crew, my mechanic I and stayed in the water. I also ordered a young and very husky Chilean lieutenant to stay with me. The only thing he said when I told him to stay was, "Si, Señor."

I asked those in the rowboat to throw their life jackets to us, but no one did. They were so scared the rowboat might overturn any minute and they would find themselves again in the water without life jackets, that apparently the weaker side of their nature won out, and they simply pretended not to hear my appeal.

One of the higher officials of the Chilean Air Force ordered the fishermen to row quickly back to the shore. Then our friend, the agent of United Aircraft Exporting, took up a boat hook and flatly declared that it did not matter who gave such an order, but if anyone tried to row away from us three men in the water and leave us there alone, he would smash that man's head with the hook. So the boat stayed right there, and although we could not climb into the overloaded craft we could hold on to the boat and rest in this way.

By this time the side float to which we had been holding had sunk and there was nothing else which could help us to keep afloat.

In about fifteen minutes more the second rowboat arrived, and we were all taken in the direction of the naval air base. About halfway to shore we were met by a motorboat from the base which was cruising around in the dark with a small searchlight, looking for us.

We were all transfered to the motorboat and rushed to the base. By the time we arrived a crowd of people was waiting for us at the pier. Everybody had a blanket or an old coat or a pair of trousers, our own clothes were in an awful state. Besides being wet they were all in rags, having been torn to pieces while we were struggling through the windows and out of the wreck.

When we arrived at the barracks we got several drinks of straight whisky. Then we were given a very hot meal. Everyone took a steaming hot bath and went immediately to bed. Out of the eleven of us, no one even caught cold.

The next morning we were driven to the nearest railroad station, where we took a train to Santiago. By this time all the Santiago papers were full of descriptions of our accident. A huge crowd was waiting at the railroad station.

I recognized our military attaché, Captain Wooten, and the naval attaché, Commander Hunter, who had come out there to meet me. They arrived in the embassy Packard, and were both in full military dress, having just arrived from some official reception. My own dress consisted of a pair of very disreputable-looking trousers and a very small overcoat, probably a child's, and no shirt. The sleeves of the overcoat barely covered my elbows. I was photographed standing between these two good-looking and smartly dressed attachés, but I was never very proud of this picture.

When I arrived at my hotel in Santiago, after being driven there in the embassy Packard, the first thing I asked the manager of the hotel was to put some extra heat in my room because I was still feeling very cold. That feeling prevailed for about four days. I was never warm enough. Even while sitting in a hot bath I was chilly.

Naturally I reported the accident by cable to our company and also reported the loss of my traveling advance. The necessary amount to cover all the bills and traveling expenses for the party was immediately cabled to me, and in a few days we started on the Grace liner *Santa Maria* from Valparaiso to New York.

Looking at the charts of that particular part of the sea, I realized that at the spot where I landed there was a very sudden break in the depth. Up to that point from the shore the depth was about 50 fathoms, then there was almost a vertical underwater cliff and the depth increased to 225 fathoms. I suppose that the rising of the tidal wave at this particular spot was due to this sudden change in the depth. When the onrushing tide met the underwater cliff, it just rose that much higher and then dropped down. Such a combination might happen only once in a hundred years. It was just our bad luck that we happened to be at exactly that spot at that moment.

Soon after our return to the United States the great aerial maneuvers of the U.S. Army started. Not only military aircraft were taking part in these but also some of the big civil transport airplanes joined the maneuvers. I was assigned one of the twin-engined Sikorsky amphibians to carry Assistant Secretary of War for Aeronautics Trubee Davidson.

In the morning I would call for Mr. Davidson at his estate near Peacock Point on Long Island, and then we would fly to the spot where the maneuvers were being conducted. It was a most thrilling and fascinating experience to take part in these maneuvers, with over 700 planes in the air at the same time. On some occasions I had a full load of newspapermen in the plane, and that was a very cheerful crowd.

In the course of the maneuvers we flew to Boston, Springfield, Hartford, and many other places. It was great to feel myself again under military command, when all the orders were so short, clear, and definite. Everybody knew their place, their task, and everything went on with the precision of clockwork. I was really sorry when the air maneuvers were over, and I had to return to the everyday routine.

But I had a very interesting plane being completed at this time at the factory. It was the first of the three huge, 40-passenger [S-40] Clipper planes with four Hornet engines. I had to make the test flights in this monster of the air. The Clipper was the largest amphibian in the world and second only to the largest plane ever built in the world, the German flying boat DO-X.

It was a thrilling experience to take the controls for the first time in this huge

The Sikorsky S-40

The success of the Sikorsky S-38 in service with Pan American led the airline to commission a larger, longer-ranged transport for its expanding service to Central and South America. The choice of Sikorsky reflected more than the success of the S-38. Frederick Rentschler had bought United Aircraft and Transport in 1929—a company that included Sikorsky, Pratt and Whitney, and Hamilton Standard—and Rentschler was a member of the executive committee of Pan Am's board of directors. Moreover, Igor Sikorsky and Charles Lindbergh were the best of friends by 1930, and Lindbergh was Pan Am's technical adviser.[1]

Despite these ties, the design of the S-40 was not a simple process. Juan Trippe, the hard-driving boss of Pan Am, wanted the big plane as soon as possible. Lindbergh wanted something as sleek and strutless as the record-breaking monoplanes that Lockheed was producing (he soon bought a Lockheed for himself). Sikorsky proposed an enlarged, four-engined version of the S-38, arguing, "This we know we can do," and Priester supported him.[2] Lindbergh was dismayed when he first saw the plans for the S-40, saying, "It will be like flying a forest through the air," but Pan Am's pressing need for the big plane won him over.[3]

The S-40 did indeed have dozens of struts and wires tying its components together in the familiar Sikorsky pattern. All the bracing was needed, for the 17-ton amphibian, with its four engines and boat hull suspended beneath a 114-foot parasol wing, was the largest airplane yet built in the United States. The springs in its retractable landing gear were of a type normally used for railroad cars.[4] Not surprisingly, its four engines were Pratt and Whitney Hornets driving Hamilton Standard propellers.

Sikorsky wanted the pilot's cabin placed at the bow, for the best visiblity. Lindbergh wanted to put the pilot aft of the wing; this had been the safest position when he had flown the air mail in open-cockpit DH-4s a few years earlier. But the memory of spray-blinded takeoffs in the S-38 persuaded Lindbergh to compromise and the cabin was placed toward the bow, where the pilots had a clear forward view.

Three S-40s were built for Pan Am, for $125,000 each. Boris Sergievsky identified the big boat's flaws, which were mostly minor maladjustments of rigging and trim. He found the ailerons required considerable strength to move, even though they were equipped with booster tabs, and Pan Am's check pilot Basil Rowe agreed, calling them "exceptionally heavy." Rowe opted for a greater gear ratio on the ailerons, saying, "The trouble with our compromise was constant winding of the wheel, but it was better than doubtful control in rough conditions." Everything else about the S-40 impressed Rowe most favorably.[5]

Once the S-40's flaws had been identified and fixed, Pan Am took them over. The first, christened the *American Clipper* on October 12, 1931, was the first of many aircraft to bear Pan Am's illustrious "Clipper" name, later made famous around the world. Lindbergh and Rowe piloted the *American Clipper* on its maiden voyage from Miami to the Canal Zone on November 19, and Igor Sikorsky joined the 32 paying passengers. Each night, the three aviators dined together and sketched on menus the plane that was to succeed the S-40: an airliner that could fly the Atlantic.[6]

Long after that successor took wing as the Sikorsky S-42, the three S-40s, converted to flying boats, sailed on across the Caribbean and down the east coast of Latin America. In their first two years on Pan Am's routes, they arrived on schedule 99 percent of the time—a record no modern airline can match. They served faithfully and efficiently for a decade, carrying hundreds of thousands of passengers without incident over an estimated ten million miles of flight, until they were scrapped early in World War II.[7]

AF

29. The S-40 towers over its creator, Igor I. Sikorsky, on the left, and his good friends racing pilot Roscoe Turner, center, and Boris Sergievsky, on the right. *Courtesy of National Air and Space Museum.*

plane. Nobody yet knew whether it would fly at all, or how it was going to fly. Its dimensions were so unusual, its weight so great, that even the slightest mistake in balance or in the control system might be too great to be overcome by the strength of the man at the controls. I realized the full amount of responsibility resting upon me when I was entrusted with such a plane to test. I had to feel my way about carefully to find the proper manner in which to handle it.

The very first flight of the *American Clipper* was made in front of the Stratford lighthouse in Long Island Sound and lasted only a few minutes. I found the controls not properly balanced and the effort that had to be applied in pulling the plane out for a landing was so great that the plane could not be considered satisfactory.

The necessary changes and adjustments were made in a few days and dur-

Sikorsky III: The Dream Comes True

Igor Sikorsky often accompanied Boris Sergievsky on test flights of the giant S-40, looking for ways to improve its handling in the air and on the water. Sergievsky noted that the aileron controls were too heavy, but they were not geared down until Pan American's pilots requested the change, to reduce the muscle power required for banking. Hull design was still an art, too, even though Sikorsky's engineers attached scale-model hulls to outriggers on speedboats and sped up and down the Housatonic River, looking for hull designs that would rise quickly and smoothly onto the surface of the water with minimal spray.[1] Sikorsky described his participation in these tests, and a revelation that occurred during Pan American's celebratory acceptance flight of the first S-40.

> During the fall of 1931, after a series of extensive flights, Sikorsky Aircraft delivered to Pan American Airways the S-40, a four-engine flying boat, which was christened the *American Clipper*. This plane was the first of a series of large flying clipper ships that have been used successfully for long-distance air travel to South America and which eventually started the transpacific airline and the transatlantic air route.

> I did a considerable amount of flying in this plane but was usually so busy making observations, watching the instruments in the pilot's cabin, and solving various engineering problems that I had little opportunity to get an impression of the flight as a passenger. Furthermore, all the preliminary flights were made with the structure bare—that is, without any interior arrangements, trimmings, or seats. In this state the cabin was very noisy, and it was difficult to move about because the temporary floors were covered with a number of sandbags to represent the useful load. Finally, all tests were completed successfully and the ship returned to the factory for the installation of seats, tables, trimmings, carpets, and other fittings.

> Upon acceptance of the plane by Pan American Airways, I was invited on a flight over New York with several members of the board of directors of that organization and a few other guests. The Pan American pilots and crew were now in charge of the ship. I had no duties on board and was able to enjoy the flight

30. Igor I. Sikorsky, seated in the walnut-trimmed lounge of the S-40 in 1931, three decades after he had dreamed of flying in such a cabin. *Courtesy of Igor I. Sikorsky Historical Archives, Inc.*

over New York, which was made partly above the clouds. We admired the scenery of the clouds against the setting sun and the city, which could be seen from time to time between the clouds.

On the way back to Bridgeport, the pilot throttled the engines and gradually brought the ship down to a lower altitude. The sun was already below the horizon, and as the ship descended, it became quite dark. The air was calm and the plane moved very slowly, with the engines running as reduced power. I was in the front cabin at the time and decided to see what was going on in the other cabins. While I was walking toward the smoking lounge, the cabin steward turned on the lights, and I stopped with a feeling of suprise. Some twenty feet ahead I saw the walnut trimmings and the elegant entrance to the smoking lounge. The bluish electric lights from the ceiling appeared bright and attractive. Usually I had been too busy to see the cabin with the lights on. Now looking at it for the first time under these conditions, I could well appreciate its fine appearance, for it was much larger than that on any other plane at the time. But I was surprised by another thought. I realized, at that very moment, that I had already seen all this a long time ago, the passageway, the bluish lights, the walnut trimmings on the walls and doors, and the feeling of smooth motion, and I tried to recall when and how I could have received such an impression, until finally I remembered the details of my dream of some thirty years before.[2] (See p. 22.)

AF

ing the second flight the controls were quite satisfactory. During the test flights of every new type of plane a lot of things are usually found out and constant improvements are going on.

Flights were continued almost every day for several months; every time something was changed and improved until we had the plane perfect enough to submit it to the trials in the presence of Department of Commerce Inspectors.

There is always quite a series of test flights required for a new type of plane before the government inspector will approve it and send his approval to Washington. Only then will the Washington office of the Aeronautics Branch of the Department of Commerce issue an "Approved Type Certificate," which is not a license for the particular plane, but a license to build planes of this type. At the same time, the individual license for the plane would be issued, and it would be allowed to operate commercially.

After exhaustive tests by ourselves, the Department of Commerce inspectors, and the pilots sent over by Pan American Airways, the first Clipper was taken to Washington, where it was christened by Mrs. Herbert Hoover the

American Clipper. This christening, occurring during Prohibition, was made by smashing a bottle of water from the Caribbean Sea against the bow of the plane.

Meanwhile, the work on the second Clipper was proceeding rapidly. It was almost completed when we received an order to work day and night if necessary, and have it ready to take the Foreign Minister of Italy, Signor Grandi, from New York to Washington. Lindbergh was supposed to pilot the plane, but I had to deliver it to New York and be in the control cabin during the flight.

The factory worked day and night to complete the plane and it was ready only at five o'clock in the morning of the day when the flight had to take place.

The weather was awful, but in spite of bad visibility and light rain we started for New York, having on board, among other people, our President, M. F. W. Neilson. When we were already in the vicinity of North Beach, approximately around City Island, the weather closed in on us completely. The fog dropped down to the surface of the water, and if we would have had to make a weather report it would have been, "Visibility Zero and Ceiling Zero." Under such circumstances I could fly blind, but I could not land.

I turned back and found a spot where I could see the water. That was in front of Whitestone, Long Island. I landed there, and taxied to North Beach on the water. In the fog we barely missed one of the College Point ferry boats while taxiing. It took us only fifteen minutes to get from Bridgeport to City Island and fifty minutes from Whitestone to North Beach. If we could have flown, we would have made that distance in less than five minutes.

In spite of the bad weather, Lindbergh arrived at North Beach in his Lockheed monoplane a couple of hours after we managed to get there, but the fog over New York harbor was so thick that the whole flight had to be cancelled, and I had to fly the big plane back to Bridgeport, which I did the next day when the fog lifted.

Between the tests of the second and the third Clipper there was a gap of time of quite a few months and I was offered an extended vacation without pay.

Fortunately for me we sold one of our deluxe S-38s to a young Englishman, Captain Francis-Francis. He requested that I accompany him as his pilot and personal instructor on a trip to the West Indies. He was himself a British licensed pilot, but he had no experience in large planes, and wanted to get practical instruction from me.

Captain Francis-Francis brought with him from England his own mechanic, who also was getting acquainted with the plane, and in this way we had two

A Test Pilot's Report

Boris Sergievsky describes how the Sikorsky factory worked day and night to have the second S-40, the *Caribbean Clipper,* ready to fly the Italian foreign minister, Dino Grandi, to Washington, D.C., saying that the giant plane was "ready only at five o'clock in the morning of the day the flight was to take place" (the flight was scheduled for November 16, 1931). In fact, some workers were racing to install the luxurious interior of the big boat, while others were correcting some aerodynamic maladjustments. Sergievsky had taken the *Caribbean Clipper* up on a trial flight on November 11 and had found some serious—though easily corrected—flaws. Here is his report.[1]

INTER-OFFICE CORRESPONDENCE
SIKORSKY AVIATION CORPORATION

To: Mr. F. W. Neilson
   cc. Mr. I. I. Sikorsky   Mr. G. A. Meyrer
   Mr. M. Gluhareff   Mr. S. Gluhareff

From: B. Sergievsky
Subject: First Test of S-40 - mfg. #2001

   The ship is very nose heavy. For level flight at 1,750 r.p.m. the stabilizer had to be taken all the way out. It is left wing heavy. The aileron controls are excessively heavy—heavier than the first ship. Longitudinal, directional, and lateral stability seem to be all right.

   After the take-off the right outer engine dropped revolutions to 1,500 wide open. There is an excessive fuel pressure on the right outer engine, more than the dial could indicate.

   The pilot's chair is too close to the pedals and to the control wheel, so that the pilot's legs, in the most forward position on the pedals, are at right angles at the knees, and in order to move the wheel back on landing it is neccessary to spread the knees apart. Such a position of the chair is very uncomfortable and makes the pilot tired even after a very short flight.

B. Sergievsky
BS/mg

AF

---

pilots and two mechanics to take care of the plane. On the passenger list was Mrs. Francis-Francis, her mother, their maid, Captain Francis-Francis's valet, one bulldog, and two Pekinese.

Before departing for the West Indies we made quite a few flights around New York and then started on our way south. Making one overnight stop at Charleston, South Carolina, we arrived at Palm Beach.

Captain Francis-Francis was a very versatile sportsman. He was a wonderful horseman, a captain in the Royal Horse Guards, one of the finest fencers in Europe, one of the amateur golf champions, and fond of many other sports, but of all the sports he liked flying the most.

His desire to master his new amphibian was so great that he did not allow enough time for other pleasures or even for rest. After arriving at Palm Beach we started practicing every morning and every afternoon. In a few days there was hardly anything more I could teach him, and it seemed to me that he was still keeping me in his employ mostly for the trip to the West Indies, where I could help him in navigating and also in obtaining all the necessary papers, clearances and permits.

We stayed several weeks in Palm Beach and spent another two in Miami, practicing ground landings at the Pan American airport. Then we flew to Havana.

We obtained a special permit to land and keep the plane at the military airfield of Campo Columbia, which was very close to the city and much more convenient for our purposes. It was very hard to obtain such a permit because the former President of Cuba, Machado, had passed a law that all the privately owned planes had to be kept at another airport farther inland, which was privately owned by Señor Machado himself, and which charged an outrageous amount for storage.

We enjoyed all the pleasures of Havana and were getting ready to start for Puerto Rico, when a cable arrived about the suicide of the Swedish financier Kruger. A substantial amount of money belonging to Captain Francis-Francis was invested in Kruger enterprises and his immediate personal attention was needed. A man in charge of part of his business had to meet him in Florida, so we made a hurried flight back to Miami.

By this time Captain Francis-Francis had mastered the art of flying the amphibian plane, and I was feeling completely useless to him. He could not, however, pilot the plane himself in the United States on his British license.

I suggested that he should pass an examination for an American license and I arranged an appointment for him with the government inspector in Palm Beach. We flew there and the Captain very successfully passed his examination. I could not be of any more use to him and told him so. He answered that my term of employment had been much shorter than either of us had expected, and he did not see any reason why I should suffer financially simply because I was such a good instructor and had taught him to fly the plane more quickly than usual.

He asked me if I would do him the favor of accepting a month's salary in advance. It was not hard for him to pursuade me. I left the captain and his party in Miami, taking a boat to New York.

Soon after my arrival in Bridgeport, the case about the crash of the Andian National Corporation plane came to court in Bridgeport, and I was called to testify not only as a witness but also as an expert concerning the circumstances of that crash. All the circumstances of my resignation from the company, my recommendations to them, the warnings that were given by our company to Andian National, were revived during the trial. My testimony took several days, and it was amazing to me how the late Chief Justice George Wheeler went deeply into even the finest details of the science of aeronautics during the trial. I understand that he had no mechanical interest whatever, never even drove his own car, and still he was so eager to get at the complete truth of the case that by the time it was over he could be considered almost an aeronautics expert.

I understand also that he had written his decision in the case in his own shorthand, but had died before he had time to sign it.

The case had to be tried all over again, but the cost of the trial for both sides was so excessive that they arrived at a satisfactory settlement out of court.

During this trial I was very much pleased to face the man who was in charge of aviation at the Andian National Corporation and who really was responsible for the whole mess. It seems to me that he realized during the trial that the crash was mainly due to his obstinacy and lack of judgment.

The reason why the Andian National Corporation had put him in charge of their aviation department was that although he was just an accountant in their organization, he had attended a flying school in Canada during the war. According to his own story, he had been dismissed from the school as incapable of flying. Yet such a record was regarded by the Andian National Corporation as sufficient to put him at the head of their aviation department.

The construction of the third S-40 Clipper was completed in the summer of 1932, and I was called for active duties again by the Sikorsky Company. As I was not on a salary, after one test flight, which took altogether only fifty minutes of flying, I was asked, "How much?" I answered, "$500." "What, for fifty minutes of flying!" "No sir, for twenty years of experience incorporated in the fifty minutes of flying." Without further discussion I got the amount I asked for.

Late in 1932, Martin Johnson arrived with Mrs. Johnson at Bridgeport to make a personal appearance for their picture, *Congorilla,* which was being shown in the Fox Poli Theater. Being interested in aviation, they visited the Sikorsky plant. When they saw the kinds of planes that Sikorsky was building, they realized that these were ideal for their work in Africa.

At first they wanted to buy one plane, but when they counted the amount of equipment and all the members of the expedition that they were planning, they realized that one plane would not do, and they purchased two, a twin-engined S-38 and a single-engined S-39.

Mr. Johnson had contracted their former instructor in flying, Vern Carstens, to be their regular pilot on the expedition. Vern was an excellent pilot, but he was from Kansas, and as we know, there is no ocean in Kansas, and he hadn't had the opportunity to fly seaplanes or amphibians before. So it was decided at the last moment that an experienced seaplane man should go along and stay with the expedition as long as necessary to train Carstens and Mr. and Mrs. Johnson in the proper way to fly amphibian planes.

I was chosen for the job. I had only a few hours to get my things ready and to get my passport stamped with visas so that I could leave with the expedition.

Flight over Africa

On December 31st, 1932, the oil tanker *City of New York* sailed from New York for Cape Town, South Africa. Among the twenty-four passengers on board were eight members of the Johnson expedition, setting out for a two-year journey to hunt and film in remote parts of East and Central Africa. Besides Mr. and Mrs. Johnson, the following people belonged to the expedition: Vern Carstens, pilot; Robert Moreno, engineer and sound man; and Hugh Davis, photographer. The temporary members were: A. D. Sanial, sound technician; A. E. Morway, airplane mechanic; and I—as flight instructor. The last three of us were to return to the United States as soon as we had finished our specified jobs.

Two airplanes were securely fastened to the deck of the ship. The more powerful S-38, intended for passengers, was called *Osa's Ark*, in honor of Mrs. Johnson, whose first name was Osa. It was painted in zebra stripes. The other plane, a single-engined S-39, with a cabin the size of a normal automobile passenger compartment, held four or five passengers. It was painted brown and white in giraffe style, and was called *Spirit of Africa*. Except for their wings being removed, both airplanes seemed almost ready to take off from the deck, rise up into the sky, and fly across the ocean to the Dark Continent, searching for adventures and new experiences on rivers and lakes over which no airplane had yet flown.

Our first several days at sea were windy, and the ship rolled so heavily that you could move around only by holding onto railings and walls. My cabin was right next to the dining room, and one morning I was awakened by a terrible crash of breaking glass and the sound of falling metal. It turned out that all of the table settings had fallen on the floor because of the strong rolling. However, after five days the sea grew peaceful. It was already hot, and, to the delight of the passengers, a swimming pool was set up in the hold.

I began every morning with a dive into the pool. After a light breakfast, I made a two-mile run around the decks (twenty-eight times around the upper deck). Then, having played several games of deck golf and deck tennis, I again

Hollywood Meets Africa

Martin and Osa Johnson, whom Boris Sergievsky flew half the length of Africa, belonged to the golden age of professional adventure travel that flourished between the turn of the century and World War II. Fast steamships could carry enterprising writers, lecturers and filmmakers to far corners of the globe—but no jetliner excursion fares allowed their audiences to vacation cheaply in the same places. Bulky, high-quality movie cameras had been developed—but not the home video camera. Furthermore, this was an era when few of the folks back home let issues like colonialism or endangered species mar their appetite for films of pygmies or elephant hunts.

Martin Johnson (1884–1937) and his wife, Osa (1894–1953), were voracious travelers and shrewd entrepreneurs who saw this historical window of opportunity and used it to the full. They also had a keen sense of show business, and of the American appetite for the exotic. Separately or together, and with considerable help from ghostwriters,[1] they produced seventeen books, more than eighty magazine articles, and countless films—often edited in one version for movie theaters and in another for their lecture tours.

In his youth, Martin Johnson had crossed the Pacific as a crew member on Jack London's sailboat. Returning home, he married Osa, then brought her along on a tour of vaudeville houses. To illustrate his adventures with London in the South Seas, she sang and danced in a grass skirt. For the rest of their life together, they alternated between traveling to distant corners of the world and lecturing at home. "When Martin and Osa did return to the States, it was usually because of finances, or, rather, no finances," one of their biographers writes, "These visits lasted only long enough to accrue sufficient funds for another expedition. As soon as possible, the Johnsons were off to the wilds on a well-planned trip that would last until the last dollar had been spent."[2]

During and after the First World War, the Johnsons went back to the South Pacific, and then on to Borneo, Ceylon, and India. They were the first Europeans to land on some of the islands in the Solomon and New Hebrides groups. They photographed shrunken heads and, they claimed, at one dinner they were invited to they barely escaped becoming the main dish. On their return home, the films poured forth: *Cannibals of the South Seas, Jungle Adventure, East of Suez*. The Johnsons never let the facts get in the way of a good story. In the New Hebrides Islands, Martin Johnson claimed, there were "monkey people" who lived in the trees, who could be the long-sought missing link between apes and humans.[3]

Between 1921 and 1935, the Johnsons traveled mostly in Africa, where for a time they had a house in Nairobi. Their safari headman had done the same job for Theodore Roosevelt. Martin operated the movie camera, and Osa, who was a better shot, killed a lion or elephant if it charged them. Such episodes thrilled wide-eyed lecture audiences back home. Part of the films' appeal was that even in these exotic settings Osa Johnson was, images hinted, still a safely traditional wife. She was shown cooking in camp, dressed in a safari hat and apron. The petite Osa was nearly a foot shorter than her husband; whether astride a live camel in the desert or beside a dead elephant in the jungle, she was always poised, trim, and with perfect make-up and coiffure.[4]

The Johnsons' 1933 trip with Boris Sergievsky was the first time they filmed in color—and the first time they used airplanes. The Johnsons knew that the airplane would be a novel platform for landscape and animal photography. And they knew that visiting remote places by plane would be vastly easier than carrying all their food and film equipment on foot: one earlier safari had required 235 porters. After Sergievsky got the Johnsons from Cape Town to

Nairobi and taught them how to fly their new aircraft, they spent many more months filming in Africa.[5]

Back in the United States in 1934, Sergievsky helped out the Johnsons once more: he flew them and a collection of African mammals, including a baby elephant named Toto Tembo, from New York to St. Louis, where the animals were destined for the zoo.[6]

Soon after, the Johnsons took one of their airplanes to Borneo, where they flew more than 30,000 miles over some of the world's most inhospitable terrain without a major mishap.[7] Ironically, they both succumbed to dangers elsewhere. In 1937, just as they were beginning a U.S. lecture tour about the Borneo trip, their scheduled commercial airliner crashed while coming into Los Angeles, and Martin Johnson was killed. Osa survived. But her bouyant presence on the lecture platform had concealed a manic-depressive condition she suffered from for most of her life, and alcoholism hastened her own death in 1953.[8]

AH

swam in the pool before lunch. They fed us magnificently on the *City of New York*. The menu contained a large variety of elaborate dishes, capable of satisfying the most demanding gourmet. After lunch we usually began playing some game, while the other passengers played bridge, read, or walked on the deck. About 4 P.M. came the favorite exercise of all. The Captain of the ship, George Winship—probably one of the youngest officers to command a large passenger vessel—appeared at this time of day with a heavy "medicine ball." One hour with this ball or playing deck tennis was enough to make us ready for another refreshing swim in the pool. After that it was time to get dressed for dinner. After dinner everyone gathered in the smoking room, where coffee was served, and where the passengers played different games until nightfall.

A few days out of New York, the atmosphere on board was like that of a private yacht. By now all the passengers knew each other and had established friendly ties. We all knew we would be spending twenty-three days at sea, and we were quick to use that time for a full vacation.

They told us that the voyage from New York to Cape Town was the longest shipping route in the world without an intermediate port. We did put in at one port along the way, the island of St. Helena, the famous spot where Napoleon spent the last years of his life.

On the morning of the sixteenth day of our sea journey, our ship approached the rocky shore of the island of St. Helena and dropped anchor in the harbor. They told us that the ship would stay there long enough for the passengers to have a look at most of the island, especially the places connected with Napoleon's stay as a prisoner of the British.

The passengers divided into several groups and headed off in horse-drawn carriages to look at the historical sights of the island. At first we stuck to the road winding up the mountainside, then, to make the ascent easier, extra horses were waiting for us at the foot of the steepest ridge. The weather was wonderful, and from the upper slopes of the mountain we had a view of the whole island and the surrounding blue ocean. The first historic site on our trip was Napoleon's first tomb. Before his death, he himself chose this spot, foreseeing, however, that there would come a time when his remains would be taken to France. No imagination could picture a more ideal spot for one's eternal rest than this little valley, with marvelous green grass beneath Norfolk pines and cedars! A simple iron fence around a simple white gravestone without any inscription on it—all this created an atmosphere of bliss and peace. Some weeks later I was to see the present resting place of Napoleon in Paris, under the cupola of Les Invalides. But it seems to me that this valley, secluded on the heights, on an island lost in the ocean, would be a more fitting place for the remains of Napoleon than in the center of gay and noisy Paris. Napoleon had the habit of stopping in this little valley during his daily walks, resting and meditating there, and quenching his thirst from a spring behind one of the rocks.

All of us found ourselves under the deep spell of the simple beauty of this spot. A sort of mystical feeling affected us, as though we were in the presence of one of the greatest figures in human history. To show more clearly this strange feeling of fascination that seized each of the visitors to this spot, here is one conversation I accidentally overheard between two of the tourists:

"George," said one of the two, "I just sent home a letter where I wrote that I was about to see Old Napy's tomb. Now that I've seen it, I feel ashamed before him for that lighthearted letter. I'd like to find it in our ship's mailbox and destroy it. This place with its memories of him somehow affects you, makes you think of many things about life . . . "

From the tomb, we went to Longwood House—the last residence where Napoleon lived. It was a one-story building, not too big, with a small garden. Only two rooms were open to visitors. The rest of the house is now occupied by the French Consul. The two rooms open for view were devoid of furniture—which had all been taken to France, to the museum at Les Invalides. In the bedroom, in the very place where Napoleon's deathbed stood, was a statue of him—the one object in the room where he lived and died. How much better it would have been to have kept these rooms inviolable, with all the furnishings and personal belongings of the Emperor, just as they had been during his lifetime! Now his desk, chairs, and various other pieces of furniture are preserved in the halls of the museum at Les Invalides in Paris. They don't appear in the right place and don't produce that impression which they undoubtedly would have on visitors if they were found in their original surroundings.

When we raised anchor at the end of the day and began to leave the island, I looked back on the high rocky cliffs, falling almost vertically to the sea, and quickly decreasing in size in proportion to our distance from shore. When these cliffs had almost dropped out of sight, I saw a vision: in the dim dusk of evening, above the summit of one of the mountains, was outlined the familiar silhouette of a man in a long gray military frock coat, in a black three-cornered hat, with his arms crossed on his chest, standing with his face to the ocean and looking with burning eyes in the direction of France, the place of his past glory . . .

After seven more days' journey through the warm South Atlantic, we arrived at Cape Town. Immediately on arrival, our airplanes were lifted from the ship's deck by cranes and deposited on the pier, noses to the water. All the members of the Johnson expedition busied themselves with the assembly of the two amphibians, beginning with the smaller of the two. After four hours' work, the *Spirit of Africa* was again lifted up by a crane and deposited in the water.

Besides me and my mechanic, on board were Mr. and Mrs. Johnson, wanting to take part in the first flight of their plane over Africa.

Cape Town harbor was too small to take off from, so I had to taxi out to the roadstead. A strong wind was blowing, and the sea was too stormy for the small amphibian. I turned into the wind, looking forward and expecting the series of waves which would be rolling over any expanse so big. When I saw several uniformly sized and not too big waves in front of us, I pushed the throttle to full power, and in less than ten seconds we took off—and came, the back way, into Cape Town airport, which was ten miles from town.

The next day we finished assembling our larger airplane and flew it to the airport. This time, films were taken of our landing and shown that very evening, along with shots of other events of the day, in all the movie theaters of Cape Town.

The following morning, we headed off in our airplanes for the long flight to Nairobi (3,161 miles). Since our engines were equipped with superchargers, we had to add a certain amount of liquid ethyl to our gasoline. Several crates con-

31. The route of Sergievsky's travels with the Johnson expedition, from Cape Town, South Africa, to Kisumu, Kenya. *Courtesy of Barbara Jackson, Meridian Mapping, Oakland, Calif.*

taining bottles of ethyl had been bought by Mr. Johnson in New York and were supposed to have been stowed in the hold of our ship. But after all our baggage was unloaded and checked, the ethyl wasn't there. It finally turned out that two crates of ethyl had by mistake been put in storage, together with other things of Mr. Johnson's that had not been needed for the expedition. This lack of ethyl would have made our flights into the interior of the continent impossible, but to our good luck, we found out that some years before, two barrels of ethyl had been sent from the United States to the Vacuum Oil Company in Cape Town. Again to our good luck, the local agents of Vacuum Oil, confused by the complicated instructions about the use of liquid ethyl, and not needing any, had stored these barrels in a company warehouse, where they had waited seven years, untouched until our arrival in Cape Town. Taking all necessary precautions, Carstens, Morway, and I, with the help of workers from Vacuum Oil, extricated one of these barrels from the warehouse. Putting on waterproof gloves and using a heavy hammer, we unscrewed the lid. Laboratory tests showed that the ethyl was in good condition.

On our flights, we would have to cross over high mountain ranges and take off from fields and lakes far above sea level. Because it contains lead, liquid ethyl is very heavy. We decided to take with us only the amount necessary to get us to Nairobi, where the Shell Company already had sent a big supply of gasoline for our engines, together with the necessary quantity of ethyl. Besides the weight of this ethyl, we also had to think about the containers for transporting it in the planes, because in that concentrated a state, any kind of leak or spill would destroy any cloth it touched. The containers offered us by Shell were solid steel cylinders, too heavy for carrying by air. Finally, Mr. Johnson and I went to the largest hardware store in Cape Town and bought all the metal canteens with screw-on caps that they had in stock. There were enough canteens so that we could bring on the flight all the necessary quantity of ethyl.

We were in Cape Town from January 23rd to 31st. During this time, Vern Carstens learned to fly *The Spirit of Africa*, which he was to transport to Nairobi, while I was to fly *Osa's Ark*. Being a talented pilot, Carstens quickly mastered the techniques of flying the plane. Practicing approaches and landings on water, we made several flights over the twelve miles between the airport and a freshwater lake. I also gave several lessons to Mr. and Mrs. Johnson. Both of them had private pilot's licenses and had done several hours of solo flying, but neither of them had had the chance to fly seaplanes or amphibians. At these first lessons, both husband and wife displayed boldness, a good understanding of the material, and a strong desire to work on their piloting technique. Mrs. Johnson, especially, showed herself to be a thoroughly able young pilot, quickly and easily absorbing all that I showed and explained to her.

We divided all the expedition's baggage into two parts. The first, consisting of photographic, movie, and sound equipment, and essential personal baggage, had to come with the members of the expedition on board the two planes. The remainder of the equipment and personal baggage was sent on by steamship from Cape Town to Mombasa, and from there by train to Nairobi. When we weighed everything that had to go on the planes, we realized we had a significant overload: the total weight of baggage and equipment on board the planes was 1,150 pounds. Before dawn on the morning of January 31st, we all came to

The Sikorsky S-39

The success of the S-38 inspired Igor Sikorsky to sketch a smaller and less expensive version, the five-place S-39, for sportsman pilots and corporate executives. Boris Labensky, in charge of design and development, translated Sikorsky's sketches into a twin-engined "kid brother" of the S-38, differing only in its smaller size and lack of a lower wing. Boris Sergievsky took the S-39 up for its first flight on December 24, 1929. On the third test flight, a week later, the fuel pump failed on one of the British Cirrus Hermes engines and Sergievsky was forced to land on rough ground short of the Stratford runway. The S-39 flipped on its back. Sergievsky and his passenger Serge Gluhareff were unhurt, but the S-39 was demolished.

Work began immediately on a new S-39, powered by a single 300-horsepower Pratt and Whitney Wasp Junior. Igor Sikorsky resisted the idea of a single engine, but United Aircraft now owned both Sikorsky's company and Pratt and Whitney and insisted on marrying the two corporate products. The crash of the twin-engined S-39 undercut Sikorsky's arguments about twin-engined safety, and the dependability of the Wasp Junior eventually affirmed the single-engine choice. (Unfortunately, the high cost of the engine forced Sikorsky to price the S-39 at $21,500, and as the Great Depression deepened, few could afford to buy it; S-39 production was halted after the first batch of 20 was completed.)

Boris Sergievsky took the single-engined S-39 up for the first time in February 1930 and later wrote to Igor Sikorsky, Jr. that "during the first flight I looped the loop with it." A few flights later, the wing "gave out with a loud groan and started to buckle," but the S-39 landed safely. A stronger wing was introduced on production models, along with an all-metal fuselage, making the S-39 the first all-metal Sikorsky airplane.

Pilots loved the S-39; Vern Carstens, who flew the Johnsons' S-39 across Africa, later said, "The S-39 was excellent. It landed slowly and takeoffs were clean. The hull design was somewhat different than the S-38 and no spray was thrown over the windshield."

The Johnsons' S-39 *Spirit of Africa* (c/n 914, NC 52V), with its brown and white "giraffe spots" painted on fuselage and floats, was the most famous S-39 of all, thanks to Osa and Martin's popular movie shorts of their trips across Africa and Borneo in their Sikorskys. Their S-39 was powered by Wasp Junior No. 2, the first of these famous engines to fly. Pratt and Whitney, eager to win both fame and production orders for their new engine, loaned or rented No. 2 to several famous fliers. No. 2 powered "Speed" Holman's Laird *Solution* racer, won the 1931 Thompson Trophy race for Lowell Bayles in the Gee Bee Model Z, and powered the Gee Bee R-2 racer flown by Lee Gehlbach before it was installed in the Johnsons' S-39. Despite its wide-open racing career, No. 2 never faltered as it took the Johnsons over the jungles of Africa and Borneo, where engine failure would almost certainly have had fatal consequences.[1]

AF

the airport before sunrise to load the planes, pull them out of the hangers, and warm them up.

Taking into account the better payload capacity of *Osa's Ark*, we carried on board all the baggage and equipment. Besides the members of the crew—myself and Morway—Mr. and Mrs. Johnson, Hugh Davis, and Wah (Mrs. Johnson's monkey) also flew on *Osa's Ark*. The *Spirit of Africa* carried Carstens as pilot and

32. Osa Johnson and Boris Sergievsky lean against a Packard roadster in front of the giraffe-spotted S-39, *Spirit of Africa*. Sergievsky's suit and vest suggest that the picture was taken in the cool Kenyan highlands. *Courtesy of the editors.*

Sanial and Moreno as passengers. When the sun came up, we were surprised to see low, dark clouds beneath the heights of the mountain ridge to the northeast, which we were going to cross. The airport chief told me that if we succeeded in flying across the first ridge, the weather on the other side would be clearer, since the clouds were held back by the first range of mountains.

I gave Carstens the signal to follow me, took off, and put *Osa's Ark* on a course for Victoria West, our first scheduled refueling stop, 365 miles northeast from Cape Town. Throttling back to the slowest safe cruising speed, I intended to give Carstens the chance to follow me, at least until we had crossed over the mountains.

Gaining altitude to the maximum allowed by the level of the clouds, we climbed to around 4,000 feet. We flew together, Carstens following right on my tail in the direction of the mountain. When we got close to it, we saw that the clouds were lower than any of the peaks or the passes between them. Directly above us was a whole billow of clouds, and in front of us the wall of the mountainside. Not knowing the topography and altitude of the peaks before us, to attempt to fly through the clouds on instruments would be too much of a risk. I changed my course to the west, following the ridge, and looking for some kind of opening through which I could fly. After twenty minutes, I noticed a very narrow canyon crossing the ridge, with patches of sunlight at its far end. Through this narrow entrance, both planes flew.

But before us rose up a second ridge, its heights covered with black clouds. We had to look once more for some kind of opening. This time we flew in an easterly direction, compensating for the deviation from our original course. Finally I saw a patch of blue sky above the mountain barrier, and pushed my hardworking engines to gain altitude, to reach this one opening in the clouds. During this climbing turn, I lost sight of the *Spirit of Africa,* which could not gain height as quickly as *Osa's Ark.* It needed to make several altitude-gaining circles in order to reach that opening which I could reach in straight flight. But I didn't worry about Carstens, knowing that he clearly saw which way he had to go, and seeing now in front of me a beautiful, wide valley, free from any obstacles, leading straight to our destination.

Approaching Victoria West, we saw the town's name in huge letters on white cliffs next to the town. This sign was visible for many miles, and, like all such landmarks, was a big help to aviators in their flights over unpopulated areas with few airports, with practically no roads and railroads. The importance of these signs on air journeys like ours was inestimable. Before landing at Victoria

West's airport, I circled over the center of town, to signal the Shell agent and his crew to come to the airport and help us refuel.

Osa's Ark took on fuel for the next 220 miles of the flight to Kimberly, and we impatiently waited from one minute to the next for the arrival of our smaller plane. But it was so delayed, that even allowing for its slower speed and slower rate of climb, we soon understood that it must have come down at some spot between where we had seen it last and Victoria West. Just at that moment, we were happy to learn by telephone that the other members of our expedition were all safe at Beaufort West, the last landing field before Victoria West, taking on a supply of gasoline. Carstens told us he had to land there because he had lost too much time crossing the second range of mountains and wasn't sure that he had enough fuel to make Victoria West. Now he asked us to wait for him, so he could follow us to the last scheduled stop of the day, Kimberly. With at least an hour at our disposal, we took a taxi to have lunch in Victoria West. Soon after this, Carstens arrived, and we reached Kimberly without further adventures.

During this first day's flight across South Africa, we realized that our engines were overheating significantly more than they had in the United States—or even in the tropics of South America, where Pan American Airways and local governments had used many Pratt and Whitney engines. Here, our oil temperature reached 96 to 97 degrees Celsius [205 to 207 degrees Fahrenheit], and the oil pressure began to drop. And while all this was going on, we were still far from the Equator, and we had yet to fly over the hottest areas! We had to do something about this. Local pilots advised us that the best place to solve our problem would be the main base of the Royal Air Force in South Africa, at Roberts Heights, near Pretoria. This military airfield was open to civil aircraft only by special permission. We telegraphed Pretoria for permission.

Most of the airports in South and Central Africa are high above sea level. Roberts Heights, at 5,600 feet above sea level, was no exception. The density of the air decreases with height, and with the decreasing density, the lift of an airplane's wings is less. In tropical and Equatorial Africa this decreased air density is aggravated by high temperatures that have the same effect on the lifting ability of airplanes as does high altitude because they also lower the density of the air.

In the "Notices to Pilots" issued by the British government, there were warnings about the effective altitude of airports, which was calculated by combining real height above sea level with the temperature equivalent in altitude. For example, the airport at Bulawayo in Southern Rhodesia, at 4,400 feet above sea

33. *Osa's Ark* and the *Spirit of Africa,* above the clouds. *Courtesy of Igor I. Sikorsky Historical Archives, Inc.*

level, had an effective altitude of 8,000 feet when you took into account the density of the air between 1 and 4 P.M. Livingstone, near Victoria Falls, was 3,000 feet above sea level, but had an effective altitude of 7,100 feet. Such conditions made pilots treat their planes carefully, allowing much more distance and time for takeoff, and landing at significantly higher speeds.

When we arrived at Roberts Heights, the technical personnel of the Royal Air Force base quickly set about making the necessary measurements for installing oil coolers on our engines. This installation and testing took three days, which we spent looking at Pretoria from the ground and from the air. With its numerous beautiful government buildings and gardens, Pretoria was undoubtedly one of the most splendid cities of South Africa. The government of the Union of South Africa is based part of the time at Cape Town and part of the time at Pretoria. Carrying out our test flights before leaving Pretoria, we took up in our planes many officers and mechanics from the Royal Air Force, especially those who had been working on our oil coolers. The workmanship and conveniences of our planes produced a great impression on these passengers. We heard many compliments on this score, and we, for our part, expressed our heartfelt admiration for the system of oil coolers installed by the Royal Air Force. Thanks to them, the temperature of our oil was reduced by 25 to 30 degrees from what it had been before.

Early in the morning on the 4th of February, we set off from the airport at Pretoria. Our first stop was at Pietersburg, where we refueled and concluded the necessary customs and immigration formalities for leaving the Transvaal and arriving in Southern Rhodesia. Our second stop that day was at Bulawayo. But the Imperial Airways agent at Bulawayo warned us that after a heavy rain the day before, Livingstone airport, which was the airport for Victoria Falls, would be all mud. Because of the overloading of our larger plane, we preferred not to risk the possibility of getting held up at Livingstone, and took a northerly course to Salisbury, where, according to information we'd gotten, the airport was definitely in better condition.

When *Osa's Ark* landed at Salisbury, it was already 5:30 P.M. As is well known, in the tropics there is almost no dusk, and after sunset darkness falls quickly. At that moment, when the sun was almost ready to vanish over the horizon, there was still bright daylight, but the sun had barely set when darkness began to fall. When, after twenty minutes the *Spirit of Africa* had not appeared, we all began to worry, knowing that in fifteen minutes it would be completely dark.

I went to the chief of the airport with a request to turn on some lights. In Africa, it appeared, the lighting of airports for night flights was something very rare, but to our good luck, Salisbury turned out to be an exception. With the coming of darkness, the boundary flares and airport beacon lights were quickly lit. Besides this, lacking searchlights, we turned on all the headlights of automobiles at the airport, at the same time putting out on the right side of the field a T-shaped array of kerosene flares to show the direction of the wind. Having done everything that was in our power to do, we waited long and tensely for our smaller plane with its pilot and two passengers. It arrived at about 6:45 P.M., when it had become completely dark, mad one circle around the airport, and came in for a perfect landing. It turned out that a strong crosswind had delayed them, pushing the airplane off course, and the pilot had not allowed enough for this drift. The new arrivals told us how much their spirits had been lifted when they saw the lit-up airport. If not for the lights, they would have had to land in complete darkness on forested mountains. It would have been death for them all.

On our next leg, we had to fly across the Zambezi River. Mr. Johnson, who was a passionate fisherman, wanted to make a two-hour stop on the river. Before leaving Salisbury, we agreed that this stop would be at a spot where the Zambezi was joined by one of its tributaries. But as we approached the Zambezi River valley, we entered a tropical storm with heavy rain and continual lightning. Heavy, dark clouds hung low, covering the tops of the last mountain range, blocking our route to the river. Fighting the storm, and being forced at the same time to search for a route across the mountains, I had to change our course and fly much farther to the west. When at last we reached the Zambezi, the weather was not good for fishing, and we flew on to our destination for the day, the airport at Broken Hill. At the time that *Osa's Ark* was going around the center of the storm to the west, *The Spirit of Africa* took a route more to the east. We arrived at Broken Hill almost at the same time, coming from opposite directions.

What we had to attempt on the following day showed that strong tropical storms and the high-altitude locations of most African airports were far from being the only dangers to aviators flying across the Dark Continent. The worst of our enemies turned out to be inexact and incomplete aerial maps of Africa. The one map we had at our disposal was of a large scale—1:2,000,000. And it was full of mistakes, sometimes showing completely nonexistent landmarks on the ground and sometimes completely omitting noticeable landmarks which ought to have been recorded on any decent map.

On this clear and beautiful day, the 6th of February, for example, we intended to stop and refuel at a town named Mpika. On the map, Mpika was marked with a little dot indicating a small city or a decent-sized village. Also, the Mpika airport was shown as the crossing of two roads, one of which was the Great North Road, leading from Cape Town to Cairo, Egypt. We eventually discovered that neither the town nor village of Mpika existed. All that existed was a little strip cleared from the bush, used by Imperial Airways as a refueling stop. At this station there was only one house, where a crew of seven men lived, and this house was half hidden in the surrounding trees. Around the airfield there were no roads, and the Great North Road was many miles to the west of where it was shown on the map.

Led into confusion by all this, we flew straight over the airport at Mpika, taking it for one of the intervening emergency landing fields. When I realized, because of the passage of time and calculation of the distance our flight had covered, that somehow or other we had bypassed Mpika, our gas tank had almost run dry, and the fuel gauge showed empty. Around us—as far as could be seen on a completely clear day from a high-flying plane—was an endless expanse of forest without any sign of habitation and without one place where we could make a safe landing. Later Mr. Johnson told me that if we had been able to land somewhere in this territory, we would have had to walk three months before arriving at the smallest civilized spot! But he assured me that there would have been no danger of dying from hunger there, since we had rifles and cartridges with us on the airplane, and around us was an endless array of wild game.

I opened the throttle and climbed, to get a wider view, and to search for places to land the plane with the least possible harm. Reaching a height of almost 14,000 feet, I saw a small lake to the east of our course. A lake meant a surface for a safe landing, and the near-certainty of finding people on the shore. I headed for the lake, gradually descending, saving every possible drop of gasoline and waiting for our engines to start coughing at any moment and to shut down from lack of fuel.

Approaching the lake, we saw next to it a beautiful stone and brick house with a red and black roof, a house that could only belong to white people. After our agony of the last few hours, this sight was wonderful! Landing on the lake, I turned toward the shore, as close as possible to the big house. While turning, I noticed that my altimeter showed 6,200 feet. Just off our left float appeared the huge head of a hippopotamus, who seemed a bit angry at this foreign invader trespassing in his domain, and it slowly slipped under water. Reaching the shore, we saw on the beach a picturesque crowd of native men, women, and children; the men were armed with arrows and spears. When the nose of our plane touched the shore, the whole crowd went down on their knees, bowing low, clapping their palms to their heads. It was later explained to us that this was the highest form of greeting, with which this tribe expressed its respect, pleasure, and happiness.

Suddenly the crowd divided and a white man came forward. He wore a khaki shirt and shorts, his legs were bare, and in his eye there was a monocle. He came straight out into the shallows of the lake toward the plane, not paying the slightest attention to the black mud sucking at his bare legs. We introduced ourselves. He turned out to be the owner of this splendid home, of the lake (named Shiwa) with its six hippopotami, and of the land surrounding it. His name was Colonel Gore-Browne. He, his family, and his former orderly—now the foreman of his farm—were the only whites for 250 miles around. He agreed to give us some gasoline, but first he invited us all for lunch at his home. And it was a luxurious lunch in a luxurious house! Our host and hostess charmed us, with the characteristic hospitality of the English landed gentry. During lunch we agreed that I would take the entire available supply of gasoline on the estate, which would be enough to get me to Mpika. It was further decided that in case our other plane was already there, we both would take on a full supply of gasoline in Mpika and would bring both planes back to the lake. After this, all the members of the Johnson expedition were invited for dinner and the night at the home of Colonel Gore-Browne.

Running on Empty over the Jungle

In the books they published about their African travels, the explorer-adventurers Martin and Osa Johnson each describe the harrowing occasion Sergievsky mentions on p. 196–97, when the plane Sergievsky was piloting overshot Mpika and almost ran out of fuel. Here is how Martin Johnson tells the story:

> In the big ship, besides the five of us, were a dozen well-filled suitcases, a dozen boxes of supplies, aerial cameras, emergency food, a couple of rifles, plenty of reading matter, and in addition to still other belongings, a sixth passenger in the form of Wah, our pet gibbon ape from Borneo. Wah was the most enthusiastic flyer of us all. He loved to look out the windows and watch the landscape glide past. He never worried about getting lost, and trifles such as empty gasoline tanks troubled him not at all. He divided his time between looking out the windows, begging for food, going from one of us to another in order to be petted, and perching on the steering wheel as Boris piloted the ship. . . .
>
> We followed the line of a road we could see beneath us, expecting to land at Mpika within three hours, but shortly we became conscious of the fact that the road and the map did not agree. Three hours passed and Mpika did not appear. Four hours. Still no Mpika. . . . We turned back in an attempt to find some landmark or other. No luck. The country below us was now a mass of mountains, deep canyons, and little streams. Here and there some native village appeared, but not a thing could we see that we could locate on the map, and there was not an acre of open space on which to land.
>
> The gasoline gauge sank to zero, and once again we listened tensely for the spluttering of the motors that would tell us that the flight was about to end. . . . I can assure you that it is neither humorous nor pleasantly exciting to sit in such a plane and watch, with one eye, a gauge that marks an empty gas tank, and with the other to look out the windows, down onto seemingly endless mountains and gorges, rocks and trees and cliffs, among which a safe landing could not possibly be made. . . .
>
> Wah, quite unworried by the danger that stared us in the face, climbed down from his perch on the steering wheel to curl up in my lap. I paid no attention to him, but he chattered gently, begging to be petted. I stroked him once or twice, glanced at the gasoline gauge again, and stared through the window at the endless ruggedness below us.
>
> Ten minutes passed, and even Boris found it harder to keep up his flow of humorous and entertaining comment. Wah was with Osa by now, and she was quietly stroking him, saying nothing, and thinking I don't know what. We were all growing more nervous by the minute. . . .
>
> I tensely watched the clock on the instrument board. . . . For a moment the bright light outside prevented my seeing clearly, but as I blinked my eyes I thought I saw the reflection of light in the distance. I blinked them again and looked. There was something, certainly. I reached for my binoculars and looked, and managed, somehow, to speak to Boris quite calmly.
>
> "There's a lake over there, Boris," I remarked.
>
> He glanced quickly in the direction in which I was pointing, and nodding casually changed the course of the ship toward the lake, which appeared fairly clearly now. . . .
>
> I'm sure I held my breath. It was only a matter of seconds that would tell us whether we would reach the water and land safely, or whether the motors would stop and we could crash on the very edge of safety."[1]

AH

After lunch, we set about letting the gasoline out of all the colonel's automobiles, trucks, and tractors. Acquiring enough gas by this means, I flew to Mpika, while all my passengers remained with the Gore-Brownes.

Landing at Mpika, I found out that Carstens had been looking for us everywhere, making flight after flight, returning to the landing field only to take on gas and search for us again. I didn't have to wait long for Carstens, and we quickly filled both planes with gas for the flight on the following day. In addition, I put some fuel in containers, so as to pay back my gasoline debt to the colonel. We then both flew back to hospitable Lake Shiwa.

I thought that because of the high altitude of Lake Shiwa (6,200 feet), takeoff from the water by the fully loaded planes would be difficult. For that reason, I decided to land on a field near the lake. Despite the fact that this field wasn't a real airport, it was big enough, and the surface was hard enough, for landings and takeoffs. And so both planes landed on the field, where the Gore-Brownes and the Johnsons met us. During my flight to Mpika, Mrs. Johnson had made a very successful fishing expedition on the lake, and, as an addition to our dinner, we were treated to freshly caught fish. After dinner we chatted pleasantly over coffee in the parlor, and separated early for bed, since we had to start at dawn the next day.

Near midnight, I was woken by the rumble of thunder and the sound of rain striking the roof. I quickly remembered our field. Not having any drainage, after such a rainstorm it would be soaked! I cursed myself for not having left the planes on the lake, but it was too late to correct this mistake.

We had to wait until morning to try to move the big plane. Its wheels had sunk in the earth almost as far as the axles. The smaller plane was in significantly better shape, weighing only a third as much as the big one and having pneumatic tires with a wider tread. There could be no question of the big plane taking off from the ground with a heavy load. Mr. Johnson immediately understood the seriousness of the situation and asked me to take into account only everyone's safety. He told me that he was not in any special hurry to get to Nairobi, and that in case we had to, he was ready to wait a week or more for the field to dry out. Colonel Gore-Browne invited the whole Johnson expedition to stay with him as long as we wanted.

But I felt that since I had insisted on landing on the field, I had to correct my mistake. And so I ordered all the baggage and equipment to be unloaded from the big plane and carried to the shore of the lake. Then I arranged with the

Colonel to mobilize not only his servants, but all the tribespeople from the nearest village. Under the Colonel's command, this whole crowd of savages began to rock the plane, at the same time as I started the engines and opened the throttle wide. The cries of the savages were louder than the roar of the motors, and to the accompaniment of this music the plane slowly moved forward, gradually picking up speed. As the speed increased, one wing began to lift and partly relieved the pressure on the wheels. Then, with several heavy bumps, the plane took off from the field, grazing the trees on the other side of the clearing with its chassis. Landing on the lake, I took on board the passengers and baggage, and we said good-bye to the pleasant and hospitable owners of Lake Shiwa. Having practically no help from the wind, I had to travel almost a mile over the lake before I succeeded in getting off the water.

Setting course for Mbeya, in Tanganyika, the former German East African colony occupied after the war by England, we flew over parts of Northern Rhodesia and Tanganyika that were rich in all types of large mammals. Mr. Johnson, knowing Africa well, pointed out to us spots where wild animals could most easily be seen. Over such places we flew low, sometimes only 100 feet off the ground. If I had not seen it with my own eyes, I would never have believed that there existed such an array of wild game! We saw thousands of zebra, hundreds of giraffes, and herds of elephants and rhinoceroses forcing their way through thickets. Frightened by the noise and sight of the airplanes, herds of ostriches ruffled their feathers like large angry turkeys, and scratched the ground with their powerful legs, raising clouds of sand.

It was very amusing to see how different animals reacted to the noise of the engines and the appearance of the plane, which they obviously took for a huge bird looking for prey. The small gazelles and deer seemed especially frightened, running away with huge, graceful leaps when we appeared. We also saw a group of lions, whose light and powerful movements brought to mind a cat's spring.

On February 7th we covered about 600 miles, making one refueling stop along the way at Mbeya, and stopping for the night at Dodoma, which was 410 miles from our final destination. Between Mbeya and Dodoma we had to fly through several rainstorms. As we approached the airport, we saw a sheet of water covering it, and I began to wonder: How should I land an amphibian on such a field—with wheels or floats? But the runway of the Dodoma airport, despite being flooded with water, appeared solid enough. We taxied both planes to the Imperial Airways office and tied them down there for the night.

The following morning we began the last leg of our flight to Nairobi. There was a light ground fog and low-lying clouds. From our maps we knew that the highest mountain in Africa, Kilimanjaro, 20,000 feet high, was 160 miles south of Nairobi, almost directly on our course to the city. This made me think about how to overcome the unfavorable ground fog, the low clouds, and the likelihood of rain. I knew that the height of the storm clouds would hardly exceed 12,000 to 14,000 feet. Climbing above the clouds to a height of 16,000 feet, I quickly saw Kilimanjaro. An extraordinary and magnificent sight opened out before me—an endless sea of white clouds, sparkling in the sun like a snowy field, and on the horizon a perfectly formed cone, its summit covered with a hat of snow. Then, below the snow line, a band of bare rocks, and below that a sharply outlined covering of greenery on the sides of the cone.

I headed on a course a bit to the west of Kilimanjaro, and after two and a half hours we passed close by it. Thanks to this, we did not drift off course. If we had not had Kilimanjaro to steer by, then, flying the whole time in the clouds, we would not have been able to calculate our drift, and we would have been taken off course, not knowing by how much.

Leaving Kilimanjaro behind, we continued to fly for some time on the same course, searching for an opening in the clouds so we could slip through and finally land at Nairobi. Such an opening appeared about forty minutes after we had left Kilimanjaro behind. We went through and found ourselves beneath the clouds. We continued on our compass course, the only difference being that now the whole time we could see the ground. Flying a short time this way, we crossed a road and railroad marked on our map, and this gave us our position. It turned out that we were exactly where we had planned to be, and that our three-hour flight above the clouds had not taken us off course.

I knew that in several minutes we would see Nairobi. At this point Mr. Johnson sat down up front, changing seats with my mechanic. He seemed a bit uneasy and depressed, and asked me how much fuel we had left. I answered that the gauge showed that we still had an hour's fuel supply in our tanks. Mr. Johnson said he was convinced we had made a mistake. His words surprised me and even seemed funny, since I knew our exact position. But Mr. Johnson continued to insist that he knew the part of the country near Nairobi very well. He confessed that he had never seen it from the air, but was certain that he would quickly recognize it. He even suggested that I land somewhere, near some village, and find out our exact location. I told him, "Mr. Johnson, in four

34. The Johnson expedition in front of the zebra-striped S-38, *Osa's Ark,* at Nairobi. Martin Johnson stands behind Osa, Vern Carstens stands to her left in a light-colored suit, and Boris Sergievsky sports a pith helmet. *Courtesy of the editors.*

minutes, I'll show you Nairobi!" But I was mistaken. We saw Nairobi in two and a half minutes!

Mr. Johnson's anxiety immediately changed, and he praised me and my knowledge of navigation. While we made a circle over the city, he showed me where their house was located. When we landed at the airport, we were met by a whole crowd of spectators and the Johnsons' friends waiting for our arrival. We had just succeeded in taxiing our plane to the spot airport workers directed us to when our second plane came in for a landing. Our two planes had finished their 3,200-mile flight from Cape Town in 37 flying hours.

We allowed ourselves one day of rest in Nairobi. Then I went to work with Vern Carstens, teaching him how to fly the larger plane. Carstens had now had excellent experience flying the smaller plane in all conditions of weather and terrain. Since the controls of both planes were identical, he didn't need much time to learn how to fly the larger plane. To practice landings and takeoffs on water, we flew to Lake Naivasha, around 50 miles northwest of Nairobi. The whole Johnson expedition accompanied us on this flight. While Carstens and I worked at perfecting his water landings, the remaining members of the expedition went fishing in small rowboats. Flying low over a valley near Lake Naivasha, we again saw an unbelievable array of wild game. Game was so plentiful even in Nairobi that heading across town towards the airport, we always saw animals close to the road, sometimes even grazing on the airport grass.

In the course of my last several days in Nairobi, I taught Mrs. Johnson how to fly the smaller plane. She turned out to be such an able young pilot that after three lessons I considered my work finished. I was ready to go home with the full knowledge that I was leaving both planes in the hands of competent, expert pilots.

However, one of our flights almost ended in tragedy. It happened two days before my departure from Nairobi. Mrs. Johnson, the mechanic Al Morway, and I set out early in the morning from the airport for one of our last flying lessons. Warming up the motor, I tried to make the usual movements of all the controls on the ground, testing them before takeoff.

I was sitting on the right side of the plane, with the control stick in front of me. Mrs. Johnson sat on the left side behind the steering wheel, which had much better leverage. When the controls would not move, I looked across at her and saw that she was holding tight to the steering wheel. That explained the immobility of the controls, and I told Mrs. Johnson to get under way and take off. Evidently when *she* had tried to operate the controls they hadn't moved—but she saw that I was holding onto the stick. I'm not trying to justify myself: It was all my responsibility and my fault, I confess. But I'm only trying to explain how it happened that our controls turned out to be tightly fastened with a special bolt. We discovered this, however, only when we were 100 feet above the airport, in a spiraling, uncontrollable descent, banking at a 45-degree angle.

The problem was that because of a shortage of hangars at Nairobi, we had had to keep the planes out in the open. To avoid having the ailerons flap in the wind all the time, our controls were locked by a special device. Since our smaller plane had no such device, our mechanic had bored a hole in the plate with which the controls were fastened to the right side of the cabin. In this hole he had put a bolt, making impossible any sideways movement of the control stick. The mechanic had done this work in my absence, so that I didn't know why the controls were locked, or why we had been placed in such a difficult position.

At just the moment when we seemed in a dangerous position with too steep a bank and too little altitude to maneuver, Mrs. Johnson got control of the plane. I had been astonished that someone I considered such a good pilot could bank so dangerously, and I was already getting ready to take command, when she turned toward me, white from fear, and said, "Captain, something's not right! I can't straighten out!" I said, "Let me take her!" and took the stick, only to discover that it would not move from side to side. Although people usually disapprove of aerobatics, pilots know that it is necessary to be able to do all possible maneuvers. And they know how often the aviator's life may depend on the ability to do these in unforeseen emergencies. Using rudder pedals in place of the frozen aileron controls seemed to me something which at this moment might save the plane, and maybe the lives of those in it. It worked. Taking control of the plane and circling upwards, I reached 6,000 feet before trying to discover what our problem was or to set it straight. At 6,000 feet, I began to carefully dismantle and examine the aileron control system, and in a few seconds found the locking bolt. It took me five minutes to remove it, and to be really able to control the plane. That evening we dined at the Johnsons and celebrated our escape from death.

If this event almost ended in tragedy, the last lesson I gave Mrs. Johnson ended in comedy.

After Mrs. Johnson became qualified as a pilot of an amphibian, we decided to finish our last lesson by looping the loop. Inside the watertight hull of every amphibian there inevitably collects oil from the engines, fluid used to lubricate the controls, and a little water—seawater, lake water, rainwater. From time to time all this is drained off and the inside of the hull is cleaned. But this cleaning had not been done since our arrival in Nairobi, and, in addition, under the floor of the plane was a fairly large accumulation of waste and garbage. At the moment when we found ourselves at the high point of the loop, all this garbage rained down on us—on our faces and over our fine white flying suits. Looking at each other, we laughed until we were exhausted, and almost lost control of the plane. After our landing, we didn't even try to clean off, but simply set off for the Johnson house, where everyone laughed heartily at the sight of us.

This looping-the-loop ended my work as a flight instructor and aviation advisor to the Johnson expedition. I had intended to get a seat on the Imperial

Airways plane flying north to London, and then to go home via steamship from Southampton. But all seats out of Nairobi were reserved for several weeks ahead; there remained only a seat from Kisumu, on Lake Victoria, from which larger airplanes flew. Mr. Johnson kindly let me use the smaller airplane for the flight to Kisumu, taking Carstens to fly it back to Nairobi. At the last minute, Mr. and Mrs. Johnson decided to fly with me to Kisumu to see me off, and then to practice water landings and takeoffs on Lake Victoria.

On the morning of February 18th, I took the controls for the last time for the flight to Kisumu. The 185-mile flight from Nairobi to Kisumu took us over such wild and dry land that an emergency landing would have been impossible; the airplane would have been torn to pieces. It was a big relief to fly over this territory in an airplane with such reliable engines.

On arrival in Kisumu, we sat down together for our farewell lunch. Then we enjoyed ourselves for several hours on the lake, while Mr. and Mrs. Johnson took turns at the controls of the plane, showing each other the art of seaplane piloting. At the end of the day I said good-bye to the Johnsons and to Vern Carstens, and we all wished each other "happy landings." When the *Spirit of Africa* lifted into the sky, I watched it until it disappeared over the mountains to the south. I remembered all the pleasant, happy hours spent in this group during these two months.

The following day I flew low over Lake Victoria, then straight along the Nile River, this time as a passenger in an Imperial Airways four-engined Handley-Page 42. The flight to Cairo was very pleasant and interesting, but without any adventures. Flying high over the Nile, we could not fail to see the vital importance of the river for Egypt and the Sudan. The silvery-blue ribbon of water stretched out before us—the great Nile, bordered with wide bands of dark green gardens, carefully worked fields and other vegetation, all extending as far as the reach of irrigation ditches with Nile water. Beyond the borders of this living green, on both sides, stretched the endless yellow sand of the African desert.

In Cairo I had a look at a mosque and visited a picturesque Eastern market before I set off by train for Alexandria, on the Mediterranean. The following morning I took a four-engined Short Kent flying boat on a six-hour nonstop flight across the Mediterranean to Athens. Along the way we flew over the eastern tip of Crete. In Athens, I spent several hours in the Acropolis and in the theater of Dionysus, admiring the genius of ancient Greece.

Our next flight, of 380 miles, to the town of Brindisi in Italy, took us over the dark blue Adriatic Sea, over small islands charmingly strewn with white villas. At Brindisi we took the train for Paris. During the first day, our route took us along the shore of the Adriatic, and the view from the window was splendid. Arriving the following morning in Milan, I used the six-hour wait for the Paris train to look at the famous Milan Cathedral, the opera house of La Scala, and the monument to Leonardo da Vinci. On the journey from Milan to Paris, our train went along the shore of Lake Maggiore, through the twenty-one-mile Simplon Tunnel, and then along the shore of Lake Geneva.

On arriving on February 28th in Paris, I found out that my steamship would be leaving from Southampton on March 3rd. Thus I had three whole days at my disposal. The first one I devoted to the Louvre. An elementary tour of this museum demands several days, if not several weeks. But since I had already been to the Louvre more than once previously, this one day was enough for me. The second day I spent looking at Les Invalides. Impressions of the island of St. Helena had not yet slipped from my memory, and I wanted to see the present-day resting place of Napoleon, and his furniture and personal items that had been removed from the small house on St. Helena. I also wanted to look at all the trophies and other important artifacts from the extraordinary life and career of this great man.

I won't try to describe all the valuable exhibits collected at Les Invalides, for that would demand a whole book. It's enough to say that I spent the entire day there, completely forgetting about food. Moving from one great hall to another, I mentally retraced the military history of France, beginning with the first French warriors, clothed in raw sheepskin and armed with bows and arrows; then the knights of the Middle Ages, on horseback in their suits of armor, taking part in the Crusades. I experienced the glory of the Kings of France, of the French Revolution, of the Napoleonic Wars with their hundreds of banners captured from all countries, and finally of the last war, 1914–18.

Impressive exhibit halls showed material from the Allied armies of America, England, Belgium, Italy, Serbia, and Romania, wonderfully displayed in rows of exhibit cases that showed uniforms, arms, pictures, and statistics. They even had a room dedicated to such Allies as Japan, Portugal, and Poland, although Poland was a highly doubtful Ally in the Great War. Except for the United Army of General Haller,[*]

* Polish General Józef Haller's United Army fought for the Allies in France until the November 1918 armistice. General Haller then moved his 50,000 Polish troops across Europe to Poland, arriving in April 1919, in time to support General Pilsudski's spring campaign against the Bolsheviks.

Pilsudski's troops fought on the German side. For that reason, both the Germans and their opponents could correctly claim Poland as their ally.

I was strongly and sorrowfully struck by the fact that among the ranks of the Allies there was no reminder of Russia. I understand that it would not be possible to ask today's government to supply exhibits of the uniforms and equipment of the Imperial Army. Such a request would be a joke for the Soviets, since they despise everything connected with the old Russia, its strengths, traditions, and glory—so much so that the very name of Russia is forbidden, and the country calls itself the U.S.S.R. In spite of this, comparing today's Red Army with the old Imperial Army would be disadvantageous for the Soviets, and they should fear to discover the difference.

But whatever the case, the Allies' debt to Russia was so great that elementary feelings of truth and justice towards a former Ally should induce those responsible for this exhibit to set aside a separate hall for Russia, displaying the tricolor flag and a sign that the rest of the exhibit would be in place when the curators could succeed in getting the material.

The statistics about Russian participation in the war are known. All who are interested in military matters know that Russia experienced the greatest casualties of any of the armies, and by the end of the war had 11 million men under arms. It is also well known that Russia captured more prisoners in this war than all the other Allied armies together. The French Marshall Foch and the German General Ludendorff agree in their memoirs that the French won the Battle of the Marne only because of the Russian invasion of Prussia, where several Russian army corps were knowingly sacrificed to the goal of saving France.

Each country pays tribute to its "Unknown Soldier." There cannot be any doubt that this tribute is fully deserved by the five million* Russian known and unknown soldiers who gave their lives for the larger Allied cause, but who are completely forgotten and ignored by those who actually owe them their victory! I said good-bye to France with a feeling of indignation and repugnance over this unbearable insult to my native land.

The flight from Le Bourget to Croydon, London, was mostly blind, on instruments, without any sight of land, water, or sky. Taking off into low-lying clouds from the French airport, we gained altitude quickly and saw land only

---

* Sergievsky apparently is adding his own estimate of Russian Civil War casualties to those of the First World War, in which an estimated 1,650,000 Russian soldiers were killed in action or died of wounds. This was the highest death toll suffered by any of the Allies.

after having crossed the English Channel, several minutes before landing at Croydon. Taking the train to Southampton, and then the steamship *Deutschland* of the Hamburg-America Line, I arrived back in New York on the 10th of March after a very pleasant crossing of the Atlantic.

In two months and ten days I had covered approximately 25,000 miles by steamship and airplane.

From a World's Fair to World Records

Upon my return from Africa in the spring of 1933 I found two projects in progress at the Sikorsky factory. One was the construction of a new flying boat type, the S-42, which was designed for Pan American Airways to cover nonstop the distance from America to Europe.

The other project was the preparation and overhauling of two S-38s for the Chicago World's Fair. The Pal-waukee Airport, Incorporated, got a concession at the Chicago World's Fair to carry passengers over the fairgrounds. They purchased two S-38s and started to operate them from the fairgrounds, carrying passengers from nine o'clock in the morning until eleven o'clock at night. The pilots employed by the Pal-waukee Airport were both veteran Sikorsky pilots and good friends of mine—Frank Ormsby, "The Admiral," and Carl Vickory.

In the middle of June, only a few weeks after the World's Fair opened, we got a very distressing message from the Pal-waukee Airport. Carl Vickory, his mechanic, and nine passengers had been killed in an accident during one of the sightseeing trips over the fair.

The Pal-waukee Airport purchased one more plane to replace the destroyed one and temporarily engaged me to fly it to Chicago and pilot it there. It was agreed with the Sikorsky Corporation that as soon as the S-42 was ready for tests, I would be relieved of my duties at the Fair and would report at the factory.

The Sikorsky Corporation loaned me to the Pal-waukee Airport very willingly, knowing that, having tested every S-38 that ever went out of the Sikorsky factory, I knew very well all the good qualities as well as the limitations of the S-38. By safely operating it at the Fair, I could restore the confidence in the Sikorsky planes which was perhaps somewhat shaken by the dreadful accident that happened to Carl Vickory and his passengers.

The investigation into the accident showed that Vickory had landed on the lake in front of the Pal-waukee ramp when the wind was blowing pretty strongly, and the lake suddenly got rough. In this landing he damaged the right pontoon, and there was some danger that the damaged pontoon would fill up with water and cause the plane to overturn.

This would mean considerable damage to the plane itself and a rather unpleasant swim for all the occupants of the plane. There was no danger of drowning, because there were many motorboats right where the plane landed and in a few seconds everybody would be rescued.

But Vickory did not want to make such a poor demonstration right in front of the fairgrounds. He decided to take off immediately, as soon as he realized that his pontoon was damaged, fly to the Pal-waukee Airport, which is about 35 miles northwest of Chicago, and replace the damaged pontoon with a spare one. There is only one thing he did not take into account: If the shock was strong enough to damage the pontoon, it was probably strong enough to also damage the wing or the attachment of the wing to the body of the plane.

He took off all right and was within a few miles of the airport and already coming down for the landing when a gust of wind overstressed the damaged wing. The plane fell to the ground, all its occupants were instantly killed, and their bodies were destroyed by the fire that followed the crash.

The proper course for the pilot in this case would have been not to take any chances in trying to fly after the pontoon was damaged. He should have let the passengers swim and have a swim himself. He might have been criticized for it, but it is always much better to be criticized alive than praised after death.

In delivering the new Pal-waukee plane I got permission to carry with me to Chicago my friends Mr. and Mrs. Hollister Sturges, whom I met on the way to South Africa, and with whom we became very friendly on the boat and later in South Africa while we were together there.

I landed near their estate at Kingston on the Hudson to pick them up, and then we flew on to Cleveland, where we stayed overnight and arrived the following morning, July 4th, at Chicago. We had a telegram from the president of the Pal-waukee Airport, Mr. Jones, stating the exact hour of arrival, because they were planning to have a formal reception ceremony for the new plane.

Besides the crew and the Sturgeses, we had in the plane Mr. Igor Sikorsky and a few members of the Sikorsky Corporation, who were going to see the Fair.

As we had a strong tailwind the last leg of the trip, we arrived at Chicago ahead of schedule and had an opportunity to circle over the fairgrounds several times. From the air they were really very beautiful. Then we landed at the appointed spot and got a very cordial reception from the officials of the Chicago Air Races, which were then in progress. Mr. Sikorsky and I had to make a short speech on the radio, and only then were we free to leave the airport.

I stayed with Pal-waukee Airport Incorporated until it closed its operation on the last day of the Fair, August 31, 1933. We were flying every day, having no Sundays off and no holidays, with our only rest when the lake was too rough for operations. One plane out of the two had to go every day to the airport for inspection and overhauling after about eight P.M., the other remaining for the night work at the fairgrounds. I and "The Admiral" alternated; one of us would do the night flying at the Fair, the other would fly over to the airport. By the time we would get home from the airport it would be after ten o'clock in the evening. So our working hours were actually from nine in the morning to ten or eleven at night.

When business was really good we had as many as 500 passengers a day. We had one reserve pilot, Lieutenant Walter Brook, who relieved "The Admiral" and myself for a half an hour during lunch and dinner time. During the two months of my work there I carried 7,000 passengers.

Most of these passengers, I should say about 95 percent of them, were in the air for the first time in their lives, and it was amusing to watch their reactions. The trip over the fairgrounds and over part of Chicago and the airport took fifteen minutes, and during this fifteen minutes the majority of the passengers got very air-minded. On many occasions they stated after the trip that from now on they would travel by air whenever possible.

On other occasions they would buy a second ride right after the first one. One family from some small town in the Middle West had four consecutive rides.

It was very tiring to make such short hops, because the pilot has to concentrate most of his attention on the takeoff and the landing and making up to fifty takeoffs and landings during one day was extremely fatiguing. But there were also many good sides to that work.

First of all, there was an extremely agreeable atmosphere in the Pal-waukee Company, where the President, Mr. Owen Barton Jones, the Manager, Mr. Duncan Hodges, the pilots, the mechanics, and the crews were just like one family.

One of the greatest days for us was the day when the Italian armada of

General Balbo arrived at the Fair.* In order not to interfere with the formation flight of the Italians, our planes were ordered to remain on the ground during their arrival and landing. But after the Balbo planes landed, we had a tremendous rush of passengers to see the Italian planes from the air.

As a veteran pilot I was invited to the reception and ball given in honor of the Italians, and enjoyed myself very much at it.

After one of our busiest days, when it was my turn to take the plane to the airport for inspection, I started there about 6 P.M., having on board two mechanics besides myself. When I was crossing the city of Chicago at an altitude of approximately 2,500 feet, I noticed an unusual motion; the whole plane seemed to accelerate slightly forward, then lose a little speed, and then accelerate again. The impression was as if a heavy pendulum were moving somewhere in the plane.

I started to look for the cause of such a phenomenon and noticed that the right engine was actually detaching itself from the plane. Hanging only on the upper bolts, it was moving gradually back and forth like a pendulum, with each motion coming slightly lower. I knew that the propeller would soon strike the boat, as the clearance between the propeller and the boat is only a few inches. Then, of course, this shock would probably tear the right wing away.

I shut off both engines to eliminate all possible vibration and started to descend, in a very gentle glide expecting to start to fall any second. Only then did I look where I was gliding to. Below me was the city of Chicago, and I would have to land on one of the streets. I could not glide far enough to be out of the town.

But looking back I realized that if I turned around I could make that part of the lake which was in front of the Navy Pier, even if I could not make it back to the fairgrounds. And so I did.

When the plane touched the water I felt as if a very, very, heavy load fell off my shouders. Both mechanics who were in the plane with me gave at the same moment heavy sighs of relief, and both simultaneously said "Gee, are we going to get drunk tonight! We have to celebrate our new birthday."

* General Italo Balbo, Air Minister in Mussolini's Fascist government, led an armada of twenty-four Savoia-Marchetti S-55X flying boats in a formation flight from Italy to Chicago and back in 1933. Leaving Rome on July 1, the fleet crossed the Atlantic by way of Iceland and Canada, arriving at Chicago on July 15, still in formation. Cheering crowds greeted this astonishing feat of airmanship and organization at Chicago and in New York on the 19th. Balbo led his formation back to Rome by way of the Azores, where one S-55X crashed. The twenty-three survivors circled Rome, still in formation, at dusk on August 12; vast crowds hailed the aviators as they paraded to the Colosseum next day.

After I landed I did not dare start the engines and taxi, because even while we were floating on the water, the right engine was still shaking back and forth, ready to fall out. We dropped anchor and in a few minutes a motorboat came alongside asking what the trouble was. Having in mind the bad publicity the Pal-waukee people had already got from Carl Vickory's accident, I did not want to state that I was losing an engine.

I simply said, "I have to make a telephone call. Can you take me ashore?" And they said, "Oh, certainly."

From the nearest booth I called up our office at the Fair. When Mr. Hodges, our manager, heard my voice he got a shock. He knew that I should be still in the air on the way to the airport. He asked me, "What happened? Where are you calling from?"

I told him that I was speaking from the Navy Pier, that the plane was sitting safely near it anchored, but that the right engine might fall off at any minute. "You had better come up in the emergency launch and bring some ropes to tie the engine to the plane."

There was a silence on the other end of the line and then a very excited voice shouted, "I'm on my way!"

We really did have to tie the engine with several ropes to the wing, and then we towed the plane back to the fairgrounds with the motorboat. We immediately ordered some spare parts by wire for the mount. They arrived with the mail plane in the morning from Bridgeport. By noon the next day, the plane was again in operation carrying passengers.

Among the passengers I carried at the Fair there were many interesting people and some very peculiar types. There were several very drunken parties that insisted that I loop the loop with them. Other passengers, who did not belong to the party, would start to argue that I should not do that, even if the other passengers were requesting it, because they had paid for a quiet ride. I always had to reassure them that I would not do any stunts with passengers on board.

On one occasion, a very old man in a Confederate uniform climbed into the plane and informed me that he was ninety-five years old, that he had seen all sorts of transportation from the covered wagon and sailboat through the railroad and steamer up to the airplane. He was going up for the first time to be sure that when he died he would have traveled by all possible means of earthly transportation. I enjoyed giving him a few minutes extra in the air, and was very much pleased that he liked travel by plane better than any other means he had tried.

The Sikorsky S-42

The Sikorsky S-42, sketched out on menus in restaurants around the Caribbean during the S-40's maiden voyage in October 1931, was one of the great aircraft of the 1930s and a technological breakthrough for Sikorsky. Setting aside the successful S-38 pattern of "airplane parts flying in formation," the S-42 linked the parts together. The four 750-horsepower Pratt and Whitney engines, in drag-reducing cowlings, were mounted on the leading edge of the 118-foot wing. Both wing and tail were mounted on streamlined pylons above the all-metal hull, which was flush-riveted to further reduce drag (the S-42 was the first American production plane to use flush riveting, which became a standard design feature of World War II fighters).

The only seeming throwback in the S-42's design was that the wing and tail were braced to the fuselage with struts and wires. But this bracing, as in earlier Sikorskys, enabled the designers to make the wing lighter and more aerodynamically efficient than the cantilever wings then coming into fashion. The pylon wing mounting lifted the propellers above the damaging spray thrown back on takeoffs; it also permitted a slim, lightweight fuselage design.

The most extraordinary feature of the S-42 was invisible; its wing loading of 28.5 pounds per square foot was astonishingly high for 1934. The figure for the Army Air Corps' hot new Boeing P-26 fighter was 19.5, and for the strikingly innovative DC-2, 19.4. The S-42 tamed this wing loading with its controllable-pitch propellers, which functioned like a car's gearshift, and with its 68-foot wing flap, which greatly shortened takeoff runs and lowered landing speeds. These and other innovations allowed the S-42 to carry a "disposable load" (fuel, oil, passengers, baggage) that was 42 percent of its maximum takeoff weight—an astounding figure in 1934. (The S-42's famous landplane transport contemporary, the Douglas DC-3, had a disposable load of only 33 percent.)

Three months after Boris Sergievsky piloted the S-42 to ten world's records, Igor Sikorsky described the design philosophy of the S-42 at a London meeting of the Royal Aeronautical Society.[1] In the discussion that followed, one leading English manufacturer of flying boats, Oswald Short, admitted that his company had been "afraid to make explorations" of wing loadings as high as the S-42's. Another engineer estimated that the S-42, with one engine stopped, could carry 1,000 pounds more load 20 miles per hour faster than Short's current flying boat, the S.17 Kent, could manage with all four of its engines running—an achievement the engineer described as "colossal."

The S-42 was created to take Pan American Airways across the Atlantic. Sergievsky's record-breaking flight on August 1, 1934, covered a distance equal to that from Newfoundland to the Azores, the longest step in that proposed Atlantic route. But the British had no transport aircraft that could accomplish such a feat, and so they refused to grant Pan Am landing rights at potential way stations in Newfoundland and Bermuda until they could provide an equivalent service.

The British response to the S-42, Short's S.23 "Empire Boats," began to appear in mid-1936. With its thick cantilever wing mounted high on its deep hull, the S.23 looked much more modern than its Sikorsky rival. But these very features required far more structure than Sikorsky's lightweight. To save some weight, Short's engineers skimped on the hull structure; five S.23s sank in 1937–39 when their hulls split open in hard landings.

When the British agreed to Atlantic survey flights in 1937, the Sikorsky S-42B *Clipper III* crossed with a crew of eight and a ton of spares aboard; the S.23s *Caledonia* and *Cambria* flew with crews of four and interiors stripped even of their floors. The S.23's flawed design had left it with a disposable load of only 25 percent.

Pan Am could have established scheduled transatlantic flights with the long-range S-42B in 1937, but with the necessary reserves of fuel aboard, the S-42B could have carried no more than eight passengers. Such an operation would have brought more glory than profit to Pan Am. The airline decided to wait for its new and much larger Boeing 314 flying boats, which could carry almost three tons of payload across the Atlantic. Because of development delays, the 314s did not begin scheduled transatlantic service until 1939.

Unable to employ its S-42s on the Atlantic, Pan Am put them to work pioneering Pacific routes instead. S-42s and longer-range S-42A and S-42B models made headlines as they surveyed the island-hopping routes across the Pacific to Hong Kong and New Zealand, only to be overshadowed by the Martin 130 *China Clipper*, which had greater range and passenger capacity for the long stages between the islands.[2]

The S-42s continued to serve Pan Am faithfully for years, flying scheduled commercial services on routes linking Hong Kong and Manila, North and South America, and New York and Bermuda. But the fame these great boats deserved was denied them.

AF

35. The hastily painted sign says it all: "Sikorsky S-42 world's altitude record with load 16608 pounds to over 16000 feet April 26 1934." Boris Sergievsky, left, NAA and FAI chief timer John Heinmuller, and Igor I. Sikorsky, right, with the measured load of sandbags and steel plates, and the thoroughbred champion S-42. *Courtesy of National Air and Space Museum.*

Many excursion groups took airplane rides to see the Fair from the air. One of them was a group of schoolteachers. They were going around the Fair in a flock, like sheep following their leader. They were from one of the Dakotas, and were typical-looking spinsters in old-fashioned clothes, the youngest being at least fifty-five.

The leader was an entirely dried-out spinster, who told me in a shrieking voice, after nine of them piled into the plane, "Now, pilot, you'd better be very careful, we girls are going up for the first time."

I replied to her very casually, "Don't you worry, Miss, I will be very careful. I am going up for the first time myself."

She jumped out of the plane, ran back to the cashier, and demanded that their money be refunded. How dared the cashier sell her a ticket for a pilot going up for the first time!

The cashier tried to argue with her, explaining that I was joking, but it was very hard to pursuade the excited excursion leader. The cashier had to get the airport manager to finally pursuade her that I was joking. She returned to the plane and apparently liked the trip.

After the Fair was over, I drove back from Chicago to Bridgeport by car. Only traveling the same distance on the ground that you recently covered by air makes clear the tremendous saving of time and effort which air travel offers to us.

Upon my arrival in Bridgeport, I found out that certain changes were being incorporated in the design of the S-42. Pan American Airways had decided to use a different type of engine than the one originally intended, and the tests were going to be considerably delayed. I started to make a preliminary study of the aerodynamic calculations of the S-42, and also of the data pertaining to the water characteristics of its boat hull, obtained from testing a model in the river and in a wind tunnel.

I wanted to have full knowledge of all the facts already known about the plane, so that when the day of the trial came I would be prepared, and know what possible problems to expect from the plane, and how to overcome them if they did arise during the test flight.

Studying all the possible data on the plane before actually taking it for a test flight is very advisable, not only for the safety of the testing personnel and the equipment, but also for a quicker solution of the problems arising during the test.

The winter of 1933 was extremely severe, and when the plane was completed to such an extent that the water tests could be started, we could not go on with them on account of ice floating on the Housatonic River and in Long Island Sound.

Finally, when the river was clear of ice, the plane was taken down the ramp and very cautiously floated on the water. It was the first check of its weight balance, to see if the actual waterline would correspond with the one that had been calculated, or if the plane would be slightly nose or tail heavy.

The first trial of the plane was to run it on the water, only increasing the speed gradually, feeling its maneuverability on the water, trying to determine the critical moment when it would be ready to rise into the air, simultaneously testing out the controls of the plane before taking it up.

During the first day of the water tests I found out a very peculiar quality of the plane. When it reached a speed of approximately 50 miles per hour it would rather violently rise off the water. The actual minimum flying speed necessary for controllable flight for a plane of such loading and flying characteristics should be approximately 80 miles per hour.

After the plane leapt into the air at 50 miles per hour, it was almost uncontrollable. Then it would fall down again and make several bounces on the water before coming to a stop. After making several runs, gradually increasing the speed up to this critical point, we made an exhaustive study of the possible causes of such behavior. We determined that the premature rising off the water was due to the dimensions and shape of a "false step." This had been built onto the second (rearmost) step of the plane to facilitate the takeoff with full load by breaking the suction of the water, always created during the takeoff of a seaplane.

After removing the "false step" we made another trial and found that the plane functioned perfectly normally, even after reaching the critical speed of 50 miles per hour on the water.

Increasing its speed to 70 miles per hour, I rose into the air without the slightest difficulty. It was a very pleasant feeling to fly this beautiful, huge plane for the first time. I had no positive method to determine my actual speed, the speed indicators being not yet calibrated, but by looking at the ground and at the water, I realized that this was the fastest large plane ever built anywhere. It behaved perfectly in the short test flight, and I made two consecutive hops.

The corporate administrators and the designers of the plane were well pleased by what they saw and what I reported to them of my observations.

There were quite a few new features incorporated into the design of the new plane. Among them is a device to decrease the run on the water during the takeoff, and also to decrease the landing speed substantially. This device, called a "flap," allows the pilot to change the curve of the wing by moving the rear part of it up and down.

The flap actually has three positions. One is the normal flying position, where it is a simple continuation of the wing; a second position, ten degrees down, is for the takeoff; the third position, up to forty degrees down, is for the landing.

Another innovation in the S-42 is the adjustable pitch propeller. Usually, if the pitch of the propeller is good for efficient takeoffs it becomes very inefficient for high speed, and vice versa, but with an adjustable pitch propeller you can have a very quick takeoff even with a heavy load, and when you are in the air, you can change the pitch for high-speed flying.

All the devices designed and incorporated in the construction of a plane have to be thoroughly tested out by the factory before the plane can be submitted for test flights in the presence of Department of Commerce inspectors, in order to obtain an Approved Type Certificate and a license.

After this there are some more tests and demonstrations to satisfy the purchaser that everything is up to the contract specifications. In other words, the test flights of a new type of plane usually take several months, because after the first few flights there are always some changes and improvements that have to be made before the next test flight can take place.

While studying the data on the performance of the plane I realized that during our test flights and contract demonstrations, quite a few of the existing world's records in the seaplane class could easily be broken. I researched the present standings in the seaplane world's records, and found out that the United States was sharing third place with Italy, behind France and Germany.

I made out a memorandum to this effect and submitted one copy to Mr. Sikorsky and one to Mr. Neilson.

The idea met with considerable interest. When the time came for our load trials of the plane, I made a trip to Washington to take up all the details with the officials of the Aeronautical Association, who are the United States representatives of the National Fédération Aéronautique Internationale. At the headquarters of the National Aeronautical Association I met with very keen interest and full cooperation from the Secretary, Mr. Enyard. I also had a nice talk with the President of the Association, former Senator Hiram Bingham.

I brought back from Washington sanction for the altitude trials and two valuable barographs, which, on the day of the flight, had to be sealed by a representative appointed by the National Aeronautical Association to act as directing official and time our record trials.

While making our full load tests at a gross load of 38,000 pounds [17,236 kilograms], we actually carried a payload of 16,608 pounds [7,533 kilograms]. A payload is that load carried by the plane in excess of equipment, gasoline, oil, and crew. For records and record trials the payload cannot include any observers or passengers; it must be all in dead weight—in lead plates or sandbags.

The record in this class of seaplanes for the heaviest payload ever taken off the water to an altitude of 2,000 meters was held by German plane with a load of 14,220 pounds [6,450 kilograms]. 2,000 meters is only 6,562 feet.

Taking on a payload which exceeded the previous record by over 2,000 pounds, I climbed to an altitude of 16,500 feet. I not only established a new world's record for the heaviest load taken up to over 2,000 meters, but also beat the payload record in the class for seaplanes carrying a payload of 5,000 kilograms. This record also had been held by Germany, at an altitude of only 2,000 meters.

Thus in one flight two new world's records were established.

But we considered it unfair to carry a load substantially exceeding 5,000 kilograms, and claim only the 5,000-kilogram record with it. So we decided to make another flight for a record carrying a load of 5,000 kilograms, and try to better our own record which we had established a few days previously.

This time the Department of Commerce inspector, Raymond Quick, was coming as my copilot, and as we had a substantially smaller gross load we could expect to rise to an altitude where oxygen would be needed.

The Experimental Department of the United Aircraft Company in Hartford supplied us with two sets of oxygen equipment, with extensions capable of taking care of four men.

The flight was made on May 17th and our altimeters showed an altitude of 21,800 feet [6,645 meters]. The day was not particularly clear, and there were quite heavy clouds in spots. In order to get through and above them we had to look for openings and found the clearest part of the sky over the Hudson River, cruising between New York City and Ossining. We saw New York, part of the Sound, Westchester County, and part of New Jersey quite well, but we were quite sure that nobody could see us from the ground at this altitude.

While I adjusted the oxygen valves, Raymond Quick relieved me at the controls.

When the ceiling apparently was reached, and the plane would not go any higher, I experimented with applying the flap in the takeoff position, and got quite a substantial climb again for at least 2,000 feet more. Then the real ceiling was reached, and no matter what I did to the controls of the plane it would not rise any higher. When pulled up it would fall off, losing speed, and then gradually it would climb up again to the same critical altitude.

After struggling with the plane for a while, being unable to gain any more altitude, I turned the controls over to Raymond Quick, who after several attempts made me a sign that he agreed with me that the ceiling was reached.

We could not talk to each other, having the oxygen mouthpieces over our mouths, but we wrote notes to each other and decided to start the descent. Although down below it was a very warm day, our outside temperature reached 20 below zero at 21,800 feet.

After these two important world's records of great loads being taken to the highest altitudes were made, we completed the remaining Department of Commerce tests required for obtaining a license and Approved Type Certificate.

Only after the plane was licensed by the Department of Commerce were the Pan American pilots allowed by their company to take part in the flights. The first Pan American pilots to be in the plane were their Technical Advisor, Colonel Charles A. Lindbergh, and their Chief Pilot, Edwin Musick.

For quite a few days Colonel Lindbergh was the guest of our factory, arriving every day in the morning in his little Monocoupe, flying from North Beach, New York. Then he would fly all day long, alternating at the controls with Musick, practicing the proper ways of handling the new S-42; and after a full day of flying he would fly back again to New York in his little plane.*

Of all the possible records which the S-42 could establish, now only the speed records remained. I designed a preliminary course for the speed record attempts and submitted it to our management. Then we got in touch with the Coast and Geodetic Survey, and they calculated a more detailed course for us, which would serve our purposes better, being exactly 500 kilometers, which is 310.7 miles. By making this course twice we could claim the 1,000-kilometer records and by making it four times we could claim the 2,000-kilometer records.

According to the rulings of the Fédération Aéronautique Internationale (FAI), there are four different classes of records for both 1,000 and 2,000 kilometers, namely, with no load at all, and with 500, 1,000, and 2,000 kilograms of pay-

* Lindbergh's "little plane," a Monocoupe built in St. Louis, now hangs in the St. Louis airport.

load. By carrying over 2,000 kilograms we would overlap all the smaller records and distances. Because the seaplane speed record in all these classes, with no load for only 1,000 kilometers, was 137 miles per hour [220 kilometers per hour], we could expect to establish eight world's records in one single flight.

The course that was finally approved, out of many submitted, went from Stratford Lighthouse, where the starting and finishing points were, to the New Jersey side of the George Washington Bridge, which was the first turning point; then down to Hudson River to the Staten Island Lighthouse, which was the second turning pylon. From there the course followed the southern shore of Long Island to Fire Island Lighthouse, from there to Block Island North Light, then to Point Judith, Rhode Island, and back to Stratford Light.

It was extremely important for us to know the exact time and exact gasoline consumption on a lap. Knowing this, we could figure out whether we would have enough gasoline to cover the whole distance of 2,000 kilometers, and also we would have an idea of what our actual cruising speed would be.

In order to determine this, and also to allow the pilots to get acquainted with all the turning points, we made a trial run of one lap on July 6th. The engineering department of the Sikorsky Corporation calculated that the total elapsed time on one lap should be two hours and fifteen seconds. When the lap was made, we were timed by a stopwatch, and the total run took exactly twenty seconds less than the theoretical calculations called for. The gasoline consumption was slightly higher than expected, but was within the possible limitations.

By this time the plane had already been accepted by Pan American Airways, and naturally they were responsible for the plane during its flight. It was agreed that two pilots share the responsibility and credit for the records; they were Edwin Musick, the Chief Pilot of Pan American Airways, and myself.

After postponing the date of the great flight several times, due to final adjustments on the plane and adverse weather conditions, the date was definitely set for August 1, 1934.

I arrived at the factory at seven o'clock on the morning of August 1. I found Colonel Lindbergh, who had arrived by car, having driven since seven o'clock the previous evening from some place in Maine. With a great deal of pleasure I found out that the Colonel was going to be on the flight.

The flight was scheduled for eight o'clock. Everything was ready to start at exactly the appointed time. The officials and observers at all six turning points reported by telephone that they were at their stations and on the lookout, but we were still getting weather reports, giving the speed of wind at different altitudes, and did not get started until an hour later.

We three pilots agreed to change places in the left seat of the control cabin every hour. In this way, two pilots were in the control cabin all the time, and the third could take one of the comfortable seats in the rear and rest for one hour out of every three. The pilot who was sitting in the left seat was actually flying the plane and making the turns.

As soon as we passed the starting line, I made out a timetable based on the expected speed and the time necessary to cover the distance between each consecutive point. This timetable indicated exactly what time we should turn at each of the lighthouses on the first, second, third, and fourth laps. With a stopwatch I was checking very accurately on the elapsed time between each two points.

I was very happy to find out that we were traveling a little faster than the theoretical calculation called for. On the first leg, to George Washington Bridge, we gained one minute, and when we completed the whole first lap our gain was over two minutes. The wireless operator handed us a radiogram from the official observers on the starting line, giving our average speed for the first lap as 160.4 miles per hour [258 kilometer per hour]. On the following laps we lost some of our advantage due to adverse winds, but we were still running slightly ahead of our schedule, and finished the whole flight with an average speed of 157.5 miles per hour [253.4 kilometers per hour], exactly 2.5 mph [4 kmh] faster than the theoretical calculations.

When we made the first half of the course I wrote on a piece of paper, "Four world's records are already ours, congratulations," and handed this message to the rest of the crew. I had the thought that even if for some mechanical trouble or for lack of fuel we should have to land before completing the second half, four world's records in one flight would not be too big a disappointment, but fortunately we completed the four laps and all eight records were ours.

During these eight hours of flying we were quite comfortable inside the big cabin. We were well provided with food and soft drinks, some of it furnished by Pan American Airways and some by Mrs. Sikorsky. She made for us quite a lot of delicious little Russian cutlets and the little bits of apple pastry we call *piroshki.*

When we finally completed the flight and came to rest in the water in front of the ramp, a motorboat came to take the pilots ashore, but no one of the three pilots would step forward first to get the welcome from the officials and the guests assembled on the ramp. So we sent the motorboat back, and all waited on board until the plane was pulled out on the ramp. Then we all went out together.*

We were immediately surrounded by officials of the Sikorsky Corporation, Pan American officials, reporters, photographers, and guests. Congratulations were exchanged all around.

For the first time in the history of aviation, one plane established eight world's records in one flight. By doing so the United States gained first place in the world as to the number of world's records held.

During the record flight we tested a mechanical device known as the "automatic pilot." When the plane was put on a straight course and the automatic pilot switched on, the pilot could actually leave all the controls. The automatic pilot would keep the plane on the same level and on the same course indefinitely, with more exactitude than any human being would be able to do. Of course, the turns around the pylons had to be made by living pilots, and for every turn the automatic pilot had to be switched off.

The automatic pilot relies on several gyroscopes to maintain the lateral and longitudinal stability of the plane, and its course and altitude.

The next morning, to my great surprise, when I opened the *Times* I found out that I was only the "copilot" on the flight. That was a bit of over-careful Pan American publicity. It seems that their publicity manager was afraid to give due credit to the non–Pan American members of the flight. The actual situation was well known to the representatives of the FAI, who had to do the timing, testify to the correctness of the payload, and make out the reports to Washington and Paris for a final confirmation of the records established.

Having no doubt of the integrity of those appointed to perform the official duties of observers for the FAI and the National Aeronautical Association, I am sure that proper credit will be given to every member of the crew.

* Lindbergh telegraphed Juan Trippe, president of Pan Am, "There is no advantage to my being on plane and I believe credit for breaking records should go to operating personnel." But Pan Am's publicists insisted that both Lindbergh, Pan Am's technical adviser, and Edwin Musick, its chief pilot, should be part of the record-breaking team. In January 1938, Musick and his crew of six vanished in the S-42B *Samoan Clipper* near Pago Pago after radioing that they were dumping fuel; apparently the vaporizing fuel, ignited by the plane's exhaust stacks, blew up the *Clipper.*

36. The record setters debark from the S-42 together after establishing eight world records in a single flight on August 1, 1934. From the left: Edwin Musick, Pan Am's chief pilot; Sergievsky; Chauncey Wright, Pan Am flight mechanic; Michael Provikoff, Sikorsky flight mechanic; Charles A. Lindbergh, and C. A. Paffe, Pan Am radio operator. *Courtesy of National Air and Space Museum.*

Flying
On

Flying On

ALLAN FORSYTH

Boris Sergievsky had good reason to feel confident that the Fédération Aéronautique Internationale and the National Aeronautical Association would give proper credit to all three pilots of the record-breaking S-42. John Heinmuller, chief timer for the FAI and NAA at all of the Sikorsky record tests flown by Sergievsky, was a friend and admirer. Sergievsky had taken him along on one of the S-38's record-breaking altitude flights in 1930. Heinmuller later wrote that,

> In my opinion Sergievsky remains the "ultimate" air record holder of today, from the viewpoint of experience and skillful piloting. I do not believe he has a peer in his field. His broad experience in flying, in all parts of the world . . . gave him thorough training and practice under all conceivable conditions. He already had rare gifts, experience and understanding, and the combination brought rich results.[1]

These "rich results" included a delightful opportunity for discreet boasting. A letter from the president of the NAA to the president of Sikorsky Aviation Corporation arrived one hour before the S-42 took off on August 1, 1934. Igor Sikorsky described the response:

> The president of our organization sent a reply to the president of the NAA, which read in part as follows: "On the morning of August 1st, I received in the mail an interesting letter from you urging the industry to . . . return to the United States the majority of the world's records in order that the supremacy of American aviation might be measured by a readily understood yardstick. At 5:30 P.M. on that same day . . . we returned to the United States eight

world's records to be added to the two already obtained by the S-42. By so doing, the United States now holds first place in the tenure of world's records. . . ."[2]

In due time, Sergievsky's Diplômes de Record arrived, with his name and records inscribed over a painting of a solemn angel with wings outstretched. All eight records were attributed jointly to Musick, Sergievsky, and Lindbergh. It must have been one of the most gratifying moments in Sergievsky's long flying career.

That career was far from over in 1934; Sergievsky continued to fly, in peace and war, for another thirty years. However, his dictated memoirs evidently did not kindle a publisher's interest in 1934. It seems unlikely that he even read them, for they contained obvious errors introduced by the stenographer, such as spelling the name of the French aircraft manufacturer Voisin as "Voisesin."

Although Sergievsky seldom wrote about his later adventures, he loved to talk about them. The recollections of Sergievsky's friends and family members thus have formed the basis for substantial parts of this epilogue, which describes both his flying career and his personal life from 1934 until his death in 1971. Whenever possible, these personal recollections have been corroborated by other sources, including government records, aircraft manufacturer's files, books, magazine articles, and newspaper accounts. All sources are acknowledged in the text that follows and in the chapter notes.

37. The Diplôme de Record awarded by the FAI to Sergievsky for flying the S-42 to a record-breaking 2,000 meters (the S-42 actually reached 4,877 meters, or 16,000 feet) with 7,533 kilograms (16,608 pounds) aboard on April 26, 1934. Sergievsky collected seventeen such certificates for setting world records during his career with Sikorsky. *Courtesy of Igor I. Sikorsky Historical Archives, Inc.*

Chief Test Pilot

For most Americans in the 1920s and 1930s, "test pilot" conjured up an image of a daredevil in leather helmet and goggles, wringing out hot new airplanes in wild gyrations to see if the wings would stay on. Boris Sergievsky certainly looked the part, but he was far from being a reckless stunt flier. In fact, he was one of the first of the modern breed of engineering test pilots, and the time was ripe for this approach. As Igor Sikorsky later remarked, "Lindbergh's transatlantic flight marked the end of aviation as a hobby and a passion, and the beginning of aviation as an industry and a profession."[1]

As airplanes grew ever more complex, testing them became a lengthy and exhaustive process. A trained and experienced engineer who had done stress calculations on many of the planes he tested, Sergievsky was a meticulous observer of the intricate machines he was flying.

When he lifted the giant Sikorsky S-40 off the water on its first test flight, many observers on the ground feared that it might be too unwieldy for one man to handle. They were almost right. As he notes in his manuscript, the plane was extremely nose heavy; "... the effort that had to be applied in pulling it out for a landing was so great that the plane could not be considered satisfactory." But even as Sergievsky manhandled the untrimmed giant through the air, he kept Pan American's pilots in mind. Knowing that they would be flying the S-40 for hours at a time, he focused his report on the need to relocate the pilot's chair to a more comfortable position.

Sergievsky spent many flying hours on such mundane tasks as recording the Sikorsky boats' fuel consumption at various weights and altitudes, but such flights did not dull his piloting skills. Sergei Sikorsky, Igor's son, says that Sergievsky's extraordinarily deft touch at the controls saved the whole S-42 program when the company's survival depended on it.[2]

In 1934, just as the S-42 was entering its flight test program, the Civil Aeronautics Administration announced new regulations for passenger-carrying aircraft. Their maximum wing loading was not to exceed 16 pounds per square foot of wing area, and the landing speed was to be no more than 65 miles per hour. The CAA would not grant an approved type certificate for aircraft that could not meet these standards. The S-42's wing loading was 28.5 pounds per square foot.

The Sikorsky team pointed out that the S-42's large wing flaps provided much greater lift during landing and takeoff than a similar wing without flaps, while the higher wing loading made the aircraft faster and more efficient than its contemporary rivals. The newly developed Hamilton-Standard variable-pitch propellers also added greatly to the plane's efficiency at cruising speed and power at takeoff. Eventually, the CAA yielded on the wing-loading rule, but it remained adamant about the 65 miles per hour landing speed.

Landing a 19-ton plane at 65 miles per hour was an extraordinary challenge, but as Sergei Sikorsky reports, "Sergievsky, with a wonderfully delicate touch, landed the S-42 at 61 or 62 miles per hour consistently on the Housatonic River" during the tests that led to the big boat's certification—and commercial salvation for the Sikorsky company.

38. Pan American Airways rose to worldwide prominence on Sikorsky wings between 1928 and 1938, as Igor Sikorsky's photo of Pan Am's Miami base in the mid-1930s makes clear. A pioneering S-38 of 1928, left, is hidden behind a 1931 S-40. A 1934 S-42 heads for the ramp, while another S-40 waits at the right. Boris Sergievsky tested every one of these planes. *Courtesy of Igor I. Sikorsky Historical Archives, Inc.*

The Sikorsky S-43

The Sikorsky S-43 followed the Sikorsky tradition of building successful designs in various sizes. The S-38, Sikorsky's first commercial success, was followed by a scaled-down version, the S-39, and an enlarged version, the four-engined S-40. The success of the extraordinarily advanced S-42 inspired a smaller, twin-engined version, the S-43, which incorporated the S-42's pylon-mounted wing, its wing planform, and its strut-braced wing and tail.

As Boris Sergievsky demonstrated in April 1936, the S-43 was a record-breaker like its big brother. (Amazingly, Sergievsky's altitude record for C-3 Class seaplanes of 24,951 feet was still standing at least as late as 1981.) The S-43's sprightly performance and its ability to carry fifteen passengers, two pilots, and a flight steward made it an instant commercial success. Inter-Island Airways of Hawaii got its first S-43 in November 1935 and flew four of them until 1947. Pan American bought fourteen S-43s for its Latin American routes, where they replaced the older and smaller S-38s. The U.S. Navy bought seventeen S-43s under the designation of JRS-1. Ten survived the Pearl Harbor attack on December 7, 1941; they were hastily equipped with bomb racks and sent on antisubmarine patrol. One JRS-1 survives still, awaiting restoration at the Smithsonian Air and Space Museum.

The other surviving S-43 was ordered by Howard Hughes for an around-the-world record attempt in 1937, but even with 900-horsepower Wright Cyclone engines in place of the standard 750-horsepower Pratt and Whitney Hornets, it was not as fast as the Lockeed 14 twin-engined landplane Hughes ultimately used for his record-breaking trip. Hughes retained his S-43 as an executive plane until he crashed it into Lake Mead, Nevada, in May 1943. The wreck was raised from 200 feet of water and completely rebuilt over the following year. Hughes soon moved on to newer planes but kept the S-43; it awaits another restoration today.

A total of fifty-three S-43s were built—fifty amphibians and three flying boats—and the last was not delivered until January 1941. Few survived World War II, and landplanes took over the postwar airline routes; the S-43 was Sikorsky's last sales success in the commercial seaplane business it had pioneered.[1]

AF

39. Sergievsky set four world records in the Sikorsky S-43 during April 1936. The S-43, a scaled-down S-42, was the last commercially successful Sikorsky seaplane; this is one of the fourteen bought by Pan Am to replace its S-38s on its Latin American routes. *Courtesy of Igor I. Sikorsky Historical Archives, Inc.*

Sergievsky's flying skills also saved the Sikorsky company from some embarassment the next year, when he took the S-43 down the Housatonic for its maiden flight on June 1, 1935. Such flights were big events when the air age was still young, and newsreel cameramen in motor launches positioned themselves to record the moment of takeoff with the stone breakwater and its lighthouse in the background.

As Sergievsky lifted the S-43 "onto the step" and the ship began skimming the wavetops, he sensed that something was not right. A quick check of the instruments showed that one of the two engines was faltering. Sergievsky reduced power on the ailing engine and trimmed the controls so deftly that the takeoff proceeded without any sign of hesitation—on one engine. The newsreels recorded a seemingly flawless debut.[3]

In April 1936, as the S-43's test flights were ending and it was about to go into passenger service, Sergievsky set out to put it in the record books. On April 14, he set two altitude records for amphibians in a single flight, reaching 24,951 feet with a payload of 500 kilograms and simultaneously setting a new record for the same height without a payload. On April 25, he set two more altitude records, for amphibians with 1,000- and 2,000-kilogram payloads, taking the S-43 to 19,626 feet with Igor Sikorsky and M. Pravikoff serving as crew members. (Sergievsky could have climbed higher without the weight of his companions, who were not part of the official payload, but taking friends along was a company tradition. Igor Sikorsky took eight devoted workers on the first test flight of the S-29-A twelve years earlier, and had to crash-land the overloaded plane on a nearby golf course.)

The S-43 was the Sikorsky company's last commercially successful airplane, in part because it replaced the faithful S-38 in the service of various customers.[4] But the Sikorsky company lost a 1937 competition for a four-engined Navy patrol boat, and only three of the commercial VS-44 transport version were built. The age of the flying boat was ending, hastened by the building of thousands of airports around the world before and during World War II, and by the production of tens of thousands of landplane transports, more efficient than any flying boat and not restricted to ice-free harbors.

In 1938, Igor Sikorsky was summoned to the office of the president of United Aircraft, who planned to close the Sikorsky division. Before he could break the news, Sikorsky proposed that he and a small team be given a modest amount of funding to develop a helicopter. The president wisely accepted Sikorsky's offer, thus putting United Aircraft in the forefront of a whole new industry a few years later, when Sikorsky perfected the single-rotor helicopter. Boris Sergievsky was not part of Sikorsky's helicopter team, however; he had already left his old friend's company to join a rival company, led by their much-admired former professor from the Kiev Polytechnic Institute, Dr. George de Bothezat.

Sergievsky, de Bothezat, and the Helicopter Corporation of America

Dr. George de Bothezat was an internationally famous mathematician, noted for his theoretical work on propeller shapes. In 1918, the Soviets let him emigrate to the United States, where he joined the National Advisory Committee for Aeronautics three weeks after his arrival. In 1921, de Bothezat was invited to McCook Field in Dayton, Ohio, the U.S. Army's aviation test center, to build a helicopter.[1]

In December 1922, de Bothezat's helicopter appeared—a cross-shaped skeleton of tubing supporting four six-bladed rotors and four smaller stabilizing fans, powered by a horizontally mounted rotary engine whirling inches in front of the pilot. Instantly named "the flying octopus," it could hover a few feet off the ground and lift several hundred pounds. However, its control systems were too complex; one test pilot complained, "It takes an octopus to fly it."

Frustrated, de Bothezat went to New York, where in 1937 he formed the Helicopter Corporation of America and invited Boris Sergievsky to be his vice president. Sergievsky had read and admired de Bothezat's paper on airplane stability as a student in 1911. In 1937, he quickly acquired de Bothezat's enthusiasm for helicopters. On May 10, 1940, the *New York Herald Tribune* announced the results of their collaboration.

NEW HELICOPTER MAKES FLIGHT AT 40-FOOT AIRPORT

A dream of inventors since Leonardo da Vinci of aircraft rising and landing vertically on the rooftops of cities came closer to fulfillment yesterday when a streamlined helicopter built by the late Dr. George Bothezat, helicopter pioneer, went straight upward in its first test flight, virtually stood still in the air, then came straight down.

The flight took place in the "postage stamp airport" of the Helicopter Corporation of America at 45-31 Davis Street, Long Island City, Queens. Located in the heart of a business section only a few steps from the elevated structure of the I.R.T. Flushing subway line, the airport is a concrete-paved backyard forty feet square. At the new aircraft's controls was Capt. Boris Sergievsky, World War ace of the Imperial Russian Armies and later a crack test pilot in the United States, who in 1934 set a world's flying record a month for four successive months.

Capt. Sergievsky made no attempt to rise more than three or four feet off the ground because of his unfamiliarity with the tricks of the new aircraft. During the tests ropes were attached to the four rubber-tired wheels of the helicopter, which is a tiny one-man affair shaped like a tear-drop and weighing less than 600 pounds. The ropes were fastened to iron rings set in the concrete runway as a safety measure in the event that the helicopter made an unexpected maneuver. At 2,500 revolutions of the craft's specially constructed engine all the wheels left the ground and the helicopter tugged hard at its moorings until Capt. Sergievsky cut the motor and landed.

Two years of actual experimental and construction work at the Helicopter Corporation's plant and a lifetime of research by Dr. de Bothezat, who died in Boston Feb.1, preceded yesterday's flight. This was intended only as a familiarization and weight-lifting test and is to be followed within a week or two by free flights of considerable altitude at Roosevelt Field, L.I.

The lifting properties of the helicopter are derived from two rotating airscrews having three blades each, which are located one below and one above the aircraft's engine above the fuselage. Dr. de Bothezat, who was regarded as one of the world's foremost mathematical physicists, worked out before his death a formula for the curves of the tapering airscrew blades, which are fourteen feet long. The airscrews are sent whirling in opposite directions by the motor so that there is no torque or twisting motion, in only one direction.

40. The de Bothezat GB-5 helicopter in a later configuration, drawn from 1940 newspaper photos. The landing gear has been made much sturdier and wider than that on the first version, probably as a result of some hard landings. *Drawing by Matei Kiraly. Courtesy of Matei Kiraly.*

Sergievsky later described the Roosevelt Field test flights of his helicopter, known as the GB-5.[2]

> For the actual free flight tests we went to Roosevelt Field, Long Island, arriving very early in the morning before any turbulent current formed. The flights lasted for months. Actually, you could not call them flights for they were really hops: never higher than five feet off the ground.

I am a firm believer in Dr. de Bothezat's theories that the helicopter is more stable than the airplane. In fact, in our flight tests, the aircraft hovered so motionlessly, I would let go of the controls, carefully climb out of the cockpit and the machine would fly itself and correct itself as I watched the incredible performance from the ground!

After de Bothezat's death, the company ran into financial problems; new management took over and de Bothezat's assistants made changes in the design of the GB-5 and its motor. The much-modified machine eventually crashed at Stroudsburg, Pennsylvania; Sergievsky was unharmed but the GB-5 was demolished. Sergievsky described the incident.

The changes made to the helicopter after Dr. de Bothezat's death gave me the feeling that the aircraft had lost the stability and had not been perfected according to the calculations and instructions of Dr. de Bothezat. In the test hops I made, the aircraft was not righting itself as it had previously. Instead of deaccelerating itself it would accelerate, and therefore, I strongly advised that the machine was unstable. However, in spite of my own protestations, I continued flying the aircraft. On this particular day, I took the helicopter aloft and when we reached about five feet—the machine crashed.

The Helicopter Corporation of America faded away slowly, although Sergievsky still listed it as his current position on his 1944 résumé for the OSS. But while Sergievsky was making the first tethered hops in the GB-5, his old friend and former employer, Igor Sikorsky, was making the first untethered flights of his first experimental helicopter, the VS-300.

Ironically, Boris Sergievsky played a role in making $50,000 available to perfect the VS-300 when Sikorsky needed it. In April 1938, Sergievsky made a visionary plea for helicopters before a congressional committee that was considering the Dorsey Bill, a $2 million appropriation "for autogyro development."[3] At that time, autogyro makers and some Army aviation officers were urging Congress to back the autogyro as a flying obervation post that could operate from any small field.

Thanks to Boris Sergievsky and other helicopter proponents, the wording of the Dorsey Bill was changed so that the $2 million was appropriated "for rotary wing development," thereby covering helicopters as well as autogyros. Two years later, Sikorsky received the last $50,000 of the Dorsey funding. The *New York Herald Tribune* for May 1, 1938, featured excerpts from Sergievsky's testimony:

FLOCK OF ONE-MAN HELICOPTERS VISIONED TO FLY OVER THE ENEMY

Battalions of flying machine-gunners, each equipped with his own silently operating helicopter and able to land secretly at night behind enemy lines—even on commanding crags and peaks impregnable to ground attack—were envisaged last week as the next revolutionary development in warfare by Captain Boris Sergievsky, Russian war ace and test pilot, before the House Military Affairs Committee. Captain Sergievsky appeared at a hearing on a bill introduced by Representative Frank J. G. Dorsey of Pennsylvania, to appropriate $2,000,000 for experimentation by the War Department with rotary wing aircraft.

He said that, as one of the organizers of the Helicopter Corporation of America, he was about to start testing a machine of this type designed by Dr. George A. de Bothezat, who fifteen years ago built the first successful American helicopter at McCook Field, Dayton, Ohio. This craft, larger than the projected one-man-and-machine-gun model, is expected to eclipse the recent phenomenal performance of French and German helicopters, Captain Sergievsky said, and to be 40 percent more efficient than an airplane of the same horsepower, besides having the ability to hover in midair and to land and take off vertically. Of the small military style, Captain Sergievsky said:

"It is possible to build very small helicopters, weighing, complete with engine, only about 300 pounds, and able to carry a man with machine gun and ammunition. This would give rise to an entirely new method of warfare, battalions of swift and silently flying machine-gunners able to land at night behind the enemy's lines, even in rough country. This type of helicopter, called a 'Heli-hop' by its inventor, has already been designed in detail and its performance rigorously estimated. Dr. de Bothezat is ready to proceed with the building of these Heli-hops."

Captain Sergievsky outlined other military applications of the helicopter:

HELICOPTER CORPORATION OF AMERICA

"Helicopters can be used to replace observation balloons, since their mosquito-like frames would be very hard to distinguish at a distance . . . The helicopter observer could hover right over the point of interest, change his position with the importance of his objectives and return to base when necessary to deliver photographs and detailed reports."

Yet Another Divorce, Yet Another Marriage

I'**m** marrying a crazy woman," said Sergievsky to Igor Sikorsky late in 1935. When his old friend raised an eyebrow, Sergievsky continued, "Well, she wants to marry me so she must be crazy!"[1] Sikorsky may have been puzzled for another reason: Sergievsky was still married to Alexandra, his wife of twenty-two years, who had once assured Sergievsky's mother that "after thirty [life] is governed by brain and duty."

41. Boris Sergievsky and his second wife, Alexandra. The photo probably was taken in Cartagena in 1928; their expressions suggest that all was not well with their marriage even then, seven years before they divorced. *Courtesy of the editors.*

42. Boris Sergievsky and his new bride, Gertrude, honeymooning in St. Moritz in 1936. Sergievsky's skiing outfit suggests that he had no intention of falling down. *Courtesy of the editors.*

Sergievsky clearly did not agree. He had pursued a well-known Russian-American portrait painter ardently until her mother, on her deathbed in 1933, made her swear to break off the romance. He dazzled his Sikorsky co-workers with a succession of glamorous girlfriends. And since 1930, he had quietly been courting Gertrude Hochschild, a shy heiress he had met while demonstrating an S-38 to her brothers at their family compound on an Adirondack lake. By 1935, Alexandra was living alone on the second floor of the Sergievsky home in Stratford, Connecticut, while Sergievsky shared the first floor with his mother and son. Orest later described the situation.

> Granny and I sensed that something was happening, not only because of Father's absence on the days when he was not away on flights, but also a few unfinished statements and his generally better frame of mind made us wonder what was going on. For months there had been talk of divorce, the difficulties of property settlement, and what would happen to Granny and me. But it always came to a dead end; no agreement could be reached.
>
> Then one day, just before I left for New York, Granny told me that she was going to have an important visitor, and that she wanted me to help her decide which dress to wear. Upon my asking who was paying her a visit, she said that she did not know, that it was someone Father had asked her to meet. When I returned later that day, Granny told me that the visitor was a lovely, gentle lady named Gertrude, who wanted to meet the mother of Boris Sergievsky, and to receive her approval to marry him.[2]

Granny must have been delighted to give Gertrude her approval, even though divorce was rare then; Gertrude was clearly a warm and generous woman. Agreements were finally reached and the *Bridgeport Post* headlined the result on December 29, 1935: "Mrs. Alexandra Sergievsky Divorces Captain at Reno; Chief Sikorsky Test Pilot to Pay $250 Monthly Alimony." Photos showed the "famous chief test pilot" in his flying helmet and his ex-wife in her pearls; she looked exceedingly mournful under a headline that said, "Wins Freedom."

The settlement was handsome—$250 was almost enough to buy a new car then. But it was overshadowed by further headlines next week: "Sergievsky, Famed Flier, Is Re-Wed in New York; Divorced on Saturday, Pilot Marries Miss Hochschild Tuesday." The brief article noted that "The wedding early Tuesday evening (New Year's Eve) was solemnized in New York in the presence of a few close friends of the couple." It did not mention that Sergievsky was late for the wedding because he had to finish a test flight of the S-43.

Sergievsky's marriage to Gertrude brought him the kind of luxury and economic security he had not known since 1914. By the summer of 1936, he was commuting daily from the Adirondacks to the Sikorsky plant at Stratford, 180 miles away, in a Stinson Reliant floatplane.[3] This may have established another record for Sergievsky. Commuter flights had carried a few Wall Streeters to and from Long Island in 1934, but Sergievsky's daily 90-minute flights each way may have made him the first do-it-yourself aerial commuter.

After leaving Sikorsky in 1937, Sergievsky flew charters and family tours in a twin-engine Grumman Goose amphibian until War World II intervened. From 1946 until he retired from flying in 1965, he flew charter flights and family excursions again, this time in a ten-passenger, twin-engine Grumman Mallard amphibian. Gertrude seemed happy to pay for it all, including the airplanes, though she often stayed home with their daughter Kira, born in 1939, while Sergievsky went roaming.

43. Dapper as always, Sergievsky stands on the float of his Stinson Reliant, in which he commuted daily between the Adirondacks in upstate New York and the Sikorsky plant on the Connecticut shore during the summer of 1936. *Courtesy of the editors.*

Sergievsky Goes to War Again

As Sergievsky gently eased the GB-5 helicopter off the ground for first time, the German Army's blitzkrieg was smashing the Allies' defenses in France. As he continued the test flights at Roosevelt Field, the Battle of Britain raged. And on June 22, 1941, when Hitler's armies invaded the Soviet Union, the community of Russian exiles in New York was plunged into turmoil. For decades, these exiles had dreamed of the day when the despised Bolsheviks would be overthrown, and the Romanov dynasty and the Russian Orthodox religion would be restored to Russia. Now the newsreels were showing Soviet peasants welcoming the Germans with flowers and kissing the crosses painted on their tanks.

Nazi propaganda was artfully crafted to play on the loyalties of Russians and Christians everywhere. It was also designed to support the Nazis' claims that they were protecting the world from godless Bolshevism—and from the Jews who were supposedly promoting both communist and capitalist plots against world order. Many exiled Russians, yearning to free their homeland from the communist terrors they knew firsthand, were swayed by this propaganda. It rang especially true to those who had brought with them the long-standing Russian tradition of anti-Semitism. By 1941, a thousand Russian fascists were holding military drills on a Connecticut estate. Compared to the American-German Bund, the American Nazi organization that drew 17,000 members to a Madison Square Garden rally in February 1939,[1] the Russian group was small. But when the Nazis invaded Russia, the Russian fascists moved to mobilize the exile community behind the Nazi "liberators."

In June 1941, Sergievsky was Commander of a Russian veterans' association in New York called Garrison 297 of the Army and Navy Union. Then as always, he was a stalwart supporter of the Russian Orthodox Church, and of anything that might put a tsar back on the throne in Russia. As news of the Nazi invasion of Russia spread, Sergievsky was visited by a former Russian army officer named Boris Brasol, accompanied by Archbishop Vitaly, head of the Russian Orthodox Church in New York. Brasol had convinced the Archbishop that the Germans would liberate Russia from the communists. Together they persuaded Sergievsky to join them in signing a letter to President Roosevelt opposing aid to the Soviets. They also persuaded him to speak to his fellow members of Garrison 297 on July 18 and ask them to cooperate with the Germans. Half of the members disagreed and began to seek Sergievsky's removal as commander.[2] This reponse apparently jarred Sergievsky into questioning the merits of working with Brasol and Vitaly, for he did no further campaigning with them.

Brasol and Vitaly were outspoken anti-Semites, supporters of armed Russian fascist groups in the United States and Germany, and closely linked with the Nazis in the United States and in Berlin. Brasol had translated the tsarist secret police's anti-Semitic hoax, "The Protocols of the Elders of Zion," so that Henry Ford could publish it in English.[3] Sergievsky's wife Gertrude and her family were Jewish and wealthy and, Sergievsky must have realized, thus prime targets for Brasol's and Vitaly's anti-Semitic plans.

The Japanese attack on Pearl Harbor on December 7, 1941, changed everything, for it brought America into the war against Germany. Any doubts Sergievsky held about opposing Germany vanished then. His adoptive country was at war and—perhaps more important to him—he saw the chance to fight again.

Sergievsky's first response was to donate his Grumman Goose to the war effort. Then he began looking for ways to join the war himself. He had become an American citizen in 1934, but like other men in their fifties, probably found that getting overseas took a great deal of string pulling. An old family friend of the Sergievskys[4] says that Lt. Col. Harold E. Hartney, then working for the Office of Strategic Services (precursor of the CIA), recruited Sergievsky for a secret mission to China in the spring of 1942. Hartney had commanded the famous U.S. 1st Pursuit Group in France in 1918 and organized the National Aeronautic Association in the 1920s. Sergievsky doubtless encountered Hartney often at the Silent Birdmen Club and other gatherings of the small aviation community between the wars.

In 1942, the OSS considered recruiting agents among the Russian exiles in China. Sergievsky's China trip most likely involved these fellow exiles. Apparently, his mission succeeded; Sergievsky officially joined the OSS as a special agent on August 1, 1944, at a salary of $4,600 a year, and on September 20 he was on his way to London. His orders assigned him to the Strategic Services Operations Office for West Europe as a morale officer.[5]

The question of whose morale he was to influence soon became moot, for Sergievsky had been in the OSS London office less than two months when a new assignment beckoned. The U.S. Army Air Force was encountering startling new Luftwaffe aircraft—Messerschmitt 262 jet fighters and Arado 234 jet bombers too fast to intercept, and rocket-propelled Messerschmitt 163 fighters, tailless interceptors that climbed five miles a minute. The Air Force wanted to get its hands on these outstanding aircraft and learn everything about them. As the Allies liberated France and pushed into Germany, all kinds of tantalizing information might be available at newly captured Luftwaffe bases—perhaps even the German jets and rocket-propelled fighters themselves. The need was urgent, for Japanese kamikazes were ravaging the U.S. Navy off Okinawa. One hope was that German advances in air defense might be used to protect the American fleet during the planned invasion of Japan in November 1945.

Sergievsky's OSS qualifications—a staunchly anticommunist test pilot fluent in English, Russian, French, and German—were even more appropriate for the U.S. Army Air Force. On October 21, 1944, for example, the Air Disarmament Command (Provisional), or ADC, pleaded for sixty instructors in German from the London office of Berlitz, but Berlitz would not release even one. On December 1, 1944, a special order of the ADC ordered "Mr. Boris Sergievsky Noo3151 Tech Rep" to report "to AAF Sta 391 for purpose of joining HQ Air Disarmament Comd." Station 391 was then at Ognon, France—presumably a forward air base on the Ognon River, near Belfort. On January 24, 1945, the OSS made it official, transferring Sergievsky to the Army Air Force with a warning that the OSS was no longer responsible for feeding him or for getting him back to the United States.[6]

The Air Disarmament Command was an operational arm of the United States Strategic Air Force (USSTAF), which was in charge of Air Force intelligence operations in western Europe in 1945. After some false starts, the USSTAF found that roving three- or four-man jeep teams had the best chance of finding and securing valuable intelligence items before they were lost in the chaos of liberation or conquest. It was no easy task. A veteran of a similar group, the Strategic Bombing Survey, remembers arriving at several vital factories, only to find that displaced persons had taken shelter there and were cooking whatever food they could scavenge over campfires kindled with top secret plans and documents.[7]

The ADC had better luck, perhaps because they were more interested in machines than paper. The ADC's orginal mission was to destroy German aircraft as they were captured, but ADC teams were soon given different colored lists of priority items wanted at Wright Field for testing and evaluation. Following hard on the heels of the advancing American armies, the ADC teams found some of the German jets on their priority lists. Bomb squads removed any booby traps and the ADC guarded their prizes until the Air Technical Intelligence (ATI) teams arrived to put the aircraft in flying condition.[8] The ATI was in charge of test-flying captured aircraft, but Sergievsky managed to fly more than one of the German jets. Sergievsky liked to talk about it in later years, and no wonder; he was 56 years old then and flying the hottest airplanes in the world.

44. Sergievsky in 1945, wearing a U.S. Army officer's uniform without insignia of rank or branch of service, but wearing his RAF pilot's wings and Russian ribbons. This uniform was appropriate as he had been granted officer status as a technical representative. *Courtesy of the editors.*

Once the fighting ended in May 1945, Sergievsky traded in his jeep for a chauffeured Army limousine and set up operations in Paris. (Though he remained a civilian, the Army granted him the privileges due a brigadier general, and he accepted them happily.) A few weeks later, Sergievsky's son, Orest, arrived in France after a rough combat tour with the Air Force in the Southwest Pacific. Orest later described their reunion.

I do not know exactly how my father succeeded in locating me. I was stationed in a chateau outside Paris. A message reached me, and a meeting was arranged through "higher ups," the high command, and I was ordered to be on my way to meet him in Paris. Being too old for active duty, my father had been appointed an advisor, dealing with Air Force planes and places and supplies that had been captured. He held a very high rank, had a car with a chauffeur for traveling in France and Germany.

Upon my arrival in the city, I called him as instructed and we arranged to meet in front of L'Opéra. It was an emotional and very theatrical meeting. We had not seen one another for over four years. Both of us were in uniform; I forgot to salute him. We saw each other at quite a distance; he had just gotten out of his military car.

As usually happens at moments like this our bodies conveyed more meaning than words could ever have expressed. No demonstrative words or gestures were exchanged between us then—or ever had been for that matter. Father was too rigidly military in his bearing for that. This reserve was very difficult for me to control; I was, after all, a theater performer who was used to displaying my emotions. But even at this special moment, I held back in respect for his military-like, unemotional relationship with me. But at that moment I saw love in his eyes, and I think pride.

After he found out that I only had an overnight pass to stay away from the chateau in which I was staying, he immediately said that he would arrange for a pass for me to stay with him at least two days. We went to the Military Police, which was operating in L'Opéra itself; the backstage entrance was the headquarters.

After seeing a few high officials and making a few phone calls, it was all arranged. Father told me we were going to celebrate our reunion. He arranged to be free, too, and with a wink and a sparkle of mischievousness in his eye he said, "And I arranged to have an Army chauffeur be our

Sergievsky's Women

Mention Sergievsky's name to men who flew with him, or built or maintained his planes, and they are likely to say, with a smile of fond recollection, "Ah, Boris . . . he had the most beautiful girlfriends." When two or more of his old companions gather, they will start to compare notes: "Remember Tanya?" "So beautiful!" "And who came after her?" Almost always they conclude that no harm came of Boris's passions.[1] And one who knew him well[2] says that Boris had a wonderful talent for "re-virginizing" his mistresses as his passion cooled and he then introduced them to men who could do well by them.

Several of these women did very well indeed, going on to marry men of wealth and power. This was hardly surprising because nearly all of them were young, clever, and beautiful. Most were ballet dancers, graceful and accustomed to admiration— and Sergievsky was a notably direct admirer of attractive women. He also had a remarkably strong and sensual physical presence, like many dancers, so the mutual attraction may have felt as irresistible as a force of nature. (One can only hope that Sergievsky did not go backstage at the famously risqué Folies Bergère nightclub when he visited Paris in 1937; among the many statuesque, near-naked showgirls there was his seventeen-year-old stepdaughter, dancing under the name of Colette Vernon.[3])

Sergievsky's physicality scarcely declined with age. At seventy-seven, he entered a party and was introduced to several attractive women. "I bet you can't do this!" he said and, standing at attention like the old soldier he was, he began to fall forward like a felled tree. Just as his nose seemed destined for a crash, he whipped both hands into the push-up position, arresting his fall inches from disaster, then sprang to his feet, flashing a delighted grin. The guests found his display outrageous but irresistible; those who knew him agreed that it was pure Boris.

The Metropolitan Opera received regular donations from him, if not regular attendance. His co-pilot enjoyed many an opera thanks to Sergievsky's tickets, while Sergievsky found more intimate entertainment elsewhere. When the opera ended, the copilot would call with details of the night's perfor-

transportation for our secret mission." It was the first time I heard Edith Piaf. We went to the best restaurant in Paris, and drank champagne at the Bal Tabarin. It was one if the few times in our lives that Father and I were on more or less equal terms.

After being with Father during that luxurious visit in Paris, returning to military routine was a dark reality.[9]

The reunion occured in the late summer of 1945, when many civilian tech reps were demanding that the Air Force take them back to the United States— and finding that they were at the bottom of the priority lists. Sergievsky, in his Paris hotel, was in no hurry; he did not return to the United States until 1946.

mance—who sang well or badly, who conducted—so that Sergievsky could go home and describe the performance as though he had been there.[4]

Sergievsky was not often this discreet. When a Park Avenue matron and family friend, seated next to Sergievsky at a dinner party, asked him to describe a high point in his life, he replied, "Bathing a princess in champagne!"[5]

Ballet was Sergievsky's favorite charitable cause. His son, Orest, who had a difficult relationship with his father, was about to accept an appointment in a famous ballet company when he discovered that his father had just donated $1,000 to the company. Orest assumed that his father was only trying to ensure his own access to cast parties, because Boris disapproved of Orest's dancing career. But the company director, learning of the relationship, began promising Orest leading roles. His pride wounded, Orest turned down the job[6]—but his pride was assuaged more than once over the years when his father eagerly introduced himself to a beautiful young ballet dancer and was asked, "Are you related to *the* Sergievsky?"[7]

Sergievsky's passion for ballet dancers was lifelong. This writer last saw Sergievsky about two years before he died, gliding by in a two-seater Mercedes convertible, top down on a chilly New York afternoon. Sergievsky was at the wheel, as always; two slim young beauties were sharing the passenger seat. All three looked more than content.

Did Sergievsky's endless succession of passions do no harm, as his old friends—nearly all Russian émigrés—maintain? His American in-laws and their friends certainly were more often outraged than accepting. And what of his third wife, Gertrude, who found ballerinas at her breakfast table and in the cabin of Boris's plane with her on vacation trips—the very plane she had paid for? Did she suffer in stoic silence through the thirty-five years of their marriage? Or did she accept Boris's mistresses as simply a part of the endless adventure that he had brought into her life just when it had seemed doomed to endless constraint and propriety? Not even those closest to her seem to know.

AF

The Mallard
Years, 1946-1965

Following his World War II adventures, Sergievsky returned to the flying boats he knew so well. He ordered a twin-engined Grumman Mallard amphibian less than three months after the first one flew, and took delivery of the third production plane, NC 2940, on October 30, 1946, at a cost of of $98,388.[1] Fast, spacious, and long-ranged, the Mallard had been designed as a ten-passenger feeder airliner—but seven of the first twelve were delivered to "sportsman-pilots" like Sergievsky. Over the years, his blue-gray Mallard's nose gradually became adorned with more than a dozen flags of countries on three continents—souvenirs of Sergievsky's flying visits.

Sergievsky quickly put his new plane to use, whether flying guests from New York City to the Adirondacks on weekends or winging across the Atlantic in 1948 with his wife and a ballerina "just for fun," as the newspapers quoted him.

This trip marked another record for Sergievsky because it made him the first private pilot to make a family crossing of the Atlantic. As late as 1939, the Atlantic crossing was a great adventure; a few airliners tested possible routes while four daredevils in three single-engined planes set out to imitate Lindbergh; all disappeared.[2] World War II turned the Atlantic into a major air route, establishing a network of airports and radio beacons in Canada, Greenland, and Iceland that made it possible for Sergievsky, and thousands of private pilots after him, to fly to Europe on their own.

Sergievsky probably established a similar first when he flew a family party to Rio de Janiero to visit a relative there. (He may have established a record of another sort during a stop in Havana when he took the family party, including his wife and her aunt, to an exhibition of sexual prowess by the fabled performer known as "Superman.")

But it was not all play for Sergievsky. He often flew charter flights in the Mallard; its long range and ability to land anywhere made it popular for fish-

45. Sergievsky, Commander of Garrison 297 of the Army and Navy Union (a Russian veterans' association he had led for at least fifteen years) leads his unit in a 1955 parade in New York City. He is wearing his Russian medals, the pilot's badges of Russia and Britain, and the winged badge of the Aéronautique International. *Courtesy of the editors.*

ing and hunting trips deep in the Canadian wilds. Sergievsky's copilot from 1947 to 1956, Elmourza Natirboff, still remembers a charter by a rich sportsman named Bob Topping, who brought four friends with him to a distant Canadian lake to hunt moose. Natirboff and Sergievsky, floating at anchor in the Mallard, were startled when their campers sent them south for another case of whisky after three days. They were more amazed when the impetuous sportsman ordered them to fly his party through dangerously foul weather to a distant town,

46. Boris Sergievsky on the left, his wife Gertrude, ballerina Marina Svletlova, her mother, and copilot Elmourza Natirboff, after crossing the Atlantic in 1948. The emblem on the Mallard's nose is a replica of the pilot's badge Sergievsky wore on his shoulder bars in World War I. *Courtesy of the editors.*

simply to see a movie that starred his favorite actress (probably Lana Turner; Topping was one of the seven men she married). Finding the theater closed, Topping bought it on the spot and ordered his movie shown. The only game bagged on the trip consisted of a moose calf, and a mouse that invaded the sportsmen's tent. Sergievsky, happy to risk losing more such charters, had the mouse's head mounted on a large plaque, fangs bared, and had a friend's chauffeur drop it off at Topping's New York apartment building.

Sergievsky's most famous charter was also the most dangerous. On July 29, 1956, the Swedish liner *Stockholm* collided with the Italian liner *Andrea Doria* in

47. Sergievsky's Mallard taxiing toward the landing ramp with its landing gear down. The waves around the *Stockholm* were far higher than this on July 30, 1956, when Sergievsky landed near it to retrieve the films of the sinking of the *Andrea Doria*. *Courtesy of the editors.*

the darkness south of Nantucket. More than fifty people were killed and the *Andrea Doria* sank early the next morning. The news media learned that a passenger on the *Stockholm* had taken movies of the disaster and they chartered Sergievsky to pick up the film. He managed to land near the *Stockholm*, amid huge swells that far exceeded the Mallard's design maximum of three-foot waves.

The films, sealed in cans and taped to a life ring, were thrown from the ship. Sergievsky taxied toward the ring while Natirboff stood in the bow hatch with a boathook. "I was drenched by the waves that broke over our bow," he said later; "I was afraid that a wave would suck me out, or flood our ship. Boris drove at the ring again and again but the waves tossed us and the ring about so much that catching it seemed impossible. Then at last I snared it." Sergievsky, timing his takeoff run to carry him between the towering swells, bounced the Mallard into the air and brought the pictures to a waiting world.[3]

The Mallard years came to an end in 1965, when the doctors proclaimed Sergievsky unfit to fly. He was seventy-seven years old and had been flying for

FLYING ON

more than half a century, in everything from spruce-and-fabric biplanes to jet
fighters. He was born when flight was an impossible dream. He stood among
the pioneers who transformed that dream into a major force in war and peace.
And he survived wars, crashes, storms, thousands of hours of flying on four
continents, even a tidal wave, and lived to see men walking on the moon.

48. Boris Sergievsky in front of his Grumman Mallard, outside its Adirondack hangar in 1949.
Courtesy of the editors.

THE MALLARD YEARS

Notes
Bibliography
Index

Notes

Out of the Blue

1. "Sergievsky" in *The New Yorker*.
2. *Ibid*.
3. Associated Press, Aug. 10, 1947.
4. Fairchild to Sergievsky, Aug. 10, 1934.

Loves and a Marriage

1. Orest Sergievsky, 21–23.

Sikorsky I: The Russian Years

1. Sergei Sikorsky in Finne, 161–62.
2. Hardesty, Cochrane, and Lee, 20–47.

More Loves, Another Marriage

1. Orest Sergievsky, 32–33.

A War of Movement

1. *American Heritage History of World War I*, 35.
2. Golovine, 97.
3. Golovine, 220–21.
4. A. I. Denikin, *Ocherki russkoi smuti*, vol. 1, part 2, 29–30, quoted in Golovine, 145.
5. Clark, 104.

An Austrian Defeat

1. Washburn, 116–18.

Hilltop Battlefields

1. Pares, 190.

2. Pares, 186.
3. Pares, 115.
4. Pares, 119–20.
5. Pares, 131–32.

While Rome Burned

1. Clark, 81.
2. Clark, 19.
3. Clark, 22.
4. General A. A. Brusilov, *Moi vospominania*, 242, quoted in Lincoln, *Passage Through Armageddon*, 238–39.
5. Rutherford, 151.
6. Lincoln, *Passage Through Armageddon*, 73.
7. Lincoln, *Passage Through Armageddon*, 48.
8. Lincoln, *Passage Through Armageddon*, 152.
9. Tuchman, 269.
10. Tuchman, 266.
11. Stone, 168.
12. *American Heritage History of World War I*, 35.
13. Stone, 169.
14. Golovine, 178.
15. Golovine, 83

The Unknown War

1. Golovine, 83ff., 97ff.
2. Churchill, 319.

John Reed Sees the Russian Retreat
    1. Reed, 143–45. (Proper name spellings modernized from the original).
    2. Reed, 155.
    3. Reed, 159.

The Air War in the East
    1. Kilmarx, 12–25; Robertson 148–50; Durkota, Darcy, and Kulikov, 9.
    2. Golovine, 150.
    3. Robertson, 158–59.
    4. Kilmarx, 26.

The Other Side
    1. Meos, 320.
    2. Schröder, 146.
    3. Schröder, 156.

Sergievsky: An Ace for the Tsar?
    1. Duz, 268; Sobolyev, 34; Robertson, 156.
    2. Durkota interview with A. F., Jan. 4, 1994.
    3. Blume letter to A. H., Nov. 8, 1992.
    4. Durkota, Darcey, and Kulikov, 224.
    5. Blume letter to A. F., July 9, 1998.
    6. Bakhmeteff Archive.
    7. Central State Military Historical Archives: 32nd Army Corps Staff records:
        F. 2008; Op. 1; D. 222V; c.22.
    8. Central State Military Historical archives: 32nd Army Corps Staff records:
        F. 2008; Op. 1; D. 170; 1. 15–20, 411–17, 755.
        F. 2008; Op. 1; D. 177; 1. 644–52.
        F. 2077; Op. 1; D. 16; c. 327–30; 550–53; 675–76.
        F. 2077; Op. 1; D. 17; c. 359–64.

The War Winds Down
    1. Churchill, 374.
    2. Middleton, 158–60.

The Russian Civil War
    1. Lincoln, *Red Victory*, 20–21, 90, 193, 307–12.
    2. Lincoln, *Red Victory*, 285, 295–299.

A Letter of Recommendation
    1. Bakhmeteff Archive.

Sikorsky II: Starting Afresh in America
    1. Cochran, Hardesty, and Lee, 62–80.
    2. New Yorker report of Aug. 8, 1926, quoted in Shoumatoff, 168.
    3. Sergei Sikorsky, Sikorsky Symposium II, June 25, 1994; Glines, 66.

Russian Contributions to American Aviation
    1. Sergei Sikorsky, Sikorsky Symposium II, June 25, 1994.
    2. Gunston, 31.
    3. Schmued's career: Wagner.
    4. Grosz, 132; Bowers, 27.
    5. Boyne, 42.
    6. Mitchell, 162–86.
    7. Bodie, 10–53.
    8. The *New Yorker,* Nov. 9, 1940, 13.
    9. Bodie, 42–45.
    10. Ralph Alex, Sikorsky Symposium II, June 25, 1994.
    11. Cochran, Hardesty, and Lee, 70; interviews, Sikorsky Retirees' Lunch, June 2, 1993.

High Life at the Sergievskys' Villa
    1. Orest Sergievsky, 116–17.

Sergievsky, Lindbergh, and the S-36

    1. Cochrane, Hardesty, and Lee, 94, 95, 196.

    2. Juptner, 155.

    3. Bender, 97–98.

Sergievsky and the Hamilton Metalplane

    1. Juptner, 209–11.

    2. Cochrane, Hardesty, and Lee, 98–99.

The Sikorsky S-38

    1. Cochrane, Hardesty, and Lee, 195–96.

    2. Cochrane, Hardesty, and Lee, 96–98.

    3. Bender, 183.

    4. Bender, 184.

    5. Bender, 186; Cochrane, Hardesty, and Lee, 99; Sergei Sikorsky, Sikorsky Symposium II, June 25, 1994.

    6. Cochrane, Hardesty, and Lee, 99.

The Sikorsky S-40

    1. Bender, 149.

    2. Bender, 186.

    3. Bender 186.

    4. Bender 187.

    5. Jablonski, 83–84.

    6. Jablonski, 89.

    7. Jablonski, 88–89.

Sikorsky III

    1. Jablonski, 87.

    2. Sergei Sikorsky epilogue in Finne, 162.

A Test Pilot's Report

    1. Igor Sikorsky Historical Archives.

Hollywood Meets Africa

    1. Imperato, xii, 90.

    2. Stott, 6.

    3. Stott, 23–27; Imperato, 67–91.

    4. Stott, 39–54; Imperato, 92ff.

    5. Stott, 52–53; Osa Johnson, 383–87; Martin Johnson, 8–24.

    6. Imperato, 184.

    7. Stott, 111–12.

    8. Imperato, 223.

The Sikorsky S-39

    1. Mayborn, 218–21

Running on Empty over the Jungle

    1. Martin Johnson, 14–18.

The Sikorsky S-42

    1. Igor Sikorsky, 194–211.

    2. Richard K. Smith, 82–94.

Flying On

    1. Heinmuller, 9.

    2. Igor Sikorsky, 209.

Chief Test Pilot

    1. Quoted by S. Sikorsky, June 25, 1994.

    2. S. Sikorsky, June 25, 1994.

    3. S. Sikorsky, June 25, 1994.

    4. Cochrane, Hardesty, and Lee, 110.

The Sikorsky S-43

    1. Adapted from Salo, 178–97.

Sergievsky, de Bothezat, and the Helicopter Corporation of America

    1. Wolf, 26–28; de Transehe, 6–11.

    2. de Transehe, 10.

    3. Frank Kingston Smith.

Yet Another Divorce, Yet Another Marriage

1. S. Sikorsky, June 26, 1994.
2. Orest Sergievsky, 137.
3. "Sergievsky . . . commutes," *New York Herald Tribune,* Aug. 30, 1936.

Sergievsky Goes to War Again

1. "Fascism in America," *Life,* Mar. 6 1939.
2. "Investigator's report on Brasol," 1–7.
3. "Investigator's report on Brasol," 5.
4. Margaret Steele Lewis interview with A. H., July 30, 1997.
5. OSS Personnel Action Request, July 3, 1944.
6. Air Disarmament Command, Roll C5035.
7. Sikorsky Symposium II, June 26, 1994.
8. Malayney, part 1.

9. Orest Sergievsky, 208–9.

Sergievsky's Women

1. A. F. interviews, Sikorsky Retirees' Lunch.
2. Ibid.
3. Orest Sergievsky interview with A. F., Mar. 1971.
4. Elmourza Natirboff interview with A. F., May 14, 1992.
5. Told to A. F. by her son, Alexander Bing, Oct. 1994.
6. Orest Sergievsky, 154.
7. Orest Sergievsky interview with A. F., Mar. 1971.

The Mallard Years, 1946–1965

1. Grumman sales order J-4.
2. R. K. Smith, "Fifty years" 96–99.
3. Natirboff interview with A. F., May 14, 1992.

Bibliography

Materials in English

"Air Disarmament Command Oct. '44–Jul. '45." Roll C5035 (microfilm). Air Force Historical Research Agency, Maxwell Air Force Base, Ala.

Allward, Maurice. *An Illustrated History of Seaplanes and Flying Boats.* New York: Dorset Press, 1988.

The American Heritage History of World War I. Narrative by S. L. A. Marshall. New York: American Heritage, 1964.

Angelucci, Enzo, with Peter Bowers. *The American Fighter.* New York: Orion, 1987.

Aviation, Apr. 11, 1927.

Bauer, Daniel. "Joe Foss: American Hero." *Air Classics,* vol. 26, no. 3, Mar. 1990.

Bender, Marilyn, and Selig Altschul. *The Chosen Instrument: Pan Am, Juan Trippe, The Rise and Fall of an American Entrepreneur.* New York: Simon and Schuster, 1982.

Blume, August G., Letter to A. H., Nov. 8, 1992.

———. Letter A. F., July 9, 1998.

Bodie, Warren M. "Republic's Battle Hymn." *Wings,* vol. 24, no. 3, June 1994.

Bowers, Peter. "Junkers Ju 88." *Airpower,* vol. 12, no. 4, July 1982.

Boyne, Walt. "Russian Refugees and Rare Birds!" *Wings,* June 1980.

Churchill, Winston S. *The Unknown War: the Eastern Front.* New York: Scribner, 1931.

Clark, Alan. *Suicide of the Empires: the Battles on the Eastern Front 1914–1918.* New York: American Heritage Press, 1971.

Cochrane, Dorothy, Von Hardesty, and Russell Lee. *The Aviation Careers of Igor Sikorsky.* Seattle: University of Washington Press, for the National Air and Space Museum, 1989.

De Transehe, N. "The Genius of Dr. George de Bothezat." *American Helicopter,* July 1957.

Delear, Frank J. *Igor Sikorsky: His Three Careers in Aviation.* New York: Dodd, Mead, 1969.

Durkota, Alan, Thomas Darcey, and Victor Kulikov. *The Imperial Russian Air Service: Famous Pilots and Aircraft of World War One.* Mountain View, Calif.: Flying Machines Press, 1995.

"Fascism in America." *Life,* vol. 6, no. 10, Mar. 6, 1939.

Finne, K. N., Carl J. Bobrow, and Von Hardesty, eds. *Igor Sikorsky: The Russian Years.* Washington, D.C.: Smithsonian Institution Press, 1987.

Glines, Carroll V. *Roscoe Turner.* Washington and London: Smithsonian Institution Press, 1995.

Gilbert, Martin. *Atlas of Russian History.* New York: Dorset Press, 1985.

Golovine, Lieutenant-General Nicholas N. *The Russian Army in the World War.* New Haven: Yale Univ. Press, 1931.

Grosz, Peter M., George Haddow, and Peter Scheimer. *Austro-Hungarian Army Aircraft of World War One.* Mountain View, Calif.: Flying Machines Press, 1993.

Grumman Aircraft Engineering Corporation. Mallard Sales Order No. J-4, Ship No. NC 2940, Aug. 30, 1946.

Gunston, Bill. *World Encyclopaedia of Aircraft Manufacturers.* Annapolis: Naval Institute Press, 1993.

Heinmuller, John P. V. *Man's Fight to Fly.* New York: Aero Print, 1945.

Imperato, Pascal James, and Eleanor M. Imperato. *They Married Adventure: the Wandering Lives of Martin and Osa Johnson.* New Brunswick, N.J.: Rutgers Univ. Press, 1992.

"Investigator's Report on Boris Brasol, Dated Dec. 5, 1941." Confidential document from files. New York: Anti-Defamation League, 1941.

Jablonski, Edward. *Sea Wings.* New York: Doubleday, 1972.

Johnson, Martin. *Over African Jungles: The Record of a Glorious Adventure over the Big Game Country of Africa. 60,000 Miles by Airplane.* New York: Harcourt Brace, 1935.

Johnson, Osa. *I Married Adventure: The Lives and Adventures of Martin and Osa Johnson.* Rev. ed. New York: William Morrow, 1989.

Juptner, Joseph P. *U.S. Civil Aircraft* vol. 1. Fallbrook, Calif.: Aero Publishers, 1962.

Kilmarx, Robert A. *A History of Soviet Air Power.* New York: Praeger, 1962.

Lincoln, W. Bruce. *Passage Through Armageddon: the Russians in War and Revolution 1914–1918.* New York: Simon and Schuster, 1986.

Lincoln, W. Bruce. *Red Victory: a History of the Russian Civil War.* New York: Simon and Schuster, 1989.

Malayney, Norman. "ATI and operation LUSTY." Parts 1–3. *American Aviation Historical Society Journal,* vol. 40, no's. 1–3, 1995.

Mayborn, Mitch. *Sikorsky S-39,* Historical Aviation Association, All American Series, vol. 14, produced by Paul Matt, 1975.

McDonough, Kenneth. *Atlantic Wings.* Hemel Hempstead, England: Model Aeronautical Press, 1966.

Meos, Edgar. "Allies on the Eastern Front." In *Cross and Cockade,* vol. 10, no. 4, 1969, 314–28.

Middleton, Edgar. *The Great War in the Air.* 4 vol. London: Waverly, 1920.

Mitchell, Kent A. "The C-123 Provider." *American Aviation Historical Society Journal,* vol. 37, no. 3, 1992.

Munson, Kenneth. *Flying Boats and Seaplanes Since 1910.* New York: Macmillan, 1971.

Pares, Bernard. *Day by Day with the Russian Army 1914–1915.* London: Constable, 1915.

Reed, John. *The War in Eastern Europe.* New York: Scribner, 1918.

Robertson, Bruce, ed. *Air Aces of the 1914–1918 War.* Los Angeles: Aero, 1964.

Rodzianko, Colonel Paul, C. M. G. *Tattered Banners: An Autobiography.* London: Seeley Service, 1939.

Ronstam-Bek, Lt.-Col. B. *Aerial Russia: The Romance of the Giant Aeroplane.* London: John Lane, 1916.

Rutherford, Ward. *The Russian Army in World War I.* London: Gordon Cremonesi, 1975.

Salo, Mauno. "The Sikorsky S-43." *American Aviation Historical Society Journal,* vol. 26, no. 3, 1981.

Schmid, S. H., and Truman C. Weaver. *The Golden Age of Air Racing.* Oshkosh, Wis.: EAA Aviation Foundation, 1991.

Schröder, Hans. *An Airman Remembers.* London: John Hamilton, [undated].

"Sergievsky." In "Talk of the Town." *The New Yorker,* vol. 16, no. 39, Nov. 9, 1940, 12–13.

Sergievsky, B. V. "The Problems of Flying in Columbia." *Aviation,* Apr. 11, 1927.

"Sergievsky, Noted Test Pilot, Commutes Too—But by Plane," *New York Herald Tribune,* Aug. 30, 1936.

Sergievsky, Orest. *Memoirs of a Dancer.* New York: Dance Horizons, 1979.

Shoumatoff, Alex. *Russian Blood.* New York: Vintage Books, 1990.

Sikorsky, Igor I. *The Story of the Winged-S.* New York: Dodd, Mead, 1939.

Smith, Frank Kingston. *Legacy of Wings.* New York: Jason Aronson, 1981.

Smith, Richard K. "Fifty Years of Transatlantic Flight." *American Aviation Historical Society Journal,* vol. 35, no. 2, 1990.

Smith, Richard K. "The Superiority of the American Transoceanic Airliner 1932–1939: Sikorsky S-42 vs. Short S. 23." *American Aviation Historical Society Journal,* vol. 29, no. 2, 1984.

Stone, Norman. *The Eastern Front 1914–1917.* London: Hodder and Stoughton, 1975.

Stott, Kenhelm W., Jr. *Exploring with Martin and Osa Johnson.* Chanute, Kans.: Martin and Osa Johnson Safari Museum Press, 1978.

Tuchman, Barbara W. *The Guns of August.* New York: Macmillan, 1962.

Wagner, Ray. *Mustang Designer: Edgar Schmued and the Development of the P-51.* New York: Orion, 1990.

Washburn, Stanley. *Field Notes From the Russian Front.* London: Andrew Melrose, 1915.

Wohl, Robert. *A Passion for Wings.* New Haven and London: Yale Univ. Press, 1994.

Wolf, William. "America's First Helicopters," *American Aviation Historical Society Journal,* vol. 33, no. 1, 1988.

Materials in Russian

In general, Russian names and words in this book are transliterated according to the system established by the American Council of Learned Societies. However, we usually have left Slavic place names spelled as they commonly appear on western maps, and we have left proper names as they were Anglicized by their owners—including Sergievsky and Sikorsky.

Belousow, Prof. Constantine and Col. Serge Riasniansky, eds. *Boris Vasilyevich Sergiyevsky 1888–1971*. New York; Association of Russian-American Scholars in U.S.A., 1975. (A Russian-language translation of most of Sergievsky's memoir, plus memorial tributes.)

Duz, P. D. *Istoriya Vosdukho-Plavaniya i Aviatsii v Rossii (Yul 1914 g. — Oktyabr 1917 g.)*. 3d ed. Moscow: Mashinostroyenie publishers, 1989.

Kiselev, Aleksandr. "Pamyati Vidayushchevosya Russkovo Cheloveka" in *Russkoe Vozvrashchenye/La Renaissance Russe* Vol. 54 (1991), 123–40. (Includes substantial excerpts from the Russian-language edition of Sergievsky's memoir)

Novy Zhurnal (New York). No. 106, 1972, 300–01. (Obituary)

Russian American Review. No. 20, Spring 1995, 157–59.

Sobolyev, Dmitri. "Moi Mechtoi Bil Malenkii Aeroplan: Boris Sergievskii—Znamenitii Ispitatyel iz SSHA." In *Krylya Rodiny*, no. 3, 1994, 34–35.

Sovremennik (Toronto). Nos. 30–31, 1976, 188–89. (Review of Belousow and Riasniansky)

Archives

Central State Military Historical Archives, Moscow.

Bakhmeteff Archive, Rare Book and Manuscript Library, Boris Sergievsky files, Columbia University, New York.

Igor Sikorsky Historical Archives, Easton, Conn.

Rodina Archive, Rodina Russian-American Welfare Association, Lakewood, N. J.

Interviews by Allan Forsyth

Durkota, Alan. Telephone interview, Jan. 4, 1994.

Natirboff, Elmourza. Telephone interview, May 14, 1992.

Sergievsky, Orest. Interview, Mar. 1971.

Sikorsky, Sergei. Interview aboard Sikorsky's boat on the Housatonic River, June 29, 1993.

Sikorsky, Sergei. Interview, Stratford, Conn., June 25, 1994.

Sikorsky Retirees' Lunch. Ansonia, Conn., June 2, 1993.

Sikorsky Symposium on Aviation History. Bridgeport, Conn., Feb. 14, 1994.

Sikorsky Symposium II on Aviation History. Bridgeport, Conn., June 25, 1994, and New England Air Museum, Bradley Field, Conn., June 26, 1994.

Index

Page number in italic denotes illustration.